ABORTION FREEDOM

ABORTION FREEDOM
A Worldwide
Movement

Colin Francome

London
GEORGE ALLEN & UNWIN
Boston   Sydney

George Allen & Unwin (Publishers) Ltd,
40 Museum Street, London WC1A 1LU, UK

George Allen & Unwin (Publishers Ltd,
Park Lane, Hemel Hempstead, Herts HP2 4TE, UK

Allen & Unwin, Inc.,
9 Winchester Terrace, Winchester, Mass. 01890, USA

George Allen & Unwin Australia Pty Ltd,
8 Napier Street, North Sydney, NSW 2060, Australia

First published in 1984

British Library Cataloguing in Publication Data

Francome, Colin
  Abortion freedom.
1. Abortion
I. Title
363.4'6   HQ767
ISBN 0-04-179001-4

Library of Congress Cataloging in Publication Data

Francome, Colin.
  Abortion freedom.
Bibliography: p.
Includes index.
1. Abortion – History. 2. Abortion – Law and legislation – History. 3.
Birth control – History. 4. Abortion – Great Britain. 5. Abortion – United
States. 6. Abortion – Europe. I. Title. DNLM: 1. Abortion, Induced –
Legislation. 2. Abortion, Induced – Trends. 3. Abortion, Legal – Trends.
HQ767.F825a
HQ767.F72   1984   363.4'6   83-15558
ISBN 0-04-179001-4

Typeset in 10 on 12 pt Times Roman by Fotographics (Bedford) Ltd
and printed in Great Britain by Biddles Ltd, Guildford, Surrey

Contents

For my children Carla Jo *and* William Robert

Acknowledgements

During the course of the research for this book I received help from many people. In particular I would like to thank David Downes and Jock Young who supervised the PhD thesis upon which much of the information is based.

I would also like to thank the many academics and activists in the field who freely gave me their time even when they knew I did not share their views. In particular I received help from Diane Munday, Bill Baird, Chris Tietze, Ellen McCormack, Phyllis Bowman, Paul Cavadino, Vera Houghton, Madeleine Simms, Judy Cottam, Sarah Waddington, Grant Harrison, Joanna Chambers, Dylis Cossey, Virginia Andary, Karen Mulhauser, Uta Landy, Emily Moore, Susan Vogel, Peter Huntingford, Sharon Spiers, Nellie Gray, Debbie Sanders, Rebecca Cook, Caroline Francome, Stephania Siedlecky, Wayne Facer, Henry David, Evert Ketting, Doris Strachan and Philip Van Praag.

The typing was by Marlene Mascarenhas and Donna Carson. The research was supported by the Lalor Foundation and the Social Science Research Council.

List of Abbreviations

ALRA	Abortion Law Reform Association (Britain) (South Australia)
	Abortion Law Repeal Association (Western Australia)
AMA	American Medical Association
BMA	British Medical Association
BPAS	British Pregnancy Advisory Service
CISA	Centro Informazione Sterilizzazione e Aborto (Italy)
ERA	Equal Rights Amendment
HIPE	Hospital In-Patients Enquiry (a 10 per cent sample of births)
IPPF	International Planned Parenthood Federation
NAC	National Abortion Campaign
NAF	National Abortion Federation
NARAL	National Association for the Repeal of Abortion Laws (until 1973)
	National Abortion Rights Action League (after 1973) (United States)
NCPAC	National Conservative Political Action Committee (United States)
NIAC	Northern Ireland Abortion Campaign
OPCS	Office of Population Censuses and Surveys
SPUC	Society for the Protection of Unborn Children (Britain)
	Society for the Protection of the Unborn Child (New Zealand)

1
The Great Change

Since the British Act of 1967 there has been a worldwide trend to relax the laws on abortion. In the period until 1982 over forty countries extended their grounds and only three narrowed them. This change has meant that nearly two-thirds of women now live in countries where laws permit abortion on request or on a wide variety of grounds. Less than one in ten live in countries where abortion is totally prohibited (Tietze, 1979). In five of the six most populous countries abortion is freely available. These are India, China, the Soviet Union, Japan and the United States (Cook, 1978; Paxman, 1980).

Laws on abortion deal with a variety of issues such as where the operations should be performed, who should perform them, whose consent is required in the case of minors, what time limits should be adhered to and what conscience clauses should be followed. The laws even between countries with liberal legislation vary a great deal on these matters. For example, in England and Wales there is an upper time limit of twenty-eight weeks, except to save the woman's life. In Scotland there is no legal upper time limit, while in France there is abortion on request to ten weeks, but after that abortion is only available in special circumstances. Sweden has abortion on request to eighteen weeks, while in the United States it is twenty-four weeks. There are also wide variations as to payment. In Italy abortions are paid for on the National Health Scheme; in Britain the chances of a free abortion depend on where you live and the attitudes of your doctor; whereas in the United States free abortion is conditional on being a medicaid patient and living in a state which finances the operations. However, an important distinction for countries with liberal laws is whether they allow abortion on request in a specified period or whether they only allow abortion to certain categories of women.

Of the countries that have changed their laws since 1967 the following twelve places have allowed abortion on request: Austria, Denmark, France, Germany (Democratic Republic), Holland,

Italy, Norway, Singapore, Slovenia (Yugoslavia), Sweden, Tunisia and the United States.

Twenty-nine countries which have extended their grounds since 1967 but not given the right to choose are: Australia, Belize, Canada, Chile, Cyprus, El Salvador, England and Wales, Fiji, Finland, Germany (Federal Republic), Greece, Guatemala, Hong Kong, Iceland, India, Israel, Korea (Republic of), Kuwait, Luxembourg, Morocco, New Zealand, Peru, Scotland, Seychelles, South Africa, United Arab Emirates, Yugoslavia, Zambia and Zimbabwe.

Hungary, Bulgaria and Czechoslovakia were countries which restricted their laws. Hungary and Bulgaria removed the right to choose for all women. However, in both countries abortion is still widely available. For example, abortion on request is available to unmarried women in Hungary and in Bulgaria to married women with two children. So even these two states imposing restrictions provide wide access to abortion. Czechoslovakia attempted to impose administrative restrictions in 1973 but by 1981 had more abortions than ever before (David and McIntyre, 1981, p. 225; Tietze, 1983). New Zealand passed a law in 1977 which was a liberalisation on the past statute. However, it at first led to the major abortion clinics closing for a time, illustrating the fact that practice can be much more liberal than officially recognised by the legal position.

This book concentrates on the reasons for this worldwide movement and looks to the possibility of further change. One striking fact that has emerged from this study is the similarity of the social forces in operation in the widely differing countries round the world. In this opening chapter I shall therefore set out the beliefs of the five main groupings involved in the abortion debate.

Neo-Malthusian

Malthus introduced his conservative doctrine in the wake of the French Revolution. He believed that there was a natural tendency for population size to outstrip food supply and hoped that the poorer groups would engage in self-restraint in order to control their family size. The neo-Malthusian movement altered his doctrine by substituting contraception for restraint and after the

Bradlaugh/Besant trial of 1877 became a major force for change. Its principles were clearly set out in each copy of their journal *The Malthusian*, as follows:

1 That population has a constant tendency to increase beyond the means of subsistence.
2 That the checks which counteract this tendency are resolvable into positive or life destroying, and prudential or birth restricting.
3 That the positive or life-destroying checks comprehend the premature death of children and adults by disease, starvation, war and infanticide.
4 That the prudential or birth-restricting check consists in the limitation of offspring by abstention from marriage, or by prudence after marriage.
5 That prolonged abstention from marriage – as advocated by Malthus – is productive of many diseases and of much sexual vice; early marriage, on the contrary, tends to ensure sexual purity, domestic comfort, social happiness, and individual health but it is a grave social offence for men and women to bring into the world more children than they can adequately house, feed, clothe and educate.
6 That over population is the most fruitful source of pauperism, ignorance, crime and disease.
7 That the full and open discussion of the Population Question is a matter of vital moment to society, and such discussion should be absolutely unfettered by fear of legal penalties.

Although between the two world wars Malthusianism was at a relatively low ebb as other organisations became much more active and the ideas of Malthus seemed outmoded, after the Second World War there was renewed concern with the size of the world's population. The sheer size of the increase was of course one factor, but the appeal was also due to the stress on population growth in the dominant economic doctrines. A good example is the argument put forward by Walt Rostow (1971). His view was that the poor countries of the world should 'take off' into self-sustained economic growth. However, he saw problems in the expanding population because if it were growing at around 2 per cent or 3 per cent per annum, the surpluses that could have been used for investment would instead be needed for immediate consumption. The clear implication of this was that the poor countries should make extra efforts to control their population size.

There was also support for the spread of fertility control from a section of the business world, and the Rockefeller Foundation helped to finance various projects. It seems that the concern about population size was much greater in the United States than in Britain. Paul Erhlich's book *Population Bomb* (1976) had wide circulation and caused a great deal of interest. It was, for example, distributed to the Hawaii legislators who were subsequently to introduce the first Act to give women the right to choose an abortion in the United States (Steinhoff and Diamond, 1977, p. 73). Erhlich later tied his concern with over-population to the ecological movement which gave it wider appeal, and in time the Zero Population Growth movement gained a measure of popular support (Erhlich and Erhlich, 1970). So variants of Malthusian ideas have continued to be important, and one of their attractions is that they offer a solution to social problems without any change in the social order. It will be shown that this was their basic appeal in the early nineteenth century, and it is still relevant today. A second reason for their appeal to the dominant members of society is that their recommendations are usually aimed at the poorer sections of the community and so are an agent of social control. In Britain in the nineteenth century contraception was regarded as a way of reducing the number of the poor working classes. More recently others have suggested it as a possible way of reducing the numbers in minority groups.

Where this pressure has been strong there has often been an element of compulsion in the spread of fertility control. There are documented cases of forced sterilisation in the United States (*New York Times*, 4 December 1977), and there were allegations that some men in India were forced to undergo vasectomies (see p. 156). So the advocates of the extension of fertility control on Malthusian grounds do not necessarily support the individual's right to choose, and in fact neo-Malthusians may argue that choice should be curtailed for the good of society. Those who regard population as the crucial problem tend not to challenge the dominant social order but regard the problems of the poorer groups as being in large measure of their own making.

Socialist/Feminist

I have used the term 'socialist/feminist' to distinguish those who while feminist may well take a conservative point of view on many issues. In contrast to the Malthusians the socialist/feminists are not concerned with the problem of over-population but instead emphasise individual rights of control. It was German feminists at the beginning of the twentieth century who first made this demand, and in Britain Stella Browne publicly advocated this position from 1915 onwards (Ellis, 1928, p. 607). The socialist/feminists demand the freedom of choice in both contraception and abortion as part of a series of changes designed to restrict the role of the state. They regard it as simply one of a number of measures which will be a step towards fundamental and large-scale changes in the structure of society.

A clear exposition of one socialist/feminist position is given by Marie Alice Waters. She argued (Jenness, 1976) that women have not always been treated as inferior to men and excluded from many productive roles. On the contrary, she suggested that in earlier societies women were equal, and

> developed or invented the basic skills that placed humanity on the road to civilisation – agriculture, tanning, weaving, pottery, architecture and much else. Women were relegated to an inferior social position only with the rise of class society . . . With the division of society into classes – those who owned versus those who did not . . . – the patriarchal family also came into existence as a basic social unit. Women were relegated to domestic servitude and second class status in society, not because it served the needs of men in general, but because it served the needs of those men who owned property. (p. 21)

Marie Alice Waters argued that the restrictions on women's sexual behaviour were designed to support the patriarchal family and to help ensure the safe transfer of property to the next generation. In her view, a revolutionary socialist society would eliminate the economic need for the oppression of women and in this society the state would not be involved in primary relationships. ' "Marriage" and "divorce" would become totally personal decisions, subject to no laws, contracts or restrictions. Abortion and contraception would be available on demand' (p. 25).

So, in this view, the fight for sex equality is part of an overall struggle for a changed society. It is not isolated from other political changes and Linda Jenness, the Socialist Workers Party Candidate for the United States Presidential election in 1972, placed these demands in perspective. She argued that by fighting for day-care facilities, equal opportunities for employment and education and for the abolition of all laws against abortion, women would not only improve their own position in society but would help to encourage the struggle of other oppressed groups. She continued to say, however, that women could not be fully liberated within the constraints of American society, but only after a socialist revolution.

The fact that socialists have stressed the priority of the revolution has meant that where fertility control has been regarded as anti-revolutionary they have opposed it. The next chapter will show that the linking of contraception to a conservative doctrine in the nineteenth century led to the socialists becoming the major opponents of the spread of birth control in Britain. Although socialists have recently supported sexual rights, they have been wary of the spread of certain kinds of commercial sexuality which they do not feel help in the development of personal relationships. For example, Linda Gordon (1977, p. 413) has suggested that some developments have been reactionary: 'The marketing of sex cookbooks for the "connoisseur" is moving, as commoditization always does, in an antihuman direction, that is, it is carving up the human experience so that sex becomes severed from economic, social, political and emotional life'. So the view of socialist/ feminists contrasts markedly with those who want liberalisation for increased opportunity for profits.

So far I have set out the position of the socialist/feminists. But how far do they differ from those feminists who work for sex equality without believing in the necessity of a socialist revolution? One debate on this subject revived the discussion about changes in oneself and changes in society which was a source of conflict between the hippies and the radicals in the 1960s (Francome, 1976a). Rita Laporte argued in the gay magazine *The Ladder* in October 1971 that 'unconsciously Marxists apply male supremacy no less than all other men. In reasoning that the means of production should be in the hands of the people, they conclude that women, as one means of production – the production of babies – must likewise be in the hands of the people'. She argued that there is no need for revolution, for 'the inner liberation of women IS the revolution'. From this analysis, women should be altering their perspective at the personal level as reflected in consciousness-raising groups. However, unlike many hippies, the women's groups have tended to combine their personal development programme with a wider strategy for change – especially on issues directly related to women.

So these are clearly contrasting positions. However, it is the socialist/feminists who have been more concerned with the wider political implications of their actions. Their perspective leads them to take a totally different position on social institutions from other groups, for example on the nuclear family. They regard it as a repressive institution which prevents full personality development and excludes those who are left outside such a relationship. They therefore welcome the extension of rights of control over fertility together with the improvement of working conditions and expansion of welfare rights. These they regard as ways in which individuals and particularly women are able to control their lives without being forced into relationships which they would not otherwise have wished to enter. Furthermore, they approve the development of alternatives outside the family, for these provide opportunities for those who are in unhappy relationships to break out of their constrictive situation.

A second important difference is that socialist/feminists do not accept that population increase is the key fact in terms of poverty. This they put down to the capitalist system and for this reason socialists in the past have sometimes opposed movements to extend fertility control. This was particularly true in Britain in the nineteenth century as will be shown in the next chapter.

In terms of their political activities the socialists, in stressing the rights of the individual, are less willing to compromise than other groups. One key issue is how late in pregnancy abortions should be allowed. The majority of groups will agree to a time limit of usually 20–28 weeks based on estimated viability. However, the socialists are much more inclined to argue for no abortion laws at all, as did Victoria Greenwood and Jock Young (1976). They stressed that a woman should have absolute control over her own body.

Another important point is that many socialists have dismissed parts of the debate that others have stressed. For example, they see as irrelevant the controversy over the change in number of illegal abortions. In general, pro-choice groups argue that legalisation reduces the number of illegal operations. However, socialists state that women should have the right to choose and the effect on the total number of abortions should not be a matter of concern (Greenwood and Young, 1976, p. 67).

The situation in the Catholic countries such as France, Italy and Spain is somewhat different from that in Britain and the United States. Later chapters will show links between the Church and the right wing. This has resulted in feminism being much more closely linked to socialism or communism.

Reformist

Those who accept a reformist position on fertility control tend to look for moderate changes. They differ from the socialist/feminists in that they accept the nuclear family and claim that abortion protects it by excluding unwanted children who would otherwise place strains upon the family unit. Historically the reformers have included people with a wide variety of beliefs, depending on the issues involved and the political situation at the time. One of the problems for reformers is that they may be willing to support a degree of social change but become unhappy if more radical developments occur.

A reformer may at one time be on the side of those working for change but at a later stage may join with the conservatives in opposition to further liberalisation. The clearest example of this was the switch in sides of Aleck Bourne. In the 1930s he had been a member of the Abortion Law Reform Association (ALRA) and worked for a liberalisation of the law. In a celebrated case in 1938 he performed an abortion for rape and was cleared in the subsequent trial, so opening the way for operations in similar circumstances in the future. However, he opposed the law being extended too far and in the 1960s he joined the Society for the Protection of Unborn Children (SPUC) and worked against the Bill sponsored by ALRA of which he had been such a prominent member.

The 1967 Abortion Act was debated in reformist terms and the kind of argument advanced was that the legalisation of abortion would help women with problems. The reformers asserted that the change they were proposing was not threatening to the social order but would help to improve it. They argued that the Act would not greatly increase the number of abortions, that there was already a high number of illegal operations, and that legalisation would transfer these to the legal sector. They also stressed that there was no attempt to give women 'abortion on demand' and that doctors would still have the ultimate control. This absence of the claim of a 'right to choose' differentiated the British campaign from those in the United States, France, Italy, Germany and other countries.

One of the crucial features of the reformist perspective is a gradualist theory of change and for this reason they tend to limit their demands to a 'realistic' level. So within a reformist campaign there may be many people holding very radical views but who for political reasons do not express them publicly. Although the British 1967 Act was argued in reformist terms, there were many in the campaign who would have liked a repeal law.

Right-Wing Groups

These have generally opposed extension of birth control and abortion rights. Right-wingers tend to value stability and oppose changes which they see as threatening to their beliefs and norms. They accept the dominant views of society that act as a method of social control and tend to regard problems as being due to deficiencies within individuals rather than structural weaknesses within the system. Poverty was traditionally regarded by conservatives as being largely due to the unwillingness of the poor to work or to their 'wastefulness'. Historically they distinguished the 'deserving poor' from the 'non-deserving poor' and their solution for the latter was to persuade them to change their ideas and to adopt the work ethic.

Jock Young (1971) has set out the conservatives' view on drug-taking. He suggests that they accept certain kinds of drugs such as alcohol and tobacco which come within their overall perspective. However, they regard others as problematical, being taken by a 'tiny minority of deviants'. So their solution to the drugs 'problem' is to persuade the non-conformists of the error of their ways by debate or punishment. However, as Young points out, some drinking of alcohol is acceptable because it is regarded as the reward for hard work and so 'deserved'.

The traditional conservative view of sexual behaviour is similar.

Sex is regarded as acceptable in certain contexts, but is also in some degree threatening. While sexuality is regarded as 'normal' within the confines of the nuclear family, it tends to be proscribed for single people who would be engaging in it without responsibility and so would not have 'earned' the right to participate. Conservatives are concerned at any extension of rights to abortion or contraception even if they take advantage of such facilities themselves. They are worried that some may enjoy sexual intercourse without taking on the responsibilities. For similar reasons they may welcome venereal disease and illegitimacy as 'punishments' for unacceptable behaviour.

Elsewhere, I have shown that in both Britain and the United States those politicians who are opposed to abortion are also likely to be opposed to homosexuality being legal and to capital punishment being abolished (Francome, 1978a and 1978b). This finding is not at all surprising in the light of the above reasoning. Those who take an extreme conservative view regard capital punishment as a deterrent to murder, homosexuality as 'deviant' behaviour in need of treatment if not punishment, and abortion as a 'prop' to irresponsibility in sexual relationships.

Conservatives tend to regard the social structure as vulnerable. They see threats in social changes and so oppose movements towards greater liberalism. However, once the changes have occurred and been seen to have limited adverse effects, they may well then be accepted and even defended. Thus the hierarchy in the Church of England once opposed contraception but now accepts the right of individuals to use it. More recently the British Medical Association opposed the passage of the 1967 Abortion Act, but when it had been in operation for a few years medical opinion changed to support the new law. As early as 1975 an editorial in the *British Medical Journal* attacked proposed restrictions in the Act. Prominent establishment groups by their perspective tend to support the status quo, but the more right wing want a greater adherence to their values. They are concerned that even those rules that do exist are not adequately followed and they may look back to a 'golden age' in the past when 'right was right' and 'wrong was wrong'. A good example of this was in 1982 when the British Junior Education Minister, Dr Rhodes Boyson, attacked sexual freedom which he said had led to personal isolation and despair. He contrasted the situation to the clear and confident virtues of the Victorian Age (*Guardian*, 20 March).

Religious Groups

In recent years the right wing have forged links with certain Protestant Fundamentalist groups. This development has been fastest in the United States with the growth of the 'moral majority'. This group, led by Jerry Falwell, has claimed that the backbone of their support has come from 'citizens who are pro family, pro moral, pro life and pro American, who have integrity and believe in hard work' (Hunter, 1981). Falwell is on record as saying that he wants to go back to the morality of fifty years ago, and this development has given a great boost to the anti-abortion movement.

Some religious groups have liberalised their position. The Church of England (Episcopal Church) used to be a strong opponent but now supports birth control and has no official position on abortion. The Methodists in Britain and the USA have supported liberal laws and opposed attempts at restriction as have other Protestant denominations. A restrictive line has been maintained by the Mormons and Orthodox Jews. However, these groups are relatively small, and the major consistent opposition to both birth control and abortion has come from the Catholic Church. One reason for this, which has distinguished Catholics from many of the Protestant groups, is that sexuality has a crucial place in its beliefs. The Church has placed a high value on virginity, and its doctrines are determined by those who have chosen to forgo sexual intercourse.

Official Catholic teaching traditionally said that the primary purpose of sexual intercourse was the procreation of children. Artificial birth control was regarded as being unnatural and against the will of God. In the 1930s it was often looked upon as murder. But with changing attitudes and the acceptance of the safe period, the Church's concern with contraception has diminished. Possibly the clearest exposition of the Church's modern theory concerning the problem of sexuality and fertility control was that put forward by Bishop Joseph Bernardin in the *New York Times* (22 January 1978) on the fifth anniversary of the Supreme Court's decision legalising abortion. He stated that he very much doubted whether 'more and better contraceptive information and services will make major inroads in the number of teenage pregnancies . . . [for] . . . It will motivate them to precocious sexual activity but by no means to the practice of contraception. In which case the "solution" will merely have made the problem worse.' Bernardin argued that the answer, although not an easy one, was to tell young people that there was no such thing as sex without consequences and, furthermore, to teach them that 'Sex is not merely for fun or for the expression of transitory affection. It is an enriching and serious business between mature people who are emotionally, socially and even economically able to accept the consequences, of which pregnancy is hardly the only one.' He then called for more education or indoctrination of teenagers in family values, stability of marital relationships and the willingness to accept the consequences of one's actions.

Leading British anti-abortion activists tend to take a similar position. Phyllis Bowman, a Catholic convert, of Britain's Society for the Protection of Unborn Children, does not see contraception as the answer. In a personal interview (14 May 1979) she told me, 'When I became involved with the Abortion Act I thought contraception was quite definitely the answer to abortion but I don't now'. She continued by saying that she felt contraception on demand would lead to an increase in abortion on demand. However, she did not oppose the right of women to use birth control: 'As far as I am concerned a girl can take pills till they come out of her ears. She's then doing what she wants with her own body.' Similar comments were made to me by Ellen McCormack, former Right to Life Candidate for the US Presidency (14 December 1979). In taking this position they were both echoing the dominant Catholic position which is to concede on the issue of birth control and concentrate on abortion. Madeleine Simms, a well known British activist, suggested to me that one of the reasons Catholicism has stressed abortion is that it is the one social issue on which regular supporters agree. She said it has helped to unite the Church which is hopelessly divided on such matters as contraception. This allegation is hotly disputed by Catholic leaders.

Although, in some countries such as Spain, Italy and France Catholicism is closely identified with the right-wing groups, there is no necessary connection in this direction. In Latin America the Church has taken a very radical stance and some priests have worked with revolutionary groups. Similarly in both Britain and the United States the dominant rationale for opposition to abortion has been linked with a radical analysis of society. Particularly in the United States, Republican anti-abortionists have been opposed to increased help to deprived groups, yet Catholics have been more likely to see the need to support these. For example John Quinn, President of the United States National Conference of Catholic Bishops, once said, 'If you want to defend the preborn effectively . . . see to it that the aged and handicapped are treated decently . . . support the rights of the hungry and disadvantaged wherever and whoever they are' (NARAL, 1972).

In Britain, too, the anti-abortion Catholics have taken a radical position on a number of issues. For example, Phyllis Bowman was an anti-Vietnam war activist and Paul Cavadino a prison reformer. Furthermore, both in Britain and in the United States the movement leans against capital punishment and for the rights of minority groups. So there are clear differences between the Catholics and the conservatives and in some cases there are strange alliances. For example Paul Cavadino, whose politics are well to the left, often used the arch-Conservative John Biggs Davidson to ask his parliamentary questions.

These, then, are five different perspectives on the issue of fertility control. They are not mutually exclusive, for some socialists have been neo-Malthusians and, possibly more importantly, some conservatives may also have religious beliefs opposing fertility control. In these cases the individuals may well be doubly motivated and spend a great deal of their time actively working for their chosen cause. There are also inevitably a number of activists who do not clearly fit into any of the groups outlined. Table 1.1 sets out some of the most prevalent beliefs more fully and shows the major differences between the groups on various social issues.

How Both Sides Have Their Own Facts

Comparison with the debate on marijuana

In his book on marijuana, Erich Goode (1970) identified some of the problems in evaluating what is ostensibly empirical information, and set out two distinct possibilities. Sometimes those on both sides of the debate on legalisation will agree upon the

Table 1.1 Perspectives on Social Issues

Perspective	Socialist/ Feminist	Radical	Neo-Malthusian	Conservative	Catholic
Social order	Needs to be radically changed	In favour of tinkering with the system. Confident of its ability to withstand some alteration	No need to change system	Concerned with instability of the social system and so threatened by any changes	Concerned with instability and so anxious to avoid change. However sometimes believe in radical changes
Concern with over-population	Deny problem	Usually somewhat concerned with problem	Very concerned	Possibly concerned with excess reproduction of 'poorer stock'	Deny problem
Solution to social problems	Complete restructuring of the social order	Minor changes in the social system	Reduce excess numbers in problem groups and so cut down extent of the difficulties	Persuade those in the poorer groups to adopt more middle-class values	Persuade individuals to change their values (aided possibly by social changes)
Family	Negative. Nuclear family is a repressive institution which should be destroyed	Positive, but regard some changes as possibly desirable	Positive. Believe birth control can strengthen	Positive, but believe vulnerable and in need of protection	Positive. Believe strong family units are crucial for the good of society

Sexual freedom	Positive. Regard it as a healthy development	Ambivalent. Regard it as being good in some cases but harmful in others	Ambivalent. Concerned that increased freedom will not harm overall case they are making	Negative. Take the view that sex should take place within marriage (especially female sex)	Negative, believe sexuality should be restricted for good of society
Sex equality	Positive	Positive	Positive	Negative	Negative
Sexual abstinence	Negative	Largely negative	Largely negative	Positive. Good to exercise self-control	Positive. Good to exercise self-control
Sexual deviation	Positive and accepting	Tolerant to some degree	Tolerant but try to minimise	Negative. Possibly regard it in need of punishment	Negative. Possibly regard it as sick
Right of fertility control	Individual's right of personal choice	Individual's right as far as society can allow	Regard as important part of society's plan for development. May enforce restrictions	Allowable so long as does not undermine family or lead to promiscuous or irresponsible behaviour	Negative. Individuals should control themselves or trust God to decide number of children
Possibility of compromise	Oppose compromise on principle	Willing to compromise	Willing to accept some compromise	Accept compromise	Oppose compromise on principle

Source: Author's doctoral research (Francome, 1980c).

facts but will make differing value judgements. He states, 'Both groups may agree that marijuana usage leads to increased sexuality but the opponents regard this as grounds for condemnation while supporters cheer society's resurgent interest in the organic, the earthy, the sensual'. On other occasions the opponents in the debate will attempt to bolster their position by seeking out facts that support their view and by negating or ignoring contrary evidence. Goode argued 'A man is not opposed to the legalisation of marijuana because (he thinks) it leads to the usage of more dangerous drugs, because it causes crime, because it produces insanity and brain damage, because it makes a person unsafe behind the wheel, because it creates an unwillingness to work. He believes these things because he thinks the drug is evil' (1970, p. 58). Goode continued with the example of a report produced by Mayor La Guardia. The proponents of marijuana took heart from its conclusions and reprinted nearly the whole of the report in its literature. However, the opponents found in the study solid evidence of the damaging effects of the drug.

The conclusions Goode drew from the marijuana debate apply equally well to the debate on abortion. For example, socialists and anti-abortionists agree on a number of facts. They concur that the extension of rights over the control of fertility increases non-marital intercourse. However, whereas the socialists approve sex outside marriage, the anti-abortionists in most cases regard it as a 'lowering of moral standards'. Both socialists and anti-abortionists believe that abortion will help in the breakdown of the nuclear family. However, whereas the anti-abortionists regard the family as the 'cornerstone' of society and see its defence as very important, the socialists are opposed to it. They criticise it on a number of grounds including the fact that it restricts child socialisation patterns, that it excludes those who are outside the basic unit and that it supports the capitalist system.

Thirdly, socialists may agree with anti-abortionists that the increase in availability of contraception will not reduce the number of abortions. They may argue that this does not matter much, for what is important is that women can control their own fertility. However, the anti-abortionists regard this as a crucial point. For if it is true it supports their view that the high number of abortions cannot be reduced by better sex education and increased availability of contraception. In these and other ways the socialists and anti-abortionists agree on certain facts but disagree on values.

How Both Sides Claim 'Facts Are on Our Side'

Within the abortion debate the most striking feature is not the limited agreement on facts, but rather the extent of disagreement between the groups. The radicals, for example, tend to disagree with all the views just given. They argue that easier abortion will protect, rather than destroy, the nuclear family. The National Abortion Rights Action League (NARAL) said in the USA in 1978: 'Legal abortion helps women limit their families to the number of children they want and can afford, both emotionally and financially, and reduces the number of children born unwanted. Pro-choice is definitely pro-family.' Radicals also argue that contraceptives stop unwanted pregnancies and that most young people are not promiscuous. Furthermore, they state that even if a few 'irresponsible' young people take the pill or have abortions this is better than them having children they cannot look after. Thus the radicals dispute facts with which both anti-abortionists and socialists agree. Furthermore, during this research it became clear that the dominant pressure groups on either side of the debate believed totally different facts about the effects of legalised abortion.

Members of both sides also believe they should publicise the facts, as the following quotations show:

Pro-Choice
Opposition is mainly based on the religious and moral convictions of a minority of the population, who try to persuade the majority with a series of arguments which frequently rely on myths about abortion ... Benyon himself stated at an anti-abortion meeting in Birmingham on 7 November 1976 that he had been convinced of the case against abortion by what he called the 'pro life' movement, because 'its members had stuck to the truth and produced fact after fact in a responsible way'. It is, therefore, worth looking at some of these alleged facts and judging how responsible these people really are. (Foreword from 'Anti-abortion myths', *New Humanist*, January/February 1977)

I always beat the anti-abortionists in debate because I give them the facts. I remember the exact references from the medical journals. (Bill Baird, United States abortion activist, personal interview, April 1978)

Anti-Choice
Pro abortionists work by propagandistic rhetoric, so their arguments are hard to dismantle. They hide the ugly facts while playing on emotions. It is a technique to use the ignorance of others by keeping the evidence of science and common sense from opening people's minds. Yet it is truth that shall make us free. (Fr Paul Marx, US-based priest, *Our Sunday Visitor*, 13 February 1977)

The only way we can get change is for people to have the facts. I am not afraid of people having facts. We are not going to be able to change the hard cases – for example doctors making money out of abortions – but people will be able to see the problems. (Ellen McCormack, Right to Life Presidential Candidate in 1976, personal interview, 14 December 1979)

The Four Main Disputes About Facts

1   The Effects of Abortion on Attitudes to Life

The anti-abortionists believe that legalisation leads to an anti-life attitude. They take the view that by legalising the right to 'kill unborn children' the way is open for euthanasia and the killing of certain handicapped groups. They often draw a comparison with the situation in Hitler's Germany which they say is the only other modern society where the right of the individual to life was systematically abrogated. A highly promoted US anti-abortion book (Willke and Willke, 1975, p. 6) states that the abortion laws 'Represent a complete about face, a total rejection of one of the core values of Western man, and an acceptance of a new ethic in which life has only relative value . . . this is a momentous change that strikes at the root of Western civilisation.'

In contrast those in favour of legal abortion dismiss the charge that legal abortion devalues life. They stress the fact that the vast majority of abortions are carried out early in the pregnancy and argue that at this stage a baby cannot be said to exist. They may give the examples that an acorn is not an oak tree nor an egg a chicken. In answer to comparisons with Hitler's Germany they point out that Hitler was opposed to abortion and argue that in many respects legal abortion can be regarded as pro life. It saves women from dying from illegal abortions and allows them to look after their chosen children more adequately.

2   The Effect of Legalisation on 'Back-Street' Abortions

There is disagreement on the effects of legalisation on the number of 'back-street' abortions. The supporters of legal abortion usually argue that before legalisation there was a division between rich and poor. Rich women were able to pay high fees for abortion from a reputable doctor while poor women were forced to make use of the services of unqualified and possibly unskilled illegal operators. Pro-choice groups argue that the major effect of legalisation is to transfer abortions from the illegal to the legal sector and in support of their case they point to the decline in the number of police prosecutions and deaths from illegal abortions.

In contrast the anti-arbortionists argue that the number of abortions before legalisation was relatively small but that the change in the law has altered attitudes. They claim that the number of illegal abortions has in fact risen, either because the availability of abortion has given rise to irresponsible attitudes towards contraception, or because of the actual increase in the number of 'promiscuous pregnancies in unmarried women' (LIFE, 1978; Willke and Willke, 1975). In order to support their case they criticise the evidence that the deaths from illegal abortion have declined. They say this reduction is due to the development of improved drugs and the fact that many deaths are not reported.

3   The Medical Effects of Abortion

A third area of disagreement is on the likely sequelae of abortion. The supporters of legalisation point to medical evidence that abortion is much safer than childbirth. For example, the United States pro-choice group NARAL produced a document, *Abortion Questions and Answers* (1976), which said: 'Approximately 87% of abortions are performed in the first trimester when it is eight times safer than delivering a baby. The death rate for legal early abortion for 1974 is 1.7 per 100,000 abortions compared to 14.6

deaths per 100,000 live births for 1974. The total death rate for legal abortion was 3.1 per 100,000.' Proponents also argue that the psychological effects of abortion are not very great. To quote the NARAL document again:

> There is no indication that abortion leads to any detectable increase in the incidence of mental illness. Any depression or guilt feelings associated with legal abortion are described as mild. One study shows an incidence of post abortion psychosis ranging from only 0.2 to 0.4 per 1,000 legal abortions as compared to a rate for post partum psychosis of 1–2 per 1,000 deliveries.

Opponents of abortion question these figures. The Willkes (1975, p. 82) claim that the extent of under-reporting is so great that the number of deaths from legal abortion should be ten times as high as those recorded. In place of the official figures for New York of 2–5 deaths per 100,000 abortions they suggest the figures 20–50 should be substituted. The Willkes also give some figures for Sweden and Denmark showing that the deathrate from abortion is higher than that of childbirth. They criticise Hungarian data showing a low deathrate and argue it is due to under-reporting and censorship by the Communist Bureaux before publication. Phyllis Bowman of SPUC argued to me that those women who die of childbirth are older and unfit whereas it is often healthy young girls who die of abortion.

4 Public Opinion on Abortion

A fourth important difference between the groups is in their perception of public opinion. The NARAL document *Twelve Abortion Facts* (undated) reported three surveys all of which showed support for liberal laws. One was a *New York Times*/CBS News poll that found that 67 per cent of Americans agreed that 'the right of a woman to have an abortion should be left entirely up to the woman and her doctor'. Another showed that the majority of Catholics did not support the Church's position that abortion should not be allowed in any circumstances. In contrast the Willkes criticise these surveys. They say polls are often wrong and draw attention to the two referendums on abortion in North Dakota and Michigan in 1972 where 78 per cent and 62 per cent respectively voted against abortion rights being extended (Willke and Willke, 1975, p. 36). A similar dispute over public opinion occurred in Britain at the time of the Corrie Bill.

Overall, the information that opposing forces on the abortion issue receive gives them a totally different perspective on the facts. At one level the pressure group operators may be criticised for lack of objectivity; but they take the view that their position is similar to that of lawyers. There are so many pieces of evidence that either side can select that which is favourable to their point of view. The first (1971) edition of the Willkes' *Handbook on Abortion* (1975) is a good example. Pro-choice people have also been selective at times. For instance, when I noticed that a Gallup study was missing from a summary of some British opinion polls and I asked the author the reason for the exclusion, she told me she did not see why she should help to 'publicise material helpful to the other side'. The leaders of the pressure groups know the views of the other side only too well because they read each other's literature and meet at debates.

Social Analysis

This introduction has set out some of the major perspectives, and the rest of the book aims to examine the contribution of various groups to the debate over fertility control. It will concentrate on abortion, but a full analysis cannot be developed if birth control is not also considered. The major interest is in the events of the 1960s and 1970s but they will be set in their historical context. This is particularly important in the case of the United States as the debate on legalisation revolved very much around the reasons for making abortion illegal in the nineteenth century. Furthermore, the analysis of the process of social change in sexual norms will facilitate predictions as to future changes.

In examining the process of liberalisation a number of different factors will be considered. It will be suggested that there is a relationship between the social climate and the development of birth control and abortion rights. Four different periods will be considered. In the Victorian era and up until the First World War it will be suggested that the general sexual climate inhibited the development of birth control practices, especially in the United States. After the First World War there was a liberalisation of attitudes toward sex and a breakdown in many aspects of Victorian morality. During these years birth control became much more readily available and there was even some pressure for abortion rights. In the third period, after the Second World War, there was no comparable liberalisation of attitudes until the 1960s and the growth of what the press was inclined to call the 'permissive ideology'. In the fourth period, after the liberalisation of the 1960s, there was a slight retrenchment in the late 1970s and fertility rights were attacked in some countries.

Although there is a relationship between the prevailing mood in a society and the possibilities for change, various other factors must be considered. The evidence will show that in a very real sense people make history. The presence of well organised groups can produce important changes while the opportunity may be lost if the necessary pressure groups or mass parties are absent or ineffective. Certain belief systems may be relevant to society at one time but become much less important when social conditions change. The predictions made by different groups will be considered in the light of subsequent events. The possibility of change also depends on the structure of the social institutions. For example, we shall see that the role of the Supreme Court in the United States was radical whilst in Germany it was conservative. This book aims to analyse these different effects and to explain the reasons for the great changes of recent years.

2
Early Debate on Fertility Control

During the eighteenth and nineteenth centuries there was a great increase in world population largely due to improvement in the death rates. There was also large-scale migration leading to great increases in population in North and South America (Table 2.1).

Table 2.1 *Population of the World, by Continents, 1750 and 1900*

	1750	1900	% increase,
	(millions)		1750–1900
Europe	140	401	186
North America	1.3	81	6,140
Central and South America	11	63	473
Australasia	2	6	200
Africa	95	120	27
Asia	479	937	96
World	728	1,608	121

Source: Royal Commission on Population, 1949, p. 7.

Table 2.1 shows that the proportion of the world's population living in Europe increased considerably. It rose from 19 per cent to 24 per cent over the period. Throughout the nineteenth century the population grew rapidly in all European countries except France, Spain and Ireland (Royal Commission on Population, 1949). In Britain the population multiplied three and a half times between 1801, when the first census was taken, and 1900, and its share in the population of Europe rose from 5.7 per cent to 9 per cent. It would have been higher but for continued emigration.

France was the country best known for successfully carrying out preventive checks and this was largely due to the successful use of coitus interruptus. It seems it was the aristocracy which first began practising the method, for in the eighteenth century their family size was less than a half of that of the peasantry and their fertility rates were remarkably low in the later childbearing years (Potts and Selman, 1979, p. 167). By the nineteenth century this knowledge had percolated through to the rest of society to such an extent that a French bishop sought papal ruling about the fact that young married men did not want to have many children and yet could not 'morally restrain themselves from the sex union'. He complained that if questioned about their practices too closely they absented themselves from mass. The Holy High Court of Doctrine ruled on 8 June 1842 that the father confessor need not investigate the matter. So the control of family size by the French received the tacit acceptance of the Church (*New Generation*, August 1922).

The French also had a liberal approach to abortion. Although the laws dating from 1810 and founded on the 'Code Napoleon' prescribed five to ten years' penal servitude, by the end of the nineteenth century, at a time when there were around 850,000 deliveries in the country, the number of abortions was estimated at between 100,000 and 500,000 per year (Potts *et al.*, 1977, p. 90). English women often travelled to France for their abortions, a process that was to be reversed in later years. The French low population growth was unique in Europe in the nineteenth century, as most countries in Europe moved towards conservative sexual attitudes. Apart from France the Scandinavian countries were also possible exceptions to this trend with chastity not so clearly accepted there as elsewhere. However in Britain, and particularly in the United States, sexual attitudes grew very restrictive (McGregor, 1957; Benfield, 1972; Perrin, 1970). Such attitudes placed great restraints on the development of fertility control and it is therefore fruitful to consider some of the reasons for their pervasiveness.

Growth of Restrictive Attitudes in the Nineteenth Century

In Britain before the nineteenth century it was mainly the middle class who had conservative sexual attitudes, often attacking the upper class for its behaviour. For example, in 1755 *The World* talked of the vices and immorality amongst the wealthy and commented, 'What should banish a man from all society, recommends him to the rich' (Thomas, 1969, p. 87). Amongst the peasant groups there was a clear recognition that young people would want to express their sexual feelings and the main problem was to enable courtship to continue without a premature pregnancy occurring. In the absence of contraceptives various garments were devised. In Wales, for example, women in their teens would be given a 'courting stocking', a garment which completely covered them from the waist down with room for both legs. Young people were allowed to sleep together on condition this was not removed, and the practice was called bundling (Baker, 1974, p. 14). This was also practised in the United States, and became common in Pennsylvania and New England where it was stated that the couple kept their clothes on to save fuel. In Britain once a couple began to court seriously the social pressure against intercourse diminished. Hair (1966 and 1970) calculated that between a third and a half of brides were pregnant on their wedding day. The evidence therefore shows that chastity was not the dominant practice nor even the dominant ideology and the change in view is linked to the social and economic changes occurring during the early part of the nineteenth century. It is possible to set out a variety of reasons for this and to explain the difference in the degree of puritanism between Britain and America.

1   The Worsening Position of the Working Class

The peasantry had been driven off the land by the economic pressures linked to the enclosure movement and pressed to work in factories where the conditions were far worse than those they had encountered in the rural areas. People were working such long hours that their homes became almost a dormitory, and in this way the factory system destroyed much of family life. There was a great amount of poverty which did not lead young people to act with forethought and restraint, and the movement from the rural setting further broke down the informal sanctions on sexual behaviour. Thus the rural norms were no longer applicable and were replaced by widespread anomy. Francis Place, not one of those inclined to bewail the current lack of morality, nevertheless commented in 1832 about the working-class poor: 'Girls become unchaste at a very early age as a matter of course; the whole family live in one room; and . . . hearing what they hear and seeing what they see;

they never arrive at any notion of self respect, and the consequences are certain' (1930, p. 326).

The worsening position of the working classes had a great influence on the middle-class groups who in many cases were insecure in their status. The changes meant that unchastity was, therefore, associated with poverty, filth, drunkenness and other features of life from which the middle classes wished to distinguish themselves. Thus there were status reasons linking the middle classes to chastity and these were buttressed by ideological factors. Many adopted the values expressed by the religious leaders and rose up the social hierarchy. John Wesley, for example, had taught his followers to work hard and be frugal: 'We must exhort all Christians to gain all they can, and to save all they can; that is, in effect, to grow rich' (Weber, 1968, p. 175). Though Wesley himself opposed wealth and gave much of his money to charity his followers did not follow his example but used it to help their rise in social status.

American commentators like Cowan (1880, p. 122) stressed the strong correlation between work and chastity. 'Everyday employment should be as much of a necessity to every man (and woman) as is eating. A man who is constitutionally lazy and careless about working is nearly always a licentious man. An idle life and a chaste and continent life cannot possibly be found in the same individual.' A combination of these status and ideological factors must count as a major reason for the strength of the belief in chastity amongst the middle classes.

2   The Changing Position of the Middle Classes

Urbanisation increased the possible segregation of the sexes. In the rural areas there had been less of a distinction between work and leisure and women often had their own tasks in the household. In the town, however, there were few acceptable jobs, and middle-class women thus spent their time in piano-playing or in other accomplishments to enhance their position in the marriage market. This sexual segregation had sometimes occurred in the eighteenth century, but the numbers involved grew and the divisions hardened. Women were, therefore, restricted in the ways they were able to develop their personalities and consequently were not valued on any grounds approaching equality. They were placed on a pedestal and were supposed to embody the virtues of society and not soil their hands with the 'evils of the world', an idealisation which led to their chastity being greatly valued. As Hannah Gavron (1966, p. 64) has rightly pointed out: 'The more a society places women on a pedestal as in modern Brazil or Victorian England, removed from the realities of life, the greater will the virginity of brides be prized. However, the less the division between male and female the less is virginity considered important.'

The movement to the towns also made it more possible for the middle classes to ignore sexuality. In the countryside this is difficult for it is ever present in the normal cycle of animal life.

3 Myths About Sexuality

One of the notable facts about the late nineteenth century was the strange beliefs about sex emanating from what were regarded as highly reputable sources. One was that men had better restrict their emissions, hence the use of the term 'to spend' rather than 'to come' for orgasm. Benfield (1972) suggests that this meant that women were a potential threat and that 'women's latent boundlessness' posed a threat to male energies, and through them to civilisation. A woman was a 'sperm absorber'. So the general idea of 'saving' transferred to the sexual field accentuated the sexual divisions.

It seems that the middle classes in the United States had an even greater fear of sexuality than their British counterparts. In 1907 Robinson noted the great fear of loss of semen amongst his patients and complained, 'A patient who notices a drop or two of semen is sure he is on the way to the insane asylum' (Benfield, 1972, p. 349). Such extreme views did not seem to exist in Britain, neither did the practice of removing the clitoris. Benfield discussed the fact that in the United States the belief existed that it was so abnormal for women to enjoy sex that clitorectomy was often performed. There is evidence of operations from 1867 at least to 1904, and he points out that in contrast the British gynaecologist who reinvented clitorectomy in 1858 was expelled from the London Obstetrical Society.

4 Effect of the French Revolution

The British upper classes were very worried by the French Revolution and some felt it was connected to immorality. The

1878 edition of the Annual Register said: 'The French revolution illustrated the connection between good morals and the order and peace of society ... The levity and licentiousness of French manners had already made alarming progress in the higher, and what were called, the fashionable circles, from whence they must pass on to the other circles' (Thomas, 1969). It is doubtful whether such an argument would encourage the upper classes to be chaste, but it is likely that it made them less open in their conduct. In this respect I would concur with McGregor's (1957) suggestion that 'Few aspects of the period are more astonishing than the successful imposition of middle class standards on the overt sexual behaviour of the aristocracy. "That damned morality" which disconcerted Lord Melbourne, covered mid Victorian England like a fog.'

5 Education and Middle-Class Values

One of the key factors in the spread of middle-class and religious ideas in Britain and the United States was the growth of the school system. In 1811 the Anglicans founded the 'National Society for Promoting the Education of the Poor in the Principles of the Established Church' which took over many of the schools. Armytage (1964, p. 91) comments, 'Its aim was heroic; nothing less than shouldering the whole burden of the national education'. By 1814 it had 230 schools and 40,484 pupils. In 1833 the government agreed to give money towards church building costs and so the first steps towards a national system of education were taken, a system which was strongly influenced by conservative attitudes and where religious instruction was prominent. In this way the restrictive ideas of the middle classes, which in early times had been minority beliefs, increasingly came to be considered as the 'proper' behaviour which should be accepted as a matter of course.

Differences between Britain and the United States

Most of the factors so far discussed applied to both countries, but two factors in particular led to the degree of puritanism in the United States being more marked than it was in Britain. America was a society with a very high proportion of immigrants and this was important for a number of reasons.

First of all the fact that the immigrants came from widely

differing backgrounds raised problems in communication. Many nuances of social behaviour could be misinterpreted, so people had to develop a directness in communication. The rules had to be spelled out and the United States has had a much greater tendency to constrain behaviour by legal means and by carefully drafted codes of behaviour. Furthermore many immigrants came from countries where the sex divisions were marked and the double standard was very strong. In this way the double standard was imported to the United States. A final point is that when the immigrants entered the society they had low status and were expected to become socialised into the American way of life. When the American middle classes saw deviant behaviour in immigrant groups they regarded it as a result of lack of knowledge. Moral entrepreneurs drew attention to the high proportion of recent immigrants in deviant activity. For example, the annual report of the Society for the Suppression of Vice in 1874 (p. 6) gave the nationality of those arrested under the pornography laws as follows: forty-six were Irish, twenty-four were English, thirty-four were American and twenty were other nationalities. It was pointed out that only just over a quarter were native born Americans and the Society aimed to educate the 'unsocialised' deviant.

A second difference between the societies was a lack of an upper class in the United States to restrain some of the excesses of the middle classes. For example, when the British Obscene Publications Act was passed in 1857 it was only the working-class literature which was to be suppressed. The upper class managed to insert a clause excluding works of 'literary merit' from the statute. Furthermore there were no laws prohibiting alcohol or pre-marital sex of the kind that existed in the United States. This evidence, therefore, shows the major differences between the two countries, and the effects of these on the debate will be considered.

Abortion Laws

During the nineteenth century most countries of Europe tightened up their provision of abortion. The Belgian law was introduced along with the French in 1810, the German law based on the Prussian Penal Code of 1851 was adopted by the German Reich in 1871 (Kommers, 1977), Portugal also made abortion illegal in 1854 and Holland in 1886 (amended in 1911). One slight legal movement in the other direction was in Sweden. In the seventeenth century abortion had been made punishable by death but an 1864 law reduced the sentence to six years (Linner, 1968).

At the beginning of the nineteenth century all countries with British common law allowed abortion at least until quickening (about four months' gestation) and possibly throughout pregnancy (Means, 1971). The British law was changed in 1803 and there were subsequent alterations until the Offences Against the Person Act, Sections 58 and 59 in 1861. The abortion provisions were:

Section 58:

> Every woman being with child, who with intent to procure her own miscarriage shall unlawfully administer to herself any poison or other noxious thing . . . and whosoever, with intent to procure the miscarriage of any woman whether she be or be not with child shall unlawfully administer to her or cause to be taken by her any poison or other noxious thing . . . with the like intent shall be guilty of felony, and being convicted thereof shall be liable . . . to be kept in penal servitude for life.

Sections 59:

> . . . of the same Act, whosoever shall unlawfully supply or procure any poison or other noxious thing . . . knowing that the same is intended to be unlawfully used or employed with intent to procure the miscarriage of any woman, whether she be or be not with child, shall be guilty of a misdemeanour, and being convicted thereof shall be liable to be kept in penal servitude for the term of three years.

The law therefore made attempts at abortion illegal even if the woman were not pregnant. The fact that it specified that abortion was illegal only if the action were taken 'unlawfully' implies that legal abortion could take place in certain circumstances, a point which was to become relevant to New Zealand and Australian law in later years. The 1861 Act passed through with no controversy and it is not surprising, for the establishment views during the large part of the nineteenth century were that even birth control was suspect, if not illegal. The British 1861 Act was subsequently introduced into the laws of the Empire.

In the United States restrictions on abortion were introduced state by state. The first law in Connecticut was passed in 1821 and codified restrictions on a woman 'quick with child'. Mohr (1978) suggests that abortion in the early part of pregnancy lasted a half century longer than it did in Britain. There is some disagreement between Mohr and Cyril Means as to the reasons for abortion being made illegal. Means's explanation was in terms of maternal health and he argued that in the early part of the nineteenth century abortion was a dangerous operation. He gave figures to suggest that the deathrate from sepsis from abortional surgery, even when performed in hospital, was over 30 per cent in 1828 when New York's first abortion law was passed (Means, 1971, p. 385). Further, he argued, this was much higher than the maternal mortality rate of below 3 per cent and this danger of the operation was the key factor behind legal restrictions. He also pointed out that at the time the New York legislature passed their 1828 Act they proposed to restrict any surgical procedure which might endanger life such as amputation of a limb 'unless it appears that the same was necessary for the preservation of life'. Although this section was not passed, Means stated that it showed the concern at the time with the dangerous nature of all operations.

Mohr documented the extent of abortion in the USA and the campaign of physicians to make abortions illegal. He alleged that the main propelling force behind their pressure was a desire to professionalise medicine. He said that the 'anti abortion crusade was nearly perfect' as a method of establishing the position of the regular physician. By raising its dangers and abuses they could encourage the state to employ sanctions against their competitors (Mohr, 1978, p. 164). In fact these two explanations are complementary and both factors could well be of importance. However, it is inconceivable that anti-abortion laws could not have been introduced for, as we shall see, in the 1870s even contraceptive information was proscribed.

Illegal Abortion

The common practice of abortion in nineteenth-century USA is well known (Mohr, 1978). It is likely that the campaign against it by the *New York Times* in 1870 was inspired by the British campaign two years earlier. In any event abortions continued,

Taussig (1910) suggesting that there were 80,000 abortions each year in New York and 6,000–10,000 in Chicago.

In Britain a common drug for the use of abortion in the early nineteenth century was savin oil of juniper. In fact the first prosecution under the 1803 Act was in 1811 when a man was accused of administering savin to his girlfriend. He argued that he had only given the drug for amusement and was acquitted (Potts, Diggory and Peel, 1977; Parry, 1932). There is some dispute about the frequency of abortion. In a lecture in 1837 Professor Thomson said that medicines taken to produce abortion sometimes worked. However he felt the incidence was rare. He commented that often unmarried women felt their disgrace so much that spontaneous abortion occurred (*Lancet*, 28 January). However, seven years later a doctor wrote to the *Provincial Medical and Surgical Journal* (8 May 1844) saying that he had attended three unmarried females who had used 'herbs' to abort and commented, 'These are not solitary cases, but I believe, they are constantly occurring and rather on the increase than otherwise'. By the middle of the century it seems that abortionists had become established. An editorial in the *Lancet* (30 July, 1853, p. 101) reported that abortion was common and that 'handbills addressed to female domestics are dropped down the kitchen areas, conveying in ambiguous but unmistakable terms, the information that pregnancy may be cut short'.

The British medical profession organised several campaigns against abortion in the period up to the First World War. From 8 February to 4 March 1868 the *British Medical Journal* campaigned against 'baby farming' which included abortion, infanticide and adoption. A female abortionist told the investigating doctor that she had been in the business for twenty-six years and that some of the patients came back six or seven times. The *British Medical Journal* series stressed that their investigators had visited the better class of establishments. In an editorial (29 February 1868) the *BMJ* drew out the implications of its findings and complained that the middle-class women were setting a bad example: 'Shall we ever be able to teach our kitchen maids that the murder of a foetus is a crime, while they know that their young mistresses can be directed by their milliners to places of agreeable retirement, with pianos, muslin blinds and jocular attendants where such a transaction is a twenty six year old tradition (p. 197).

A second campaign in the *Lancet* between 10 December 1898

and 1 April 1899 attacked abortifacient pills. It pointed to an important blackmail case that was in progress. Three brothers, aptly called Chrimes, had been advertising abortifacient pills. In the space of two years 12,000 women had replied. The brothers wrote to them under the guise of Charles J. Mitchell, a public official, saying that he was in possession of evidence that the recipient had committed the awful crime of preventing the birth of a child and stating that arrest would follow unless two guineas costs were received. The blackmail was discovered and the prosecution drew attention to the fact that the police intercepted £800 in a few days (*Lancet*, 31 December 1898, p. 1,807). The brothers were sentenced to long periods of imprisonment. The *Lancet* felt the case would have stopped the trade, but on 25 February 1899 it reported that it had over 100 newspapers before it 'in which occur the advertisements of persons of whose pretensions to procure abortion there can be no doubt'. It began an aggressive campaign of naming the offending newspapers and on 11 March, 101 were reported. Subsequent issues contained nearly 100 more.

A third campaign was against lead pills (diachylon). A woman had died of lead poisoning in 1893 (Parry, 1932, p. 36) and the issue was brought to prominence by Professor Arthur Hall in the *BMJ* (18 March 1905) and in an article with Ransom the following year (24 February 1906). The pills produced abortion but could also cause blindness and death. Women of childbearing age in some areas were routinely examined to discover if they had a blue line on their gums which was symptomatic of lead poisoning. An editorial in the *BMJ* (24 February 1906) called for legislation, but this campaign was unsuccessful and a piece of research completed in 1911 (Elderton, 1914) showed abortifacient pills to be common. Her research may have been the basis of an estimate in *The Malthusian* (14 May 1914) that 100,000 working women took abortifacient pills each year.

In France, Tardieau claimed in 1868 that abortion had 'increased into a veritable industry' and by the end of the century several observers noted the rise in hospital admissions for abortion (Potts *et al.*, 1977, p. 161). In 1907 a French physician, M. Tissier, stated that magistrates took a light view of abortion and that upper-class women had no shame in stating they had had one (*Lancet*, 4 May). In the same report Dr Blondel talked of 'sundry English women, both married and unmarried, who had crossed the channel simply to have an abortion brought on' (p. 1,257). He refused them, but by the period before the First World War it is clear that many women were successful. Mrs Burgwin visited France around 1913 and told the Birth-rate Commission (1917, p. 220) that, over and over again, doctors had told her that rich English women went to Paris for abortions. One had said: 'We have got 50,000 criminal abortions taking place in Paris in a year and we find that numerous English women resort to that city to be relieved of their pregnancy'. This trade continued into the 1930s (Ellis, 1933). There is also evidence of abortion in Italy before the First World War and in a large trial in 1904 eight licensed midwives were convicted of what the *BMJ* called 'abortion mongering' (28 May 1904).

Origins of the Debate about Birth Control

This can be traced back to the aftermath of the French Revolution and the debate which led Thomas Malthus to write his *Essay on the Principle of Population* (1798). Godwin in his *Enquiry Concerning Political Justice* (1793) had argued that the cause of injustice was human institutions which needed to be changed by the removal of the inequalities in society. Malthus attacked this view, contending that if Godwin's kind of utopia came into existence there would be such a massive population increase that the standard of living would take a precipitous fall. This argument appealed to the upper classes who were terrified that the French Revolution would be repeated in Britain and were looking for a justification of the existing order. Marx in his *Capital* rightly talked of the theory as being 'greeted with jubilation by the English Oligarchy' (1976, Vol. 1, p. 766). The solution Malthus proposed for the population increase was the delay of marriage. He believed that prudential restraint, by narrowing the supply of labour, would raise its price. People, by spending a few years working before marriage, would be able to save enough money to enter it without fear of the consequences. He argued that without controls food production only increased in arithmetic proportion, but that evidence from the United States showed that population increased by geometric proportions. He did not intend to be an apologist for poverty but was often interpreted in this way (Himes, 1930).

The conflict between the Malthusians and the socialists is still relevant today. A solution to the problem was provided by the radical Francis Place in 1822 with his *Principles of Population*. He proposed that society should both improve the material wealth of the worker and introduce contraception (Place, 1930). He argued that Malthus's opposition to contraception on the grounds that it would lead to unchastity was not very relevant to the working class, for they had little chastity either before or after marriage. He proposed that the most effective method of diminishing 'promiscuous intercourse' was young marriages. (This argument is one that the neo-Malthusians would take up in a militant fashion in the latter part of the century.) In the summer of 1823 Place began his public propaganda. He published three pamphlets on contraception and had them distributed to the working classes through radical sources. It seems that it was Place who persuaded John Stuart Mill to write and distribute literature in favour of birth control – for which he spent a few days in prison. Place wrote of his success: 'I have received a multitude of thanks from persons who have been saved from poverty and misery or whose circumstances have been improved by the practice recommended' (Place, 1930, p. 311).

Place was also influential in the early birth control agitation in the United States. He convinced the editor of the *Republican*, Carlile, to support it. Carlile advocated contraception in his journal and published a pamphlet 'Every Woman's Book' (1926). Rober Dale Owen published this at New Harmony, Indiana, and became the first neo-Malthusian in the United States (Himes, 1930). After a brief battle with a Christian group Owen published a tract entitled 'Moral Physiology' which was the first booklet on birth control printed in the United States. In its first five years it had a circulation of 20,000–25,000 copies. Owen was also important because he encouraged Dr Charles Knowlton who in 1832 published, at first anonymously, a pamphlet called the 'Fruits of Philosophy'. This was republished in England a year or two later and remained in circulation on a limited scale until the Bradlaugh and Besant trial of 1877.

Most observers have suggested that in Britain from the 1830s until 1877 there was little discussion of birth control. Although this view has been challenged by McLaren (1978), the Royal Commission on Population in 1949 reported that birth control had had little influence on the birthrate.

The British Debate

We have seen that the early history of birth control was closely linked in Britain and the United States. However, in the latter part of the century experiences diverged greatly as the British debate was transformed by the Bradlaugh/Besant trial.

Henry Cook, a Bristol bookseller, had been sentenced to two years' hard labour for issuing the 'Fruits of Philosophy' inter-leaved, it was alleged, with obscene pictures. Charles Bradlaugh and Annie Besant decided to challenge the law and republished Knowlton's pamphlet in order to precipitate a test case. They were duly charged and the trial began on 18 June 1876 (Banks, 1954). The Solicitor General argued that the real aim of the book was 'to suggest to people that they might enjoy the pleasures of sexual intercourse with or without marriage and yet avoid offspring' (*The Times*, 19 June 1876). Later in the trial he set out the criteria on which to judge the book: 'The proper test of it is this – that it is a book which no decent man would dare to place into the hands of a decent woman'.

The defendants conducted themselves admirably and used a whole battery of arguments to support their case. Their main thrust was, however, the neo-Malthusian position that the population was being restrained by the enormous mortality amongst the poor. They pointed to the fact that many of the children were unwanted and Annie Besant stressed the high amount of infanticide. However, the Lord Chief Justice in his summing up clearly stated his concern that birth control would lead to a breakdown in the social order. 'Though these means are recommended to those who are married, they may equally be used by those who are unmarried, and that if at present unlawful intercourse is restrained by the apprehension of its natural result – in the birth of offspring – the removal of that restraint may remove one of the restraints on vice and one of the safeguards on morality.' One of the witnesses was Dr Drysdale whom Annie Besant questioned about abortion. He stated that it was common among both rich and poor women, and then agreed with her comment that it was better for health if people used contraception.

The defendants were found guilty, although the foreman of the jury absolved them of any corrupt motives in publishing the book. They were sentenced to six months' imprisonment and fined £200, but were freed on appeal. The trial was a watershed in birth control history. The publicity surrounding the trial and the subsequent appeal brought contraception to the forefront of public discussion. Sales of Knowlton's pamphlet grew from about 1,000 a year before the trial to 125,000 copies between March and June 1877 (*The Malthusian*, February 1914). Branches of the Malthusian League were set up in many towns and *The Malthusian* newspaper was formed, its main slogan being 'A crusade against poverty'. The birthrate began to fall rapidly and it became rare for people to be prosecuted for disseminating information. *The Malthusian*, supported by an array of medical men and women, gave information on a continuous basis with no trouble from the authorities.

During the period 1877–1915 the neo-Malthusians were the only significant group working to propagate birth control knowledge. Their ideas spread to France, where there was a neo-Malthusian magazine and to Holland (Sutherland, 1922; Van Praag, 1977). In 1878 a Dutch clinic began giving birth control information, the first time this had happened, and in 1881 the Dutch Neo-Malthusian Federation was founded (Van Praag, 1977, p. 252). The Malthusians believed that with the universal knowledge of contraception people would have just as many children as they could afford, and poverty would disappear. This standpoint is different from that taken by Place, and subsequent history has shown that people in poverty have very little control over their lives and in general it is only when poverty is diminished that people restrict their family size by contraceptive measures.

Neo-Malthusians and Abortion

Although the Malthusians were radical on contraception, in the period up until 1915 they were totally opposed to abortion. There were a number of reasons for this, the most important being the belief that abortion was dangerous. In this respect the major piece of research quoted during the period was that of Tardieu. In May 1881 *The Malthusian* carried an article on 'an excellent pamphlet on the great danger to human life of criminal abortion'. It commented that the pamphlet pointed out that 'Dr. Tardieu, of Paris, had shown that 60 poor women had lost their lives out of 116 cases, when criminal abortion had been made use of, either from loss of blood or from inflamation'. This research was widely quoted even after the First World War and despite the fact that on

19 April 1902 the *Lancet* criticised it. Brouardel (1901) reported a series of seventy-two abortions without a death, and later observers such as Parry (1932, p. 88), talked of Tardieu having had an exceptional series. However, in the intervening period it was often believed that abortion was very dangerous and so was opposed for this reason.

Secondly, the Malthusians maintained that abortion resulted in the removal of potential life. When arguing this point of view a Mr Carpenter, lecturing to men only, contrasted contraception to abortion, for there 'the only life destroyed was that of the spermatozoa themselves tnd these were constantly being destroyed anyway' (*The Malthusian*, March 1887). The third reason for opposing abortion was a political one. The Malthusians tried to distinguish abortion from contraception in order to facilitate the wider acceptance of their arguments. In the *Law of Population* Annie Besant pointed out that Dr Fleetwood Churchill had legally given many methods of inducing premature labour and inducing abortion. She continued, 'surely the prevention of conception is far better than the procuring of abortion' (Besant, 1877, p. 36). This kind of argument, that contraception was a substitute for abortion, was one that was continuously used in the following years and is still relevant.

Opposition to Fertility Control in Britain

When the Malthusians started their propaganda they faced almost total opposition from the major bodies, despite the fact that the individual members of these organisations may well have been using various techniques in their private lives. This meant that information did not get to the poorer groups and resulted in a differential birthrate, which in turn worried many people as being anti-genetic. The Malthusians argued that it was just a temporary situation and that once the information had been adopted by the middle classes it would eventually percolate through to the working classes.

Medical Profession and Birth Control   The official attitude of the doctors in the 1860s and 1870s was totally opposed to control of births. The *British Medical Journal* (20 March 1868) reported that Dr Ewing Whittle had read a paper on infanticide and abortion to the Liverpool Medical Institution. In this he attacked a statement of the London Dialectical Society, which suggested that the medical profession should devise a scheme to limit the number of births, by quoting from the Bible passages which confirmed that large families were a special blessing from heaven. It was unanimously agreed that the profession should show its disapprobation of the subject. This argument in favour of large families was one that was stressed many times in the next sixty or so years. In 1871 (30 September) the *Lancet* called birth control 'a form of bestiality'.

In the 1890s the opposition of the medical profession began to weaken somewhat and its members began to use it in their private lives. However as late as 1905 the *Lancet* (21 October) quoted with approval Professor Simpson who had spoken against the decline of the birthrate and had praised the Jews for fulfilling the commandment 'Be fruitful, and multiply and replenish the earth'. In 1910 the *BMJ* attacked the view that there was some connection between mental disturbance and contraception, stating that if that was the case 'the proof has yet to be furnished'. The movement towards liberalisation continued through the early part of the twentieth century, so that by February 1914 *The Malthusian* could claim that medical opposition to contraception had collapsed and that the growth in the number of its medical vice-presidents was evidence that definite support had begun.

Medical Profession and Abortion The medical profession in the late nineteenth century was still firm in its opposition to abortion, but often took a more sympathetic view to the plight of the woman than might have been expected. For example, the *Lancet* in 1896 (8 August) said that while illegal abortion was wrong, it was unfair that women should have to shoulder the blame:

We believe we are right in saying that the procuring of abortion otherwise than for reasons which can be medically justified is banned by the civil and ecclesiastical law of every civilised country, and as constructive murder it is right it should be so. But the whole question teems with difficulty. It certainly appears unjust, and very possibly is actually so, that a woman who driven and harassed by shame and fear resorts to the questionable remedy of abortion should be liable to severe punishment, while the man who is equally responsible for the child goes free.

The profession was also against giving evidence to the police about abortions. In 1896 Lord Brampton told a grand jury: 'I doubt very much whether a doctor called in to assist a woman, not in procuring an abortion, for that in itself is a crime, but for the purpose of attending her and giving her medical advice, could be justified in reporting the facts to the Public Prosecutor. Such action would be a monstrous cruelty' (*Lancet*, 5 February 1916). The issue was raised again in 1914 when Mr Justice Avory had to deal with a situation where three successive doctors had attended a woman who had received an illegal operation but had not given information to the police. There were, therefore, no grounds for conviction (*Lancet*, 5 February 1916). Following this, on 27 January 1915, the Council of the British Medical Association passed a resolution: 'That the Council is of opinion that a medical practitioner should not under any circumstances disclose voluntarily, without the patient's consent, information which he has obtained from that patient in the exercise of his professional duties' (*Lancet*, 5 February 1916). Thus the doctors sometimes took a view on abortion much less vindictive than might have been the case. In fact in some ways there seems to have been a degree of empathy with the woman who often found herself in difficult circumstances.

Religious Opposition   The Church of England was initially opposed to birth control but at first does not seem to have used its institutional power to oppose its development. Some individual clergymen fought the Malthusians, however, and John Rothwell reported on particular debate:

I need hardly say that the question of limiting the population is one upon which clergymen hold opposing views. A rector, for example, favoured me with his opinion that it was the duty of a married couple to have children, even though they lived upon a small island which could only support two persons. My humble suggestion that, if they did so, either the parents must be starved outright or the whole family must be half starved, was met by the almost incredible rejoinder that, for aught I knew, they might discover how, out of the very stones of the island, to make bread. (*The Malthusian*, January 1884)

However, Rothwell recorded that another vicar had written to him saying that people should not have more children than was consistent with their circumstances and had requested birth control information.

Some institutional opposition to contraception came in May 1888. *The Malthusian* reported the Primate of all England as referring to the great evils of drunkenness and early marriage in Bethnal Green and saying, 'Self restraint was that which Christian men and women of Great Britain must bring to bear on their fellows'. When the Malthusians cheekily invited various bishops to attend their Annual General Meeting the Archbishop of Canterbury declined, as did the Bishop of Manchester who retorted, 'I fear that I am not on all points in harmony with your society' (*The Malthusian*, June 1888). However, by no means all clergymen were opposed. A youthful Reverend Dawson came out publicly in their favour and in response to his support and that of certain others, *The Malthusian* announced a 'thaw' in Church opposition and that the younger churchmen were increasingly in favour of contraception (April 1888). This optimism was, however, somewhat premature, and in 1908 the Lambeth Conference passed the resolution that: 'The Conference regards with alarm the growing practice of the artificial restriction of the family, and earnestly calls upon all Christian people to discountenance the use of all artificial means of restriction as demoralising to character and hostile to national welfare' (*The Times*, 8 August 1908). In later parts the resolution praised those medical men who had 'borne courageous testimony against the injurous practices spoken of'. This resolution coming from the bishops probably did not represent the views of the younger clergy. However, it seems that for the next six years or so the conservatives were in control and the document prepared for the Birth-Rate Commission (1917) put forward a very restricted ideal of sexuality. It suggested that in all marriages the man (sic) should go for certain periods without sexual intercourse, that for some fertile people 'a considerable proportion of married life may have to be lived in abstinence', and for others abstinence may even be permanent. 'Christian Chastity,' the document continued, 'means the power to bear all this without injury to the wife or sinful indulgence with others' and it condemned those who 'allow indulgence without fear or restraint' (Birth-Rate Commission, 1917, p. 385).

Thus in its evidence before the Commission the Church was putting forward a viewpoint very similar to the traditional

Catholic position. However, there was some fragmentation in the ranks. The Dean of St Paul emphasised the need for control of population, other ministers called for limitation of births amongst the poor and the Church newspapers began to take a more liberal line. In July 1914 *The Malthusian* (again) saw in the changes signs that the Church was coming round to its point of view and argued, 'its conversion will mark the final step in the acceptance of our doctrines'. The enthusiasm was still a little premature, but from this time onwards there were always a number of prominent clerics who were willing to take a liberal line on contraception.

There was no significant opposition from other religious groups. Catholic opposition was not important until after the First World War and the free churches took a liberal line. On 15 June 1893 the *Christian World*, for example, one of the influential voices of the nonconformist press, said in a leading article: 'There was a time when any idea of voluntary limitation was regarded by pious people as interfering with Providence. We are beyond that now and have become capable of realising that Providence works through the common sense of individual brains.' This is the earliest known support of birth control from a respected conventional religious source. Later, at the Birth-Rate Commission, W. F. Lofthouse distinguished the Wesleyan Methodist attitude from that of the Catholic Church and had an altercation with its representative Monsignor Brown. Lofthouse argued in his prepared evidence that the Catholic Church's official theology misunderstood the New Testament standpoint and showed mistaken asceticism. He stated that he could see no grounds for condemning contraceptives as immoral and that they were only wrong if they were unsafe or dangerous. In the early days, therefore, the major religious opposition came from the Church of England, but even that was weakening somewhat by the time of the First World War.

Opposition from the Socialists   The opposition of the socialists to the Malthusians in particular and birth control in general was crucial in preventing the spread of contraception to the working classes. In a letter published in 1837 Place complained that 'some who really are ardent friends of the working people, occupy themselves in persuading people to disregard me' (Place, 1930, p. 303). It was also the radicals who opposed Robert Dale Owen's work in the United States. Himes reports (1930, p. 540) that Skidmore, a land reformer and agrarian egalitarian, wrote a pamphlet entitled 'Moral Physiology Exposed and Refuted' in which he stressed the 'Iron Law of Wages' and that reduction of the size of the family would lessen the subsistence necessary to maintain workers. It would cause wages not only to fall, but to fall more rapidly than the decrease in needs, so that after the reduction in the size of labourers' families they would be less well off than before. Owen countered by arguing that the reasoning was specious and could be applied against any economy the workers might employ to eke out their wages. This debate was quite acrimonious and Skidmore's pamphlet contained a great deal of personal abuse. Van Praag (1977, p. 252) found similar opposition from socialists in Holland. Both Malthusians and socialists were committed to women's equality, both groups were alienated from the established religious groups and, most important, they both wanted radical changes in society. However, they disagreed in their analysis of the causes of the problems and therefore in the kind of action necessary to rectify the situation.

In *Capital* Marx called Malthus's work a 'shameless plagiarism' (Marx, 1976, p. 639) and in general socialists felt that the first priority was to promote a revolution, nationalise land and create a more equitable distribution of resources. This would lead to the product being transferred from unnecessary and wasteful goods towards fulfilling real needs. Socialists pointed out that the worker only received a small part of the wealth created and that the rest went to the owners of the means of production, most of whom had inherited their wealth. In the face of these necessary changes they believed that the Malthusians, by stressing contraception for the poor, were diverting attention from the real issues. They were seeking to blame the poor for having too many children when it was necessary to have a redistribution of the nation's wealth so that their children could be fed. The Malthusians, however, opposed the idea that a revolution was necessary. They felt that contraception should first of all be taught to the middle classes who would restrict the size of their families and then teach the techniques to the working classes.

The issue came to the fore with the publication of George Sims's pamphlet 'The Bitter Cry of Outcast London' in October 1883, which raised a great deal of interest in the condition of the working classes. In its December issue *The Malthusian* published the main details of the report and included a letter Sims had written in the

Daily News (14 November 1883). It alleged that the terrible condition of the poor was due to low wages and over-population and stated that those who said that drink was the cause of poverty were making a mistake, 'For, though it is a curse, it is also true to say that poverty is the cause of drink'. Sims argued that it was poverty which forced young girls, often as young as 11 or 12 years old, into prostitution, and which made young boys into thieves. He then set out to give his solution: 'If we are challenged to find a remedy, we have to go into a question which thousands of excellent people refuse altogether to discuss. The deserving poor could all be better housed now without a single brick being laid or a single Act of Parliament passed if they had fewer children.' Sims went on to suggest a gradualist approach and proposed that the slums should be weeded out by degrees. At first the most decent among the workers should be encouraged and then reformers should

> get down the lower strata step by step. Leave the poor wretches who are impossible in any but rookeries a rookery or two to finish their careers in. Encourage everything that will keep their rents down, and encourage everything that will give labour a better return. If the process of elimination is gradual, we shall in time improve the condition of all who are not beyond help. As for the rest, they will solve the riddle in time for themselves by dying off, and leaving the ground free for the well paid, well educated, healthy labourer, with two little children and a contented mind, who is the dream of the modern social reformer.

This solution was mainly Malthusian in its approach. But Sims clearly did not ignore the role of poor wages and high rents which kept the workers in poverty.

The debate between Malthusianism and socialism was a continuous topic in their respective papers. *The Malthusian* on at least two occasions (March 1884 and January 1887) even published poems setting out their differences such as:

> We neither oppose those who aim for the land
> Nor, when commonly civil the socialist band
> Their plans may be better than our plans indeed
> But ours is essential until they succeed.

This antipathy between the socialists and the Malthusians continued over the years, but one key factor leading to its diminished importance was the development of Fabian Socialism with its emphasis on gradual change.

In 1913 the Malthusians began sending a van with rose-coloured flags and lanterns into the East End of London, and in September they produced a leaflet describing the simplest methods of birth control. C. V. Drysdale described the work in *The Malthusian* (April 1914) and pointed out that despite some heckling the opposition from the socialists was much less than it had been in the early days of the campaign. In 1915 Stella Browne argued that it was possible to combine birth control and social reform, and in May 1917 *The Malthusian* published a moderately-worded defence of socialism by F. A. Wilmer in which he suggested that socialism and Malthusianism were mutually complementary. However, a crisis arose because in the same issue Drysdale set out a detailed attack on Wilmer's article in particular and socialism in general. He tabulated the differences between the philosophies in two columns and this article was something of a watershed. In the face of the changed climate of opinion it seemed singularly inappropriate and aroused a great deal of opposition. H. G. Wells, possibly the Malthusians' most eminent supporter, was absolutely furious. He said he did not want to resign from the organisation because people would say he had been converted away from neo-Malthusianism, but 'On the other hand, I cannot lend my name to back preposterous attacks on socialism. If I am not to withdraw immediately from association with the Malthusian Society, then you must permit me to say, without any ambiguous civility, not merely that I disagree with the opinion of Doctor Drysdale or anything mild of that sort, but that I think the article in your issue of May 15th utterly silly' (*The Malthusian*, June 1917).

Stella Browne defended Drysdale from this attack but from this and other incidents it was becoming clear that another organisation was needed to promote the birth control campaign. In June 1916 *The Malthusian* had announced that it had received many letters suggesting it should give up its economic doctrine, and proposed that the time was ripe for an organisation to promote contraceptives simply on humanitarian grounds. In April 1918 Janet Chance's husband Clinton suggested in *The Malthusian* that those who differed from Malthusian principles should 'so soon as the war is over definitely embark on the formation of a Birth

Control League, whose chief function shall be the spread of the knowledge of the present methods of birth control'. Chance already knew that Drysdale welcomed this, so in post-war years the way was open for a new approach to the spreading of knowledge in Britain. As far as socialists were concerned the ideological solution was that combination proposed by Place nearly a hundred years previously.

The Debate in the United States

While the thrust of the British change in the period 1870–1910 was towards greater liberalisation in terms of contraceptive use, in the United States there was a popular movement against sexuality led by Anthony Comstock. Although the British too had staunch opponents of vice, there were various differences in the social conditions between the two countries that were relevant to the changes. The fact that the puritanism was more solidly based in the USA than in Britain has already been discussed. Also important was the lack of a neo-Malthusian movement. The United States did not form the kind of social movement that had such a powerful influence in Britain and Holland, for it has already been shown that the earliest pressure for contraception originated from the debate on Malthusian ideas, and in the United States, with such a low population density, fears about over-population were less pressing.

There was practice of contraception in New England as early as 1867 (Kennedy, 1970, p. 45). But it was not advocated on Malthusian grounds, and although generally supporting birth control, Thomas Pope, for instance (1888, p. 522), commented that 'Malthus, perhaps, forgot when he wrote that almost one half of the world was unpopulated'. This argument would be supported by others. Pomeroy (1888) attacked Malthus because in practice it was the most intelligent who did not have children and so the acceptance of his views would lead to a lowering of the quality of the race. This argument was also used in Britain, of course, but it had particular force in the United States because the high rates of immigration raised fears that the newcomers would become a disproportionately large part of the society.

However, a crucial factor during the period was the relative strength of the purity campaigners in the United States and the fact that they had no effective opposition. In Britain the upper classes were willing to oppose the worst excesses of the moral entrepreneurs. Winston Churchill (1972), for example, told how in 1894 he had opposed the purity campaign of Mrs Ormiston Chant. He also reported that the popular press had attacked some of the overt manifestations of prudery. In contrast the American purity campaigners were in status terms from the highest reaches of their society and had strong support from the press. The leading campaigner in the United States was Anthony Comstock and his personality dominated the debate from the 1870s to 1915. When he began to be active, the social conditions were ripe for a purity campaign. The growth in number of abortions had led to a great deal of concern in the *New York Times*. In 1872, with financial help from Young Men's Christian Association (YMCA) members, he began to attack virtually all aspects of sexuality, not distinguishing between pornography, abortion or birth control.

One tactic he used was copied from *New York Times* reporters and their method of gaining information about abortion by pretending to seek one for a friend. In 1872, in an important case, he arranged for a police captain to knock on the door of an abortionist and to say that a previous patient was dangerously ill. They then raided the premises to find 'a young girl in a semi nude condition lying on a sofa'. She told the police she was six weeks' pregnant and had gone there for an abortion and Comstock prosecuted the doctor involved (*New York Times*, 31 August 1872). Comstock was concerned that the law was not strong enough and he agitated for a Federal statute. This was introduced in Congress by C. L. Merrian on 1 March 1873 in a speech which praised Comstock. He described how in a relatively short time Comstock had seized and destroyed 182,000 obscene pictures, more than five tons of obscene books and over 30,000 obscene rubber articles (condoms). He also announced that he had arrested over fifty dealers and six more were dead.

Comstock, flush from these successes, became America's primary moral entrepreneur, and a law was passed making the spread of birth control and abortion knowledge through the post illegal. This was a Federal statute and so applied in all the states. It gave Comstock the legal backing he needed to suppress literature and to prevent advertisements for appliances. He therefore set about preparing for a great campaign. At the first Annual Meeting of the Society for the Suppression of Vice (1874), Comstock wrote:

'The Society which has for some months past been in contemplation, is now organised and ready for aggressive action'. It had the backing of many businessmen and Comstock was the major driving force. It was not until Comstock changed the focus of his attack from pornography to birth control that he met any real opposition. The middle classes had used it for some years. The *Medical and Surgical Reporter* in 1888 carried a whole series of articles, in one of which D. E. Matteson described four procedures: the syringe with astringent, withdrawal, condoms, and finally recommended a silk sponge $1\frac{1}{2}''$ in diameter with a thread attached. Comstock did not take any action, despite the fact that this discussion was illegal. However, as the amount of overt pornography declined, he began to take a much greater interest in the activities of the birth controllers, which brought him into conflict with totally different groups. Now he was effectively attacking a segment of the middle class – and they were more willing to fight back.

Origins of the Birth Control Movement

The major early pioneer of birth control in the United States was William Robinson. He began his campaign in 1903 and in 1907 made his opposition to Comstock's activities quite clear in an article in the journal he edited: 'Unfortunately the man who is at the head of the vice crusaders is a stupid ignoramus utterly devoid of sense and judgement'. If Comstock had just attacked obscene pictures, he continued, there would be no reason for opposition, but 'He has started to prosecute retail druggists and supply houses who sell, and manufacturers who produce a certain kind of rubber or fishskin article' (*Medico-Pharmaceutical Critic and Guide*, February 1907, p. 2). This comment could have warned Comstock of the problems he would meet. He was facing a new opposition. Naturally he did not like the *Critic and Guide* but he could do nothing about it, especially as Robinson was careful not to print information about contraceptive methods.

Robinson differed greatly from the Malthusians in his general views and argument that birth control and social reform should be developed together. He also disagreed with competition and stressed that the rich usually did not become so by hard work but rather by inheritance or by unsavoury means. Thus in some ways he was more radical than the Malthusians. On other issues, however, he was rather reactionary – for example, he did not have the Malthusians' belief in female equality and would often make comments detrimental to women. He also accepted some of the common prejudices against excessive masturbation which he treated by placing nitric acid on the penis to create a sore and make an erection painful (*Critic and Guide*, 1906, p. 195). But despite his foibles Robinson was an important activist for over thirty years until his death in 1936.

On the question of abortion Robinson took a pragmatic approach. In a paper he read before the Eastern Medical Society in 1911 he said that it was much better to teach contraception, but that as long as illegitimacy was viewed as being such a matter for shame there would be a great demand for abortion (1933, p. 26). Furthermore, he stated that if the operation were not performed by a professional it would be carried out by a non-medical person and so in certain circumstances it was justifiable. But although he took this view, he publicly claimed he had never carried out an abortion and he did not regard it as the pressing issue. One of his major criticisms was that the law treated abortion and contraception as if they were the same thing. In 1916 he called for birth control to be separated from both abortion and pornography in the statute (he felt it was not politically possible to legalise it) and in his writings he continually attacked those who treated the different issues together (*Critic and Guide*, 1916, p. 125).

Thus Robinson was responsible for one of the major strands of the birth control movement. However, there was an alternative source of pressure which, in contrast to Britain, came from the socialist movement and was rooted in the subculture largely located around Greenwich Village. It was the socialists and anarchists who questioned the traditional attitudes. Emma Goldman, one of the most prominent members, had been introduced to birth control ideas when she was taken to a meeting of the French Malthusians in 1900. She became one of the major early proponents and was also in contact with Margaret Sanger who became the largest single influence in the United States. Sanger was a socialist and in the early years of her marriage she and her husband spent a great deal of their time in Greenwich Village listening to ideas of revolution, feminism and sexual radicalism.

In 1914 Sanger began publishing a magazine called *Woman Rebel* which said it would stimulate working women and encourage them to break the bonds imposed by machines, bourgeois morality and wage slavery. The magazine also announced that it would advocate the prevention of conception and would give the knowledge in the columns of the paper (Kennedy, 1970, p. 25). The *Woman Rebel* was a wildly radical magazine but did not carry much information about contraception. Margaret Sanger had decided that she would give out this information in a small pamphlet called *Family Limitation* (1915) of which she had 100,000 copies printed. With this she intended to challenge the Comstock law. However, a complication arose when she was charged by Comstock for the publication of *Woman Rebel.* She therefore decided to leave the country and go to England – a move which proved to be an important part of her intellectual and political development. She met Havelock Ellis and he directed her reading at the British Museum. The English birth controllers gave her emotional support, helped her educationally and suggested how she could be politically effective. They persuaded her to concentrate on just one issue and to leave the denunciations of capitalism, marriage and the churches to others (Kennedy, 1970, p. 30). Bessie Drysdale gave her advice on clothes, suggesting that the more radical a person's ideas, the more conservatively she must dress. She accepted this argument. Arrangements were also made for her to visit the state-assisted birth control clinic in Holland. So by 1915 when she returned to the United States she had a much clearer idea of what she was going to attempt to do. She accepted many arguments of the English Malthusians but an important difference was their emphasis on economic factors. Sanger thought that this approach on the subject was too narrow and she simply wanted people to have greater freedom to decide the number of children they wanted. This decision prevented any conflict with the socialists, and thus it was the radical groups who distributed *Family Limitation* and furthermore provided a network through which other information could be distributed.

Thus it came about that in contrast with the British situation, the early days of the American birth control movement were closely linked to the socialists. However, by the end of the First World War the United States was similar to Britain in having a birth control movement not tied to other general ideologies which would restrict the flow of information. As in Britain, there was no movement for abortion reform. Indeed, the only country known to have an active movement before the First World War was

Germany where the women's movement was calling for the 'Right to Choose' from 1897 onwards (Ellis, 1928).

3
Debate Between the Wars

In the 1920s commentators on both sides of the Atlantic became increasingly concerned with the change in sexual morality. Some United States observers dated increased freedom of sexual behaviour even to before the war. However, it was during the 1920s that the new attitudes became widely discussed. One focal point was the behaviour of young people, with the growth of youth culture and a distinctive style of dress. In the United States the young women had become 'flappers', a term coined in England and used to describe those who were assertive, independent, who had casual courtships and possibly granted 'permissive favours' to young men.

In Britain too there was a good deal of discussion about the new freedom of the young. Bertrand Russell (1929) predictably welcomed it, as did other radicals. In an attempt to keep up with the times *The Malthusian* changed its name in 1922 to *The New Generation* and in the 1920s found itself increasingly in the mainstream of thought on the matter of birth control. However, the best discussion on the changes of morals was to be found a series of articles in the *New Leader*, the organ of the Independent Labour Party. The author, a social scientist, writing under the pseudonym '27', described the basic change in the attitude of the young:

What then is this change? Let us put it in one bald sentence. Many people under 35 no longer regard the act of sexual intercourse as in itself sinful . . . [but] to refuse to regard the sexual act as sin is no new or original piece of wickedness suddenly evolved by the present generation. In almost all times and in almost all parts of the world humanity has regarded sexual experience, simply and naturally, as one of the most desirable things in life. Actually, it is only in the Britain and America of the last 100 years (and perhaps to a lesser extent on the continent of Europe) that sex has been thought of as a sin. So we must conceive of the present tendency, not as some strange aberration but essentially as a return to the normal. (*New Leader*, 30 November 1928)

In the United States the extent to which the liberalisation occurred is a matter of some controversy. Linda Gordon (1977, p. 193) says that women reaching their teens after 1910 had twice as much premarital sex as those reaching puberty in the years immediately preceding. This suggests that liberalisation may have occurred earlier in the United States and without the effect of the war. Another piece of evidence that supports this suggestion is the decline of chaperonage a common phenomenon in the nineteenth century. Ms J. Borden Harriman, describing her visit to her first ball in 1888, commented 'No girls ever went anywhere except with a chaperon or maid' (1923, p. 36). Its decline may have been associated with the rise in economic wealth, as Scott Fitzgerald's comment that 'As far back as 1915 the unchaperoned young people of the smaller cities had discovered the mobile privacy of the automobile at 16 to make himself reliant' suggests (McGovern, 1968, p. 318). However, in contrast it does not seem that chaperonage ended in England until the wartime conditions made it difficult to enforce. Vera Brittain (1934, p. 177) told of the way she was closely observed at first during the war but that 'the free and easy movements of girl war workers had begun to modify convention' so that after the war there was no attempt to reintroduce the same restrictions. 'How different was the peaceful independence of a post war courtship.'

The war, '27' suggested, was the greatest single cause of the change. He proposed that towards its end there was a revolt against the prevailing moral standards which people felt had precipitated the conflict, and that many rejected previous sexual norms. He also drew attention to the fact that young people under the age of 25 could earn three to four times more than they could before the war. This had led to the growth in cinemas, motorcycles, cars, cafés and dancing places which catered for those even with little to spend. He also mentioned the finding of a cure for venereal disease and the role of birth control (*New Leader*, 23 November 1928).

In the United States the role of the war seems more problematical. In some respects it had a conservative effect on the dominant ideology. Boyer (1968) suggests that the war was sold to the public as a conflict between good and evil. The Americans learned that the Germans were a depraved people and that a

German soldier would laugh as 'he mutilated virgins and impaled infants on his bayonet'. In opposition to this, Americans were idealised as paragons of virtue and changes were introduced to try to ensure that their soldiers did not engage in sexual behaviour or get drunk. Later the idea grew that the whole population should receive a spiritual renewal. During this period alcohol was prohibited (1917), prostitutes were harassed, and young women were encouraged to keep the soldiers on the straight and narrow path with such slogans as 'Do your bit to keep him fit'. The anti-vice societies also grew in size as conservative values received support. However, despite all the official puritanism, the reality of behaviour was somewhat different. The problems of venereal disease and unwanted pregnancy meant that in 1917 the decision was taken to give condoms to the troops and sexual behaviour became more free, and thus the gap between official attitudes and actual behaviour widened. Schmalhausen even talked of the 'sexual revolution' and stressed the strong effect of the First World War in 'remoulding the conventional mind in the direction of sexual anarchism' (Calverton and Schmalhausen, 1929). Judge Ben Lindsey (1925, p. 54) also stressed the role of the war in liberalising sexual behaviour, suggesting that many young men became 'innoculated with continental standards'. He said that before the war he had talked to a hundred boys and half admitted they had been with prostitutes in the red light district. However, with the changed conditions the boys were turning to girls in their own class.

One important factor leading to liberalisation was the findings of the anthropologists. In this respect Malinowski's *Sexual Life of Savages* (1929) and Margaret Mead's *Coming of Age in Samoa* (1943) were the most influential. Mead argued that Samoan girls had relaxed attitudes and that masturbation was almost universal amongst those over the ages of 6 or 7. She attacked the conservative views present in American culture and claimed that by their liberal approach the Samoans 'legislate a whole field of neurotic possibilities out of existence'. The book had great implications for those who wished to maintain Victorian sexual attitudes and Havelock Ellis challenged people to read Mead's book, claiming that it 'enables us to realise how rapidly a new sexual order, if on a reasonably natural foundation, may grow and become fairly stable' (Calverton and Schmalhausen, 1929, p. 25).

One final factor that should be mentioned was the increased

confidence of the upper classes in Britain to speak their mind. Bertrand Russell has already been discussed in this respect, and the role of Lord Dawson and Justice McCarthy will be considered below. In the United States, too, the elite were looking to more relaxed standards than those of the conservative middle class.

These then were the major reasons for the liberalisation. But there were limits as to how far it could spread. The conservative forces of the nineteenth century were still in operation. The Church was still largely opposed to contraception and the education system was under its strong influence. The mass media, the radio stations, the movie business and literature were under very strong censorship. Furthermore it seems likely that the great stock market crash of 1929 affected the general climate within which sexual behaviour would occur. We know that the growth of unemployment led to a resurgence of right-wing policies in some countries together with repression of women and restrictions on sexual behaviour. The effect of these changes on the debate on fertility will now be considered.

Debate on Contraception in Britain

The post-war liberalisation of attitudes facilitated the spread of contraceptive knowledge. In 1918 Marie Stopes published her book *Married Love* and in 1921 she opened the first birth control clinic in Britain. Stopes had been a member of the Malthusian League in the war years but gradually began to reject its overall theories of society. She let her membership lapse and after the war began fighting for birth control as a single-issue campaign. In *Birth Control News* (July 1922) she pointed out that all Malthusians could join her 'Campaign for Constructive Birth Control' but not all members could agree with the Malthusians.

In the 1920s some medical opposition continued, as did that in the Church of England. However, changes were afoot. At the 1921 Church Congress Lord Dawson, the King's physician, caused a tremendous stir in a speech which attacked restrictive attitudes towards sexuality. In a widely quoted passage he stated

> To tell you the truth, I am not sure that too much prudent self restraint suits love and its purport. Romance and deliberate self control do not, to my mind, rhyme very well together. A touch of

madness to begin with does no harm. Heaven knows, life sobers it soon enough. If you don't start life with a head of steam you won't get far. (*The Malthusian*, November 1921; *Critic and Guide*, 1923, p. 455)

Lord Dawson went on to call for the churches' support for birth control and this speech did much to break down the resistance of the middle classes. Most of the press comments were favourable, but the *Sunday Express* (16 October 1921) in a hostile editorial entitled 'Lord Dawson Must Go', clearly drew out the implications of the speech:

Hitherto Malthusianism has been a stealthy and furtive cult, which has never dared to show itself openly and shamelessly in the light of day. Now for the first time in our national life, it appears, of all places in the world, on the platform at the Church Congress. Lord Dawson has given it the imprimatur of medical science, the hall mark of social eminence, the sanction of the Court physician, and the aegis of the established church.

The *Express* made a correct assessment of the impact of Dawson's views and from that time on discussion could be much more open.

Dawson helped the acceptance of birth control at the Lambeth Conference of 1930 by 193 votes to 67. The statement declared that 'where there is a morally sound reason for avoiding complete abstinence, the Conference agrees that other methods may be used' (*The Times*, 15 August 1930). Lord Dawson's role in this decision did not fully come to light until 1934 when he introduced a Bill into the House of Lords to create restrictions on contraceptive advertising. At first birth control proponents were horrified that their ally had seemingly deserted them. Drysdale then proposed that Dawson had promised to introduce a Bill in order to get 'the valuable pronouncement of the Bishops at the last Lambeth Conference' (*New Generation*, March and April 1934).

By the 1930s, therefore, organised Church opposition to contraception within marriage, with one notable exception, was over. The Malthusians had become eminently respectable and their Ball of 1933 was patronised by a princess and presided over by a High Court judge. There was, however, one opposing force which could not be ignored.

Social Characteristics of the Opposition

The major opposition came from the Catholic Church which provided a basis from which opponents of change could work. Noonan (1967, p. 502) explains that the opposition of the Church to fertility control only became important after the First World War. Before that time it had not campaigned actively to persuade non-Catholics to adopt its viewpoint. In part its reaction may have been a backlash against more aggressive methods of the birth control proponents and an attempt to arrest some of the social changes that were beginning to take place. One practical reason for the Catholic Church to oppose fertility control was because a high average family size was necessary in order to keep up numbers. Sometimes Catholics argued that its view of birth control would lead to its growing faster than non-Catholic Churches. For example, a doctor speaking to the Southend Branch of the National Council of Women in 1923 asserted that 'Our people will never adopt these practices, and *we shall breed out the protestants* and England will become Catholic again' (*Birth Control News* (*BCN*), December 1923, emphasis in original).

The best known of the opponents to contraception in Britain was Dr Halliday Sutherland, a Catholic convert, who in his book *Birth Control* (1922, p. 3) warned that 'The path of the Malthusian League, although at first glance an easy way out of many human difficulties, is in reality the broad road along which a man or a nation travels to destruction'. Sutherland became famous when defeating Marie Stopes in the House of Lords in 1923 – he had alleged that her method of birth control was dangerous and she sued him for libel. After the trial he stated, 'This propaganda of birth control had spread through the country with little to stop it until it reached the invisible and invincible frontiers of the Catholic Church, but there the battle had been joined' (*BCN*, February 1924).

At first the opposition was unorganised, but in 1926 Sutherland was behind the formation of the League of National Life which aimed to be 'undenominational and non political' with a membership open to anyone, but did not disguise the fact that it was largely supported by Catholics (*Universe*, 23 July 1926). The general climate of opinion, however, was against this group. The percentage of Catholics in the population was relatively low and the teaching of the rhythm method undermined many of their arguments. This also was realised by Sutherland, and when in

1947 he reflected on the problems he and his allies had faced, he commented:

Knowing that it was useless to quote religious sanctions in neo pagan Britain, we sought to defeat the contraceptists by proving their propaganda to be contrary to the laws of biological, economic and ethical science. We failed. We witnessed the medical profession betray its trust; we saw the white flag hoisted over Lambeth Palace; we were in Whitehall in 1931 when the Ministry of Health first permitted advice on contraceptives to be given in antenatal clinics. (Simms, 1975)

Sutherland's movement was the forerunner of modern anti-abortion movements, and the kinds of argument used by opponents of birth control are still used by anti-abortionists today. One was that birth control was murder. In 1914 the *Daily Mirror* carried an article supportive of birth control. In reply the Catholic newspaper *The Universe* argued that the regulation of the birth-rate meant the killing of the unborn child and the suppression by intention of the potential child in conception: 'It is open and unashamed war upon babies . . . What care we for the future of family or fatherland? Confront the natural law of life with the hedonists' law of death. Kill, Kill, Kill, and "let us eat drink and be merry for tomorrow we die" ' (*The Malthusian*, April 1915, p. 30). Another argument was that birth control would lead to sterility. Halliday Sutherland stated in the *BMJ* that birth control practices were harmful to men and women, commenting that 'sterility is less common in countries such as Ireland and Spain where birth control is not practised' (30 July 1921, p. 169). Other people would go even further. Dr F. J. McCann, a surgeon at the Samaritan Hospital, argued during the Stopes/Sutherland libel suit that contraception was always prejudicial to a woman's health, and is sometimes dangerous to her life (*BCN*, March 1923).

A common argument was that birth control would destroy the family. In 1929 a leaflet 'Birth Prevention', issued by the British League of National Life, argued that birth control 'leads to a disintegration of the family upon which nation and Empire are founded' (*New Generation*, August 1929, p. 90). It is difficult to see why small families should be seen as destruction. There was, however, an extension of the argument. This was that the fall in numbers meant that the ends of families were not being reached and that for this reason many great men would not be born. This argument was used by the Catholic Archbishop of New York in justification of instructions from his office to close one of Margaret Sanger's meetings. He argued (wrongly) that John Wesley was the eighteenth child and that 'one of the reasons for the lack of genius in our day is that we are not getting the ends of families' (Sanger, 1932, p. 211). Against this argument the birth controllers stressed the fact that many 'great men' were born high in the birth order – for example Jesus and John the Baptist. Another argument they used was that it would have been better if some men had not been born. William Robinson wrote later in his *Critic and Guide* of the misery society would have escaped if the mothers of Dillinger, Hitler, Al Capone, Goering and Oswald Mosley had used birth control.

One argument that worried the Malthusians was that of race suicide. In August 1921 *The Malthusian* asserted that the 'only objection to birth control which has any appearance of reason is its supposed effect on the defensive power of the nation' (p. 62). The political movement to the right in Germany and Italy had led to birth control clinics being closed. An Italian law in 1926 made it an offence to distribute Malthusian teaching or any other 'means of prevention of conception or any regulation of female fertility' (*BCN*, December 1926). The birth control advocates in Britain and the United States had found a 1913 statement from Mussolini supportive of birth control and they used it to attack his change of views (*New Generation*, April 1935). However, the argument was also important in France and on 7 May 1918, as the war drew to a close, the French bishops used the military argument against birth control: 'Let the lesson not be lost. It is necessary to fill the spaces made by death, if we want France to belong to Frenchmen and to be strong enough to defend herself and prosper.' Two years later France banned birth control, and this was seen as a victory by the Catholic Church. The *Catholic Times* commented that the French Government had realised it was 'now unable to provide sufficient troops' (28 October 1922).

Mussolini argued on numerous occasions that the Italians were a prolific people and needed more land. But since at the same time he banned fertility control, it was obvious that problems were to arise. The *New Generation* had more than a hint of exasperation in the following report:

Mussolini is surely the most inconsistent of men. He has again and again told the world that Italy is terribly overcrowded, and that to accommodate her growing population she must have more territory, even if she has to get it by war. Yet he has repeatedly spoken contemptuously of Malthus, and said there is no such thing as pressure of population. Which Mussolini are we to believe? (November, 1934, p. 123)

The League of National Life was sympathetic. Sutherland called the work of Hitler and Mussolini in this area 'heroic efforts' and commended the Nazi penal code of November 1936 which made 'the public ridicule of marriage or of maternity, and all propaganda in favour of birth control and abortion into criminal offences' (Simms, 1975, p. 713).

The failure of the League of National Life was to be expected, although its pressure did have some effect on the Labour Party for a time. In 1927 the Labour Women's Conference voted by 581 votes to 74 for birth control information to be given to the poor, but the full Labour Party rejected the motion. The three main opposing speakers were Irish Catholics, and Stella Browne accused the Labour leadership of surrendering to Roman Catholic threats (*The Malthusian*, November 1927). One of the arguments was that many Catholics would leave the Labour Party if it endorsed contraception. Marie Stopes attacked this view in a letter to the *New Leader* and argued that the Catholic Church through its approval of the safe period was now in favour of birth control (28 December 1928). In drawing attention to this fact she was pointing to a problem for those defending the Church's position. Once the rhythm method was widely known to be acceptable many of its traditional arguments against birth control had much less plausibility.

Stopes, Sanger and Abortion

Marie Stopes genuinely opposed abortion, and was also concerned that the issue might harm her fight for birth control. At the time many people confused the two methods, and typical were the comments she made at a meeting in May 1923 when she insisted that her members should differentiate between birth control and abortion and let the world know that the Society for Constructive

Birth Control 'would have nothing to do with abortions, in spite of the numerous and often pathetic appeals' (*BCN*, June 1923).

In contrast, research reveals that Margaret Sanger only opposed abortion for tactical reasons. This becomes clear from an analysis of her writing on the subject. In her pamphlet *Family Limitation*, first published in 1915, she approved abortion: 'No one can doubt that there are times where an abortion is justifiable but these will become unnecessary when care is taken to prevent conception'. In *Birth Control Review* (May 1919) she pointed out that abortion could be a safe operation: 'We know that abortion, when performed by skilled hands, under right conditions, brings almost no danger to the life of the patient and we also know that particular diseases can be more easily combated after such an abortion than during a pregnancy allowed to come to full term'. A year later she again took a less than censorious attitude: 'The women who goes to the abortionist's table is not a criminal but a martyr; a martyr to the bitter, unthinkable conditions brought about by the blindness of society at large' (Sanger, 1969). She continued by arguing the case for contraception as the substitute.

The British birth controllers were critical of her stance on this matter and in February 1915 *The Malthusian*, when reviewing *Family Limitation*, criticised its passage on abortion:

It is unfortunate that in Mrs. Sanger's otherwise excellent pamphlet she tells women that if they intend to have an abortion they should do so without delay . . . Mrs. Sanger has informed us that she has not advocated abortion, but that the practice is so common in America, and so generally spoken of, that she felt it desirable to warn women against the use of drugs and against delay if abortion had been determined upon. (p. 11)

When Sanger returned to the United States to face trial for breaking the Comstock law with *Family Limitation*, Marie Stopes organised a group of nine English birth control supporters including H. G. Wells to write to President Wilson saying that the United States was the only 'civilised' country in the world where the spreading of birth control information was a criminal offence and asking for presidential action (*The Malthusian*, November 1915). The President was particularly impressed that Wells had signed it. Marie Stopes, however, was worried by the passage on abortion. She therefore wrote a further letter in which she stated:

The fact that Mrs. Sanger has even apparently condoned abortion may be seized upon as a justification for her condemnation. But, if this is truly and impartially considered, it will be seen to be, on the contrary, a condemnation of the system against which she is so valiantly fighting, a system under which it is possible for secret abortionists to have practices so flourishing that queues of poor women stand outside their doors as if waiting for a popular theatre to open. (*The Malthusian*, November 1915, p. 86)

From the early 1920s Sanger did not argue the case for abortion but simply stated that with contraceptive usage it would become unnecessary. However, this does not mean that she changed her fundamental position on the subject. In fact according to James Reed (1978, p. 118) at least from 1933 onwards she began to help patients get abortions. Reed discovered one documented case of a woman being given a pregnancy test and referred to a sympathetic physician. Given the risks involved it is surprising that evidence of even one case was available and it suggests there may have been a system of referrals. There would, for example, be very little risk in referring regular patients who had suffered contraceptive failure.

Abortion in the Soviet Union

Although there were calls for legalisation in Germany it was in the Soviet Union that abortion was first legalised in modern times, and this affected the debate in both Britain and the United States. As early as 1914 the most eminent society of physicians had called for all laws to be removed. In 1920 the Soviet Government faced with a birthrate of about 40 per 1,000 and a high number of illegal operations passed a law legalising abortion. The measure was very important for the abortion debate in other countries (*The Malthusian*, September 1926). It provided for the operation to be performed free of charge in hospitals although it seems that the shortage of facilities meant that the law could not be enforced.

This law had two main effects on the debate elsewhere. First, it was a prime example to show that change was possible, and radical groups were able to point to it as an example of what could be accomplished. Secondly, and this was probably more important, it revised the estimates of the safety of the operation. Until that time it had been widely believed that abortion was an unsafe operation. The Soviet authorities drew comparisons with Germany where in 1924 4 per cent of abortions were estimated to have resulted in death. In Moscow it was less than one-tenth of 1 per cent (*New Generation*, September 1926). The Soviets publicised their results and in 1929 sent a delegate to the First Congress of the World League for Sexual Reform in London. The figures suggested that abortion mortality and morbidity had decreased 'almost to vanishing point' and British medical men took an interest and on a number of occasions visited the country to watch the procedures. One such observer, L. Haden Guest, reported in the *Lancet* (5 December 1931) that in a Russian series of 40,000 cases there were only two deaths. A few months later the journal commented that if the evidence of the Russian experience of safe abortion were accurate: 'They will from the strictly medical point of view, deserve serious consideration by those planning new legislation appropriate to the outlook and habits of our time' (*Lancet*, 19 March 1932, p. 627). The Birkett Committee drew attention to the Soviet figures in 1939 and American medical men also made comparisons. The US-based doctor F. J. Taussig paid a visit in 1930 and devoted a whole chapter in his influential book to legal abortion in the Soviet Union (1936).

The repeal of the Soviet law in 1936 was against the wishes of the people. The *New York Times* (28 and 31 May 1936) reported strong opposition from women who felt they would be condemned to being childbearing machines, commenting that the abortion law had not prevented the creation of happy, devoted and even conventional families. The change in the law was regarded 'As the first step toward putting the Soviet Union squarely into the population race with Germany and Italy' (*New York Times*, 7 March 1937). It was accompanied by promises of large premiums for every child after the seventh and a crackdown on illegal abortions. In one case eighteen women were sentenced to one to ten years' imprisonment. The *New York Times* correspondent noted that Mussolini wanted 10 million more Italians to win the next war, but said dictatorships should look for more specialists, not more babies (31 May 1936). The restricted Soviet law continued to allow abortion if pregnancy threatened the woman's health or if there were a likelihood of inherited disease (Birkett, 1939, p. 105). The programme was initially successful and official estimates talked of a tripling of the birthrate in Moscow in the first year. In Czechoslovakia too the abortion law was liberalised in 1920 and restricted in 1936 (David and McIntyre, 1981). This suggests Soviet influence on its policy.

Abortion Movement in Britain

The first known call for a change in the British abortion laws was from Stella Browne. In *The Malthusian* in March 1915 she proposed a number of reasons for liberalisation. First, she said that a reliable contraceptive had not been discovered so pregnancy might occur even when the greatest care had been taken and there were overwhelming reasons why a child should not be born to the people concerned. Secondly, the education of young people in sexual matters was only just beginning, and she argued that it was grossly unfair to penalise ignorance. Thirdly, she stated that the laws left people open to blackmail because of the need for secrecy and the fact that the operation had mainly fallen into the hands of the criminal class. She also pointed out that those performing the operation were often unskilled and produced permanent injury although, despite these factors, those with 'any knowledge of the lives of working class women will prove that the professional abortionist is sometimes the truest friend and benefactor' (p. 22).

Stella Browne also argued that prejudice against abortion was not due to medical science but was based on Christian canon law which stated that at the time of conception there was a right of baptism. She said that thinking people would wonder why embryonic life alone should be considered sacred. She then referred to the war and suggested that the world should be made fit for children to be raised. Just after this article was published reports began to arrive of the problems of French women who were pregnant because they had been raped by German soldiers. The *BMJ* noted the claims that such women should have a right to abortion and that there was some support for a change in the law (20 March 1915). *The Malthusian* stated that it was pleased to see the question raised but that 'we have a better remedy, and it would be folly for us to waste our energy and resources in championing an imperfect one'. It claimed that when the knowledge of preventive methods became universal, abortion would only become necessary in rare cases where prevention had not been employed or had failed and where there were serious medical or eugenic reasons against offspring. In the meantime, *The Malthusian* said that it was going to confine itself to advocating contraception and that the real advocates of abortion were its opponents, on the birth control issue.

Although the Malthusians were not prepared to endorse abortion, they gave sympathetic treatment to the writings of Stella Browne and others on the subject. One of the key tactical factors which must have influenced their approach was that by the 1920s the Malthusian League was no longer the major pressure group working for birth control and so it did not have to worry about damaging this cause. Throughout the 1920s statements favouring the legalisation of abortion were treated sympathetically in the *New Generation*, although the Malthusian League did not make it part of its official policy. In the early 1930s the *New Generation* began to seriously consider the need for an organisation to fight the abortion laws. An article in 1931 commented: 'Instead of a new society being formed, it would be better if the Malthusian League were to take the matter up. It would be fitting that the first society in the world which advocated birth control should also be the first to advocate legalised abortion by a qualified surgeon' (*New Generation*, December 1931, p. 134). Although the Malthusian League did not take up the suggestion, throughout the 1920s and early 1930s it was the only organisation carrying abortion information on a regular basis. Furthermore, it was members of the Malthusian League who set up the Abortion Law Reform Association in 1936.

Justice McCardie and the Abortion Law

During the 1930s, as many European countries moved to the right, the movement for free abortions in Britain might have expected to receive serious setbacks. However, a number of factors prevented this, and amongst them were the actions of Justice McCardie. McCardie had grown convinced that the 1861 Abortion Act was out of touch with the realities of life and so, on 30 November 1931, he publicly attacked the law. Two women had come before him and pleaded guilty to aborting themselves. He could have sent them to prison for life, but instead he just bound them over. In his summing up he said, 'I express the view clearly that in my opinion the law in regard to illegal operations should be substantially amended. It is out of keeping with the conditions that prevail in the world around us.' Addressing Mrs Elsie Golding, he continued:

> Your case illustrates well what I have just said. You are a woman of most excellent character. You have been brave in the midst of sorrow to bear the burden of providing for your family. You had seven young children born in poverty and almost doomed to poverty for all their lives. You had no money. Your husband is lazy and you feared that another burden was to fall upon you. I can well believe you, because judges know more of human life than many people think. I shall not send you to prison but will bind you over for two years.

Then the Judge, turning to the jury with raised hand, said: 'A mother of seven children, gentlemen' (*New Generation*, December 1931).

Two weeks later, on 11 December 1931, McCardie went even further and refused to sentence a woman who had committed an abortion on another. He said to her:

> You are charged under an Act that was passed seventy years ago. Since then, the national point of view has been greatly changed. The knowledge of men has grown and I am glad to see that a new and a wide vision has grown up. I think these abortion cases will continue so long as the knowledge of birth control is withheld . . . In my view, and I say it plainly and publicly, the law of abortion should be amended (*New Generation*, January 1932).

These attacks on the law by McCardie were widely publicised. The *New Generation* said that the speech would make history in every country where the English language was spoken. It was influential in changing attitudes and L. A. Parry, the leading English authority on abortion at the time, told the British Medical Association (BMA) that McCardie's remarks had encouraged him to become more open-minded (*BMJ*, 31 December 1932, p. 1,192). It also seems that McCardie's actions were important in stirring the BMA. In July 1932 it passed a resolution calling on its council to 'consider the question of setting up a special Committee . . . to consider any modifications of the law dealing with abortion'. In proposing the motion Dr G. Pollock asserted that it should not be the purpose of the Association to see abortion as a solution to problems caused by moral laxity, but that 'there are many cases where the problem ought to be looked at from the point of view elaborated by Justice McCardie'. This resolution was passed and the BMA set up the Committee (*New Generation*, August 1932, p. 89).

Origins of the Abortion Law Reform Association

We saw earlier that it was the women's groups, especially in the Labour Party, that were the most forthright in the matter of birth control. Radical women were also prime movers of the pressure group for the reform of the abortion law.

A notable victory for the pro-choice groups in the early 1930s was to obtain the support of the Co-operative Women in 1934. There were 1,360 delegates to the Annual Meeting, and the following resolution was passed with only twenty dissidents:

> In view of the persistently high maternal death rate and the evils arising from the illegal practice of abortion, this Congress calls upon the Government to revise the abortion laws of 1861 by bringing them into harmony with modern conditions and ideas, thereby making of abortion a legal operation that can be carried out under the same conditions as any other surgical operation. It further asks that women now suffering from imprisonment for breaking these antiquated laws, be amnested. (*New Generation*, July 1934, p. 78)

Stella Browne was euphoric about the success of such a strong resolution and the rejection of an amendment deleting the call for an amnesty for the women in prison. Among the arguments used in favour of abortion was the case for a woman's right: 'For our bodies are our own, the rights of children to be born when they are wanted, the reduction of illegal abortions and the need for a back up method when contraceptives were to fail' (*New Generation*, July 1934). At last the pro-choice groups had found a solid basis of support amongst the women of the left.

Two years later, on 17 February 1936, the Abortion Law Reform Association (ALRA) was set up. The leaders of ALRA had been working for change for many years, and so the new association was an extension of previous activities. It was chaired by Janet Chance and to a large extent financed by her husband Clinton, who was very active in the birth control movement at the time of the First World War, and who had provided the money for Margaret Sanger to set up her birth control clinic in 1922. Stella Browne was the most militant of the three principal organisers, and the Secretary, Alice Jenkins, noted: 'Stella never wavered from her uncompromising belief in the "woman's right to abortion up to the viability of her child". Janet and I shared her opinion, but mistakenly or not, believed that we could further our views better by a less forthright declaration' (Jenkins, 1960, p. 59). This division of opinion about reducing demands for political reasons was one that became important in both Britain and the United States.

Although the movement for abortion freedom was dominated by women, there was no particular prejudice against men being involved on the grounds that it was a woman's issue. At the first conference of ALRA in May 1936, Stella Browne specifically thanked the men who had 'come forward under circumstances of difficulty and possibly embarrassment to stand beside us and express their sympathy' (Jenkins, 1960, p. 53). By 1938 ALRA had 274 members, hardly a mass movement, but a reasonable size for the kind of organisation that it was.

The Bourne Case   The greatest victory of ALRA in the 1930s was the trial of Aleck Bourne, for it extended the law to cover rape and other factors related to the health of women. There were a number of legal abortions available to rich women after the First World War, as was made clear in a speech by Thomas Eden, Consultant Physician at the Charing Cross Hospital, at the section of obstetrics at the Annual Meeting of the BMA in 1926. He stated that it was impossible to lay down rigid criteria for abortion: 'It is an ethical question of great interest to what extent we as doctors have the right to insist that a woman shall pass through an ordeal which she is unwilling to face' (*BMJ*, 7 August 1926, p. 237). He gave the example of a barrister's wife who had two children very quickly and then became pregnant again. Both she and her husband took the view that as the prospective baby was theirs they should decide whether or not she should have an abortion. Eden confessed to being shaken by their view, but when he consulted a senior colleague, the doctor agreed with the patient and her husband, and so the abortion was carried out. Furthermore, at a later stage the woman was given another abortion.

Thus many doctors took a very liberal line on abortion. However, others were concerned that the law did not specifically allow for abortion even to save the woman's life. This was changed with the Infant Life Preservation Act 1929, a law passed after many attempts, which finally made it illegal to kill a child while it was in the process of being born. This had been a loophole in the English law allowing infanticide to occur. In creating the offence an exception was made to save the woman's life, and by 1932 it was generally accepted that the 1929 Act was relevant to the abortion law (Parry, 1932). However, it was worthwhile for the pro-choice groups to try to extend the law more formally. A Committee, set up by the BMA, reported in 1936 that the law was somewhat confused and in need of clarification. Bourne, a member of ALRA's Medico-Legal Council, decided to try to find a suitable subject for a test case. The opportunity came in 1938 when a girl aged 14 years and 9 months was raped and became pregnant. Joan Malleson, who was also a member of ALRA's Medico-Legal Council, saw her and wrote the following letter on 21 May 1938:

Dear Mr. Bourne,
I have been consulted by the organiser of the Schools Care Committee about a girl of 14 [who] was assaulted in Whitehall by some soldiers. The actual facts were that she was with two girl friends, who ran off and left her, and she was held down by five men and twice assaulted.

She continued to say the girl was pregnant and asked whether

Someone of your standing were prepared to risk a cause célèbre and undertake the operation in hospital.

Many people hold the view that the best way of correcting the present abortion laws is to let the medical profession gradually extend the grounds for therapeutic abortion in suitable cases, until the laws become obsolete, so far as practice goes. I should imagine that public opinion would be immensely in favour of termination of pregnancy in a case of this sort.

Bourne replied:

> I am interested in the case of rape which you describe in your letter. I shall be delighted to admit her to St. Mary's and curette her. I have done this before and have not the slightest hesitation in doing it again.

Bourne observed the girl for eight days. The morning he performed the abortion the police arrived and he told them he wanted them to take action against him. It was not clear who, in fact, contacted the police in the first place. It seems Bourne did not do so as he had promised the girl's father that he would keep the matter as secret as possible in order to save the girl's mother from worry (*BMJ*, 23 July 1938). In his summing up at Bourne's trial Mr Justice MacNaghton stated that the traditional view was that abortion was justified only if it were done to preserve the life of the woman. However, he said that too narrow a view must not be taken of the meaning of these words. Any serious impairment of health might reach a stage where there were a danger to life, and anything which threatened such impairment of health might justify the operation. In fact he went further and asserted that it might be the duty of the doctor to perform the operation and that religious scruples would be no excuse for not doing so. 'If the life of the woman can be saved by an operation and a doctor did not perform it because of his religious views he would be in great peril of being brought before this court on a charge of manslaughter for negligence'. Bourne was acquitted, and the decision passed into English case law.

Illegal Abortions and Maternal Mortality in Britain

During the inter-war period there was great concern with the number of deaths from illegal abortion in England. There were between 400 and 500 deaths every year between 1926 and 1935 (Birkett, 1939, p. 6). The BMA set up a Committee to consider the problem in 1934 and it published a report which suggested that perhaps 16–20 per cent of pregnancies ended in either spontaneous or induced abortion (British Medical Association, 1936). The Birkett Committee (1939, p. iii) was set up in 1937: 'to enquire into the prevalence of abortion, and the law thereto, and to consider what steps can be taken to secure the reduction of maternal mortality'. The report opposed a suggestion from ALRA that there should be a general legalisation of abortion, partly because it would lead 'promiscuous sexual intercourse to be more common' (Birkett, 1939, p. 85). It recommended that the Bourne decision should be formalised in law and also attempted to estimate the total number of abortions each year. It applied the BMA estimate to the total number of annual births of 600,000 and reached a figure of between 110,000 and 150,000 spontaneous and induced abortions each year (p. 9). The British Medical Association (1936) had suggested that spontaneous abortions were a relatively small proportion of the whole. However, Birkett took the view that 'perhaps 40 per cent of the abortions in this country are due to illegal interference' (1939, p. 11).

A year later David Glass, an ALRA member, suggested that the 60–40 proportion should be reversed and that probably 60 per cent of all abortions were illegal. He argued that, taking into account under-reporting, it is 'not at all impossible that there are about 100,000 illegal abortions in England and Wales' (Glass, 1940). This figure was given great publicity in 1947 in an ALRA pamphlet *Back Street Surgery* (Chance *et al.*, 1947). On the front cover the pamphlet declared itself to be 'A study of the illegal operation, which is performed probably about 100,000 times a year in England and Wales'. Inside it gave Glass as the source, and this became the most widely quoted figure in the period leading to the 1967 Act.

Although there may be doubt as to the exact number of abortions in the 1930s, there is no doubt that it was widely used and that in Britain the illegal abortionist was often a valued member of the community. It is not difficult to see why. In 1926 Lord Buckmaster gave the House of Lords the following case history: 'A woman was married at the age of seventeen who by the age of thirty four had had eighteen pregnancies and eleven live children' (*Birth Control News*, May 1926). Buckmaster asserted that this case was not unusual. The illegal abortionist was usually only discovered if there was a death. Even then it seems that the local community often continued in support. In 1930 a woman, Mrs Lee, who charged from 2s 6d to 10s for an abortion, was sentenced to five years' penal servitude, with the following result:

A big demonstration began when Mrs. Lee was taken away from the Shire Hall. The crowd, which consisted mainly of women, cheered when Mrs. Lee, in charge of a wardress, came out of a rear door of the Shire Hall, and many crowded round the car. A sobbing woman, apparently a relative of Mrs. Lee, insisted on kissing her before she was helped into the motor which was waiting. Another woman pushed her way towards Mrs. Lee saying, 'Let me kiss her; I must kiss her.' From the car Mrs. Lee waved kisses to her friends and as the car left the precincts of the Shire Hall the cheering was renewed.

There was great anger against the witnesses who caused Mrs. Lee's conviction. The cheering was changed to 'booing' when witnesses in the case were seen at the windows of the building, and shouts such as 'Come out of it!' and 'Come down, you dogs!' were heard. (*Gloucester Journal*, 14 June 1930)

The view that abortion was accepted by the mass of people gets other support. Birkett, for example, stated that 'the law relating to abortion is freely disregarded among women of all types and classes' (1939, p. 118).

One method of abortion that shocked the medical profession in the 1930s was slippery elm bark. It was derived from a tree found in Central and North America. The bark was prepared by being separated from the trunk, having the outer corky portion removed and then being dried. It was sold in flat pieces several inches long, a few inches wide and a few millimetres in thickness, and contained material which expanded when the bark was soaked in water. Small pieces approximately doubled in size, and it was alleged to be of value in the preparation of poultices and as a 'food' in illness and debility. Small pieces were placed into the cervical canal by the woman herself or by an abortionist and the abortion was procured partly on account of the presence of a foreign body and partly because of dilation of the cervix following swelling of the bark. The first mention of slippery elm as an abortifacient in the British medical literature was in February 1929, and Parish reported it (1935) as a minor method in his study in Camberwell of women treated for abortion between 1930–4. Of 1,000 cases, 485 women admitted illegal interference and in 426 cases the method was known (Table 3.1).

In 1938 a 'moral panic' about slippery elm occurred in the medical literature and the *British Medical Journal* (14 May) contained a picture of the bark as removed from a woman's bladder.

Table 3.1   *Percentage of Illegal Abortions by Method*

	Number	Percentage
Drugs	111	26.1
Syringe	108	25.3
Syringe and drugs	170	39.9
Catheter	7	1.6
Slippery elm bark	16	3.8
Knitting needle	5	1.2
Abortionist	9	2.1
	426	100.0

Liberalisation of Abortion in Scandinavia

Iceland made abortion illegal in 1869 but liberalised its law in January 1935. The 1935 Law took account of social factors such as whether the woman's 'domestic conditions are difficult, either on account of a large flock of children, poverty or serious ill health' (Potts *et al.*, 1977, p. 383). In 1938 Iceland further liberalised its law to allow abortion where rape was proved and where hereditary disease might be transmitted to the offspring (Birkett, 1939, p. 161).

Sweden liberalised its law in 1921 but illegal abortions continued, and during the early 1930s resulted in about seventy deaths each year in a population of 6 million. A Royal Commission was set up in 1934 and resulting legislation went into operation on 1 January 1939. It allowed abortion if childbirth would entail serious danger to the life or health of the woman, if she were pregnant from rape or incest or under 15 years of age. It also allowed abortions in cases where the woman were legally insane or if serious physical or mental handicap might result (Linner, 1968, p. 76).

In Denmark a delegation of working women sought changes in 1929. In 1932 a commission was set up and recommended legalisation on various grounds in 1936. The liberalising legislation was passed on 18 May 1937 and came into operation in October 1939 (Birkett, 1939, p. 159; Potts *et al.*, 1977, p. 385). It allowed abortion for maternal health, rape, incest and potential foetal abnormality.

American Debate Between the Wars

The first modern activist for birth control, William Robinson, also became the first systematic proponent of the legalisation of abortion. This mirrors Britain where the Malthusians were the first agitators on both issues. However, it will be shown that in the United States the fledgeling abortion movement died out in the 1930s.

William Robinson seems to have taken a consistent position on abortion which from his published works can be summarised as follows:

1   Abortions occur in great numbers and the operations are usually carried out by doctors.
2   This is a situation which should be deprecated and it is much better to substitute contraception.
3   Although contraception is much better, abortion is a relatively simple and safe operation and cannot be regarded as murder, for only a few cells are destroyed.
4   The law on abortion should be repealed to allow it in the early months of pregnancy.
5   He would never perform an abortion as it would restrict his possibilities in campaigning on the issue.

Robinson's estimation of the number of abortions rose from 1 million a year in the 1910s to 2 million in the 1930s. He said he had little respect for the professional abortionist but that he was morally superior to the judges and hypocrites who condemned him: 'He has saved many a family from shame and humility, and many an unfortunate young girl from a suicide's grave' (*Critic and Guide*, 1925, p. 136). He also pointed out that 'An altruistic physician does it, when necessary for a nominal fee, and often altogether gratis' (Robinson, 1933, p. 25).

He believed that the law on abortion was illogical, so when in 1908 the *New Orleans and Surgical Journal* reported a symposium on illegal abortion he criticised it as being 'one physician vying the other in his expression of execration of the crime of abortion, the same talk that the fetus is a living human being from the moment of conception' (*Critic and Guide*, 1908, p. 380). But despite this opinion, he did not at this stage call for legalisation. His views did not become known until 1913 when he criticised the radical statements of the German Professor Kocks. Kocks called for abortion throughout pregnancy, but Robinson said that he did not agree that all restrictions should be abolished irrespective of gestation. He preferred to seek legalisation of abortion in the early stages of pregnancy, asserting that 'Abortion is a nasty business ethically, aesthetically and physically, although not infrequently it is fully justifiable as the lesser of two evils' (*Critic and Guide*, 1913). He maintained this position when an American commentator, Herman Dekker (1920), began calling for legal abortion, and gave him space to write a series of articles in the *Critic and Guide*. Dekker's basic argument was that legalisation of birth control had gone through two stages. First, although illegal it became widely used, and secondly, it became accepted legally. Abortion, he suggested, was now in the first position: 'in the process of becoming ethically approved the first stage of widespread practice has already been completed' (*Critic and Guide*, 1920, p. 336). One of the arguments underlying Dekker's proposals for abortion was that the 'lower' classes did not use contraceptives and so those of poorer quality were reproducing themselves to a greater degree. He claimed that if both contraception and abortion were practised it would eliminate the effects of what many saw as 'reverse Darwinism'. Robinson opposed Dekker's standpoint for being too radical and not giving enough weight to the possible problems of abortion. He said that it should only be used in exceptional cases where for one reason or another contraceptives had failed (*Critic and Guide*, 1921, p. 24).

This view of Robinson that abortion should only be used sparingly led him to be very critical of some young people who took a much more relaxed attitude. One day in 1929 a young woman came to his office and requested an abortion. As she had already had three, Robinson was angry: 'I do dislike a certain type of modern young woman who indulges promiscuously, uses contraceptives rather reluctantly, preferring repeat abortions, which she regards as lightly as tossing down a cocktail or a glass of whiskey' (*Critic and Guide*, 1929, p. 428). From the 1920s Robinson took the view that the birth control issue was won, and so he felt able to permit himself to devote some energy to the subject of abortion. In his book *Sex, Love and Morality* (1928) he made a forthright call for legalisation: 'Abortion up to the end of the third month should be made perfectly legal, when performed by a physician and at the request of the woman'. Five years later he devoted a whole book to abortion in which he reiterated his earlier views (1933).

By the early 1930s other doctors like Rongy (1933) were supporting Robinson's call. There was also some pressure for the reform of the laws from a women's group who formed the Association for Reformation of the Abortion Law in 1932 (Taussig, 1936, p. 426). This aimed to broaden the grounds to include cases of rape, seduction, infirmity, likely handicap, destitution and divorce. However, it does not seem to have been very strong and could have had little hope of success in a society which had not even legalised the spread of contraceptive information. There was never anything in the United States of comparable influence to ALRA, for reasons which are partly historical and partly due to the social conditions. In Britain the neo-Malthusian movement had by the 1920s lost its role as the major organisation pushing for birth control reform and was looking for a new issue. It was therefore able to alter its policy on abortion and provide an immediate structure within which pro-choice agitation could operate. In the United States no similar organisation existed. William Robinson and subscribers to the *Critic and Guide* played a similar social role to that of the Malthusians, but Robinson was a lone organiser and when he died in 1936 his magazine closed.

Perhaps a more important factor was, however, the failure of the birth control movement to break down the Comstock Laws until 1936, and the fact that the American Medical Association did not accept contraception until 1937. If this breakthrough had come at a time when Margaret Sanger was younger, she may well have been the person to launch off in a new direction. As it was, she went into semi-retirement. Planned Parenthood's leadership saw its major task to be· spreading of contraceptive knowledge. Adoption of abortion as an issue would frustrate the main aim – a view it shared with Marie Stopes and the Family Planning Association in Britain. For this reason the United States was lacking the effect of an active pressure group for abortion. However, although abortion was a statutory offence in every state, there were wide variations in penalties, and provisions were not uniform. In six states there were no legal exemptions. In thirty-nine states abortion was allowed to save the life of the woman and a further three states and the District of Columbia also allowed abortion if there was a threat to the health of the woman. In Mississippi alone the operation was legal at the discretion of the medical practitioner (Birkett, 1939, p. 165; Taussig, 1936).

Conclusion

At the outbreak of the Second World War there was no country in the world where women were expressly given freedom of choice on abortion. However, apart from those discussed, various other countries did allow abortion in certain circumstances (Birkett, 1939, pp. 158–65). In Yugoslavia a 1929 law allowed abortion to protect the health of the woman, as did an Argentinian law of 1921. The Argentine's Act also allowed abortion for rape or the 'violation of an idiot or insane woman' (Birkett, 1939, p. 158).

In some countries, notably France and Norway, there were no specific exceptions to the abortion law, but practice was more liberal. Birkett (1939, p. 159) reported that the French 1923 law did not specify legal abortion but that 'French medical journals frequently contain accounts of abortions induced for serious medical reasons'. In Germany there were at first no exceptions, but later the Courts ruled that abortion to prevent serious injury to the woman's health was not unlawful. This exception was codified in the 'Law for the Prevention of Hereditary Disease in Posterity' 1933, as amended in 1935. This law also allowed abortion for eugenic reasons with the woman's consent (Birkett, 1939, p. 160). In Poland a 1932 law allowed abortion for the sake of the woman's health and for rape and incest. A Latvian law of 1932, as amended in 1935, allowed abortion not only on the same grounds as Poland but also to 'prevent the birth of a child with serious mental or physical defects' (Birkett, 1939, p. 162). The only other place known to have changed its law during the inter-war period was a region of Spain, Catalonia, which in 1936 allowed abortion for foetal deformity, rape or 'sentimental' reasons in the first three months (Anderson, 1980). These examples show that, while abortion was not freely available under the law, many countries made at least some provisions.

4

Legalisation of Abortion in Britain

The British Abortion Act (1967) was a watershed which influenced the law in many other countries. Amongst the reasons for the legalisation, three groups of factors are relevant – the general climate of opinion, the relative strength of the pressure groups, and the composition of the House of Commons.

Climate of Opinion

In previous chapters the changes in attitudes towards sexual behaviour have been observed and in particular the liberalisation after the First World War. However, after the Second World War such changes do not seem to have occurred, and with some exceptions the period of the late 1940s and 1950s was not one of tremendous upheaval in terms of sexual morality. The war produced deep-seated social changes in British society, and did much to reduce the social class difference (Titmuss, 1963, pp. 75–87). The position of women in society also improved (Myrdal and Klein, 1968). But in the case of sexual morality it appears that the closing of the social distance between the classes meant that chastity which, as has been shown, is mainly associated with the middle class, became a normative value of the working class, too (Pierce, 1963).

In the early 1950s even some social commentators were likely to accept chastity as an ideal and to assert that the problem of morality was being able to persuade young people to accept it. In fact Rowntree and Lavers (1951) put the causes of promiscuity down to the poor conditions of the working class and suggested that, if these were improved, a well conducted campaign in favour of chastity might lead to a great improvement in the nation's moral fibre. This argument would seem very old fashioned within fifteen years but it reflected the dominant middle-class view at the time. The problem was seen to be to persuade the working classes to accept the middle-class value of deferred gratification. There were obviously some opponents of this view amongst the radical members of the middle classes, but in the major countries of Europe chastity was accepted as the ideal pattern of behaviour. Even in Sweden the sex education programme introduced in 1955 was instructed to teach chastity.

Attitudes in Britain, the United States and most of Western Europe changed in the 1960s with the growth of what was popularly called the 'permissive ideology'. A complete explanation of these changes and the way they differed from country to country is beyond the scope of this book, but in the case of Britain some points are worth noting. We have seen that in the nineteenth century the growth of the belief in chastity was linked to the increased power of the Church and the education system. However, after the Second World War the influence of these two sets of institutions changed. By 1962 nearly one third of people were married in civil ceremonies and so were not directly involved with any religious injunctions to chastity (Martin, 1967). Attendance at the Church of England declined and, whereas at the turn of the century 70 per cent of people were married in an Anglican church, by 1962 it was below a half. There was also a change in doctrine and a movement within the Church against the idea that life should be governed by strict rules. Bishop John Robinson's book *Honest to God* (1963, p. 118) challenged many of the religious assumptions and said that it could not be argued that 'sex relations before marriage' are wrong, for the only intrinsic evil is the lack of love. This decline in the practice of religion and change in emphasis meant that the conservative influence of the Church of England declined a great deal during the 1960s.

Other religious groups also began to challenge the contemporary standards. The report *Towards a Quaker View of Sex* (Heron, 1963) stated unequivocally: 'We reject almost completely the traditional approach of the organised church to morality with its supposition that it knows what is right and wrong'. The report continued by proposing that the new morality should be based upon tolerance and understanding of the issues of homosexuality, pre-marital and extra-marital sex. These challenges to the traditional position were opposed by the Archbishop of Canterbury in September 1963 and the Convocation at York, but their opposition just served to suggest that the Church was divided on the issue (Eppel and Eppel, 1966).

The nature of the education system also changed. The number of students in higher education in Britain began to rise just after the war and by 1967–8 had surpassed all the targets of the Robbins Report (King and Moser, 1979). Students before the war constituted only 2.7 per cent of their age group but by 1967 the proportion had risen to 11 per cent of the total (Francome, 1976a). Furthermore, the baby boom of the late 1940s meant that the absolute number of young people rose in the 1960s, and in 1967 the total of those in higher education had risen by over 300,000. The atmosphere at colleges and universities is generally much more liberal than in schools, and so the expansion of higher education meant that many young people were ending their education in a more radical way. This too, served to diminish the conservative influence of both the Church and the education system.

One factor leading to the 'new morality' was thus the changed nature of the traditional conservative forces, but even more important was the growth in strength of new radical groups within the middle class. The mass media managed to break free from some of the constraints it had faced in earlier periods. In terms of literature a key factor was undoubtedly the trial of Penguin Books for publishing D. H. Lawrence's *Lady Chatterley's Lover* which ended with acquittal in 1960. This well publicised case led to a re-evaluation of ideas about what it was permissible to publish and a liberalisation of standards in other media. In 1967 the musical *Hair* introduced nudity to the London stage, and this and other changes were largely the result of the middle-class media feeling free to challenge prior restraints.

There was, too, a growth in the size and strength of radical middle-class youth. The young people in the 1960s had been brought up with little knowledge of the post-war privations. As I have analysed more fully elsewhere (Francome, 1976a) the whole issue of youth changed from its position in earlier years. In the 1950s when people talked about the problems of youth and the generation gap they were often referring to the fact that 'teddy boys' and girls were not following the middle-class patterns of deferred gratification. However, in the 1960s the 'generation gap' referred to the differences in values between the younger middle class and their parents' age group. A significant minority of these young people had the confidence to challenge many of the assumptions of the dominant ideology, and with the development of the 'pill' and the opening of birth control clinics for single people in 1964 they were able to engage in pre-marital intercourse with fewer worries. George Carstairs (1962, p. 51) was able to say in his Reith Lectures: 'It seems to me that our young people are rapidly turning our own society into one in which sexual experience with precautions against conception is becoming accepted as a sensible preliminary to marriage, a preliminary which makes it more likely that marriage, when it comes, will be a mutually satisfying partnership'. This statement was given a great deal of publicity. When previous writers had challenged the belief in chastity their views had not gained widespread acceptance. However, by the 1960s the climate of opinion had changed sufficiently for it to be socially acceptable to challenge tradition. Just as after the First World War, people were talking of the 'new morality', and the liberalisation of attitudes provided an environment within which changes could be brought about.

Apart from the general climate there were a number of events specifically relevant to abortion and these had an important impact on public opinion. A crucial one was the drug Thalidomide which was first marketed for morning sickness in 1957 and was, by 1962, known to be responsible for deformed children. An American, Sherri Finkbine, focused attention on the drug when she was refused termination in the United States and had to fly to Sweden for an abortion (Guttmacher, 1967). In July 1962 questions were raised in the British House of Commons and the House of Lords as to whether women who had taken Thalidomide could get legal abortion. The minister replied that abortion was legal on the grounds of physical or mental health of the woman, but not on the grounds of possible deformity of the foetus (Hindell and Simms, 1971, p. 110). The *Daily Telegraph* attacked Lady Summerskill for daring to ask the question, but the opinion polls at the time revealed that there was public support for abortion for foetal deformity (Hindell and Simms, 1971, p. 110). Thalidomide was thus a reason for many people becoming concerned with the abortion law. Diane Munday, arguably the most effective activist to take up the cause, told me (22 June 1979) that this was the reason she began campaigning:

I joined at the time of Thalidomide. I was offered it when I was carrying Nick, my third son. I was sleeping badly and I had two babies at the time to look after. I was nearly going mad and my doctor actually gave me a prescription for it. It sat on the mantlepiece of the living room downstairs. Sometimes I was very tempted to take it after a sleepless night and then I realised what could have happened.

She learned that if she had taken the drug she could have been carrying a badly deformed foetus with no access to a legal abortion. So she decided to join ALRA to work for a change in the law. Others were similarly influenced, and Thalidomide was thus a key factor in both showing the inadequacies of the law and in galvanising public opinion.

Support for the Change in the Law

The major pressure for change in the law came from the liberal left, but during the period up to the passage of the 1967 Act is was ALRA which dominated the campaign. It was the only pressure group solely concerned with abortion, and in some senses the 1967 Act shows what it is possible to achieve in the right social conditions with good organisational skills even without mass mobilisation.

During the early 1960s younger members of the organisation began to become increasingly involved in it and during a few months up to March 1964 the leading positions on the ALRA executive committee changed hands. The chair was taken by Vera Houghton, wife of a prominent Labour politician, who had been actively involved with International Planned Parenthood (IPPF) for many years, and Madeleine Simms and Diane Munday also joined (Hindell and Simms, 1971). The new composition of the committee led to a much more energetic approach. The three women mentioned worked closely together and Dylis Cossey was the secretary and is still active. Madeleine Simms, an active Fabian, was in terms of her personal behaviour and outlook the most conservative of the women. She recalls how she was appalled when Diane Munday told her that she had had an abortion, for that was the first time she had met anyone who had admitted to one (personal communication, 1977). She drafted the newsletter and did the major part of the writing for the Association. Diane Munday combined a flair for public speaking with enormous tenacity, so she did the larger part of the broad-casting. There were inevitably tensions within the organisation, and one of the most important roles Vera Houghton played was to reduce the conflict. She also helped mould the executive committee by giving each member an area of responsibility. Hindell and Simms (p. 118) say of her: 'Cool, detached, objective, and tolerant, within a short space of time she had acquired an unquestioned authority over all the disparate elements on the committee'.

The committee also contained a number of men who made an important contribution to its work – Alastair Service, for example, was the main political lobbyist – and this involvement of men is an important part of ALRA's tradition. Later commentators have criticised the ALRA leadership at the time of the Act for not being sufficiently committed to feminism. Madeleine Simms commented that one of the benefits they had at the time of liberalising the Act compared to the feminists who became responsible for defending it was that they were supported by their husbands. They were, therefore, relatively free to work for the cause (personal communication, 1978). In later years the increase in female employment meant that there were fewer supported women to take an active role, and full-time workers had to be paid.

Reform or Repeal?

One of the crucial decisions ALRA had to make was whether to aim for the total repeal of the abortion law up to a specified time in the pregnancy, or simply to reform the law by increasing the categories of women eligible for abortion. This question was brought to a head by the suggestion of Professor Glanville Williams at the Annual General Meeting in October 1963 that abortion be legalised on request until the thirteenth week of pregnancy. This proposal was not as radical as that of Stella Browne, but would have been a very great change (Jenkins, 1964). In support Williams claimed that limited changes related to the 'hard cases' would leave untouched the mass of illegal abortions in the country, and he had some support for this proposal. Lord Gardiner agreed with him, as did Dorothea Kerslake, ALRA's most prominent female gynaecologist. He also had backing from regional groups, one of which passed the following resolution by 14 votes to 1:

The North West London Group of ALRA supports Dr. Glanville Williams' view as expressed in his recent address to the AGM that 'doctors should be authorised to terminate any pregnancy of less than thirteen weeks' and that this should become the official aim of the Association, if the medical, legal and political authorities connected with the association agree that this is tactically advisable against existing aims. (3 December 1963)

The full executive had to decide whether or not to back this proposal. On 14 February 1964 Vera Houghton wrote to Madeleine Simms and Diane Munday with suggestions as to the future aims of the organisation for consideration at the next meeting:

The Association's aim is to secure such changes in the law as will provide that a registered medical practitioner may lawfully terminate or advise termination of pregnancy up to the 13th week if he considers it to be in the best interests of the patient. Terminations after the 13th week would only be undertaken to preserve the life of the mother ... To the question Does the Association advocate the complete freedom for women to decide whether or not they will bear a child, the answer is 'Yes', provided that there is a clear indication that this is what the public wants.

However, four days later the executive reversed the last sentence and its reply became 'No, it depends on the medical opinion of the doctor, not the personal opinion of the patient'. With this decision ALRA therefore turned its back on a woman's right to choose, and it seems that it was a tea party at the House of Lords (12 February 1964) which decided ALRA against taking such a step. In a letter (23 March) Vera Houghton said of the event: 'It was pretty clear from the discussion which followed that the Association would not stand a chance of getting a bill introduced, in the present climate of opinion, along the lines recommended by Dr. Williams'. Thus, the main aim became to introduce a 'reform' rather than a 'repeal' bill.

Tactics of the Pressure Groups

ALRA used various tactics to garner support for change, one of which was to gain as much institutional backing as possible. Even before ALRA was revitalised there had been support from a number of different organisations. The Magistrates Association had passed a resolution in favour of reform as early as 31 October 1955 (Hindell and Simms, 1971, p. 83), and by 1963 an ALRA leaflet claimed backing from:

The National Council of Women
The Family Planning Association
The British Social Biology Council
The Eugenics Society
The Women's Co-operative Guild

However, others were needed.

In August 1964 a special leaflet was prepared by ALRA which said:

We feel sure that recent articles in the Press and feature programmes on television and sound radio about the social problem of illegal abortion will not have gone unnoticed and that they reflect a growing public awareness of the unsatisfactory state of the law. We are therefore writing to voluntary organisations, particularly women's groups, which have shown an interest in our aims, to suggest to them that now is the time to make their feelings more strongly known about the need to revise the hundred year old Offences Against the Person Act, 1861.

May we count on your organisation to support us in this renewed fight for a more humane law? If so, would you consider whether you can help us in one or more of the following ways:

1   By submitting a resolution along the lines attached to your next Annual Conference. If this has already been done, would you kindly send us the terms of the resolution? If put to a past conference, please let us know with what result.
2   By circulating copies of the enclosed leaflet 'What is ALRA?' to your members. We need more new members to build up our strength. Please let us know how many copies you will require and we will do our best to supply them. Also enclosed are samples of two further leaflets, 'A Clergyman's View' and 'What Help can ALRA Give?'
3   By becoming a regular contributor to ALRA. Your organisation could do this by applying for affiliate member-

ship, the annual fee for which is one guinea which entitles affiliated bodies to send one member with voting power to General Meetings and to receive two copies of the ALRA newsletter; or, if affiliation is not feasible, by a donation or an individual subscription (minimum 10/– a year).

Our overheads arc kept to the absolute minimum: we have no office premises and no salaried staff, all work in a voluntary capacity. This enables us to devote all our resources to the main task. Any help that your organisation can give will therefore contribute to the extension of our work.

In the next three years support was gained from many organisations, whose resolutions fell into two main categories. A few were calls for repeal of the law up to a certain stage in the pregnancy. For example in 1964 the University Humanist Group Federation Annual Conference supported a resolution which called for it to be lawful to perform an abortion 'on any grounds provided that the termination of pregnancy is performed before thirteen weeks of pregnancy are completed'. The following year the Socialist Medical Association passed a similar motion and called for 'Legislation to enable abortions to be carried out under the National Health Service before the twelfth week of pregnancy' These two organisations specified that the abortion should be carried out early, but this was not the case with the resolution of the Progressive League at its AGM in 1964. This simply called for a change so that the 'termination of pregnancy by a qualified medical practitioner if the expectant mother so requests should be lawful'. However, these kinds of resolutions were in the minority, and far more common were the ones calling for limited extension. Typical of these was that of the National Union of Townswomen's Guilds which in 1965 urged

Her Majesty's Government to introduce legislation to legalise abortion, when personally desired by the woman concerned and when advised by a medical panel and performed by a suitably qualified member of the medical profession in the following circumstances:

1   Where it is necessary to preserve her physical or mental health.

2   Where there is serious risk of a defective child being born.
3   Where the pregnancy results from a sexual offence such as rape or incest.

These conditions were the same as those contained in ALRA's aims. Other organisations which passed similar resolutions to this were:

1965   National Women Citizen's Association AGM
1965   National Secular Society
1965   National Association of Women's Clubs Annual Conference.
1965   Scottish League of Young Liberals
1965   Church Assembly Board of Social Responsibility
1966   Free Church Federal Council National Congress
1966   Co-operative Women's Guild Annual Conference
1966   National Council for Civil Liberties ('supports efforts already being made')
1966   Church of Scotland General Assembly Moral and Social Welfare Board
1966   Royal Medico-Psychological Association (memorandum)
1966   Conservative Political Centre
1966   Congregational Union of England and Wales – Christian Responsibility Committee
1966   Methodist Conference
1967   Law Society and British Academy of Forensic Science Joint Committee
1967   British Council of Churches
1967   National Conference of Labour Women
1967   United Free Church of Scotland General Assembly

Although during this period there was a widespread movement for change, there were differences in the degree of support. The British Council of Churches resolution, for example, called for a clause in the Bill so that the Act could be reviewed after a period of five years, and others were worried lest reform went too far. In 1966 the Free Church Federal Council objected to a 'severely overstrained mother' clause in David Steel's Bill. However, even with such reservations there was growing and solid support.

A second task of the organisation was to build its individual membership. In the early 1960s it had had less than 200 members, but with the impetus of the new leadership and a more aggressive approach it grew steadily, and by 1966 had passed the 1,000 mark. The membership was of course atypical in comparison with the general population. Nearly two-thirds were women, two-thirds had a higher education and a fifth were doctors or para-medical. A third of the women had required an abortion at some time, and politically there was a higher than average number who were left wing. Overall 51 per cent were Labour supporters, 21 per cent Conservatives and 13 per cent Liberal. A fifth were members of the Fabian Society (Hindell and Simms, 1971, p. 120). But although the membership was to the left, there was also support from the right wing. For example, David Steel's medical adviser Peter Diggory was a member of the Conservative party. This kind of support was valued by the ALRA executive as giving a broader base upon which to campaign.

As there was not mass membership, ALRA tried to show the support of the public through opinion polls. One in 1962 found that 72 per cent of the population agreed with abortion for foetal deformity. Three years later NOP found that 70 per cent agreed with abortions if the woman's health would be seriously affected, and only 24 per cent said it should be illegal in all cases. In the following year three-quarters felt that abortion should be easier to obtain. ALRA also tried to monitor clergy and medical opinion to show their support. In 1966 the South East London ALRA group distributed a questionnaire to non-Catholic clergy. The 450 replies showed that a huge majority favoured a change. Only 6 per cent said they were satisfied with the law, and 89 per cent said they were not happy with it. A medical survey carried out by NOP in 1967 gave the first and major clause of the Bill and asked doctors if they agreed with it. A total of 1,180 interviews were reported and the results showed that 65 per cent thought the new grounds were satisfactory or too restricted, 21 per cent felt the proposals were too liberal and 10 per cent disagreed with all abortions (4 per cent were undecided). So with these results ALRA was able to claim widespread support for change.

ALRA used a variety of techniques to keep abortion in the news. Sometimes it would simply exploit an event, as with Thalidomide, but on other occasions it actually set out to make newsworthy discoveries. A good example of this was a study of the abortifacient drugs racket in 1965 under the direction of Dr Martin Cole. Three investigators, two women and a man, visited forty shops in London and Birmingham asking for products to bring on a delayed period, and a twelve-page report was produced. This said: 'The impression was gained that this sort of request was so common as to occasion no distinctive reaction' and that, while the preparations were never labelled 'abortifacients', they made claims such as bring 'swift and blessed relief'. The findings showed that the use of abortifacient pills was still being tried by women unable to obtain a legal abortion (Hindell and Simms, 1971, p. 34). ALRA was able to make political capital out of this fact, and Madeleine Simms wrote in her press release: 'Our present antique abortion laws have the effect of encouraging women to resort to drugs when the wish to end unwanted pregnancies, instead of consulting their doctors to discuss the problem. It is suspected that these drugs rarely produce the desired results but may sometimes poison the mother or damage the foetus if taken in large doses' (undated). ALRA could, therefore, argue that a change in the law would lead to a great improvement in the health of women who would not need to resort to such remedies.

Those in favour of change stressed the fact that they were not particularly radical on other issues. When speaking they dressed conservatively in order not to alienate the support of the majority. A large part of the ALRA public speaking engagements, both to local groups and for the media, were fulfilled by Diane Munday, and her lecture notes are indicative of the issues in the campaign. The major points she made were as follows:

1 In a survey over half the doctors polled said they did not know how to interpret the current law.
2 Rape and incest are far more common than expected. Yet the law does not specifically allow abortion in these cases.
3 Arguments against abortion used by the opposition:

   a) There are many physical dangers of the operation;
   b) Abortion leads to depression and guilt;
   c) Abortion leads to promiscuity.

4 Present situation – There are now 1,500 abortions on the National Health Service compared to 100,000 illegal ones.
5 The Catholic Church is not consistent in its teaching. From 1211 to 1869 it recognised two types of foetus. It taught that the male foetus became animated at 40 days and the female at 80

days. Furthermore, until 1869 the Church allowed abortion until quickening.

6   The same arguments previously used against contraception are now used against abortion.

7   Anti-abortionists are trying to impose their law. In contrast the proposed liberalisation would be permissive and nobody would be forced to do anything against their conscience.

The facts she used show clearly the approach taken by the supporters of change. They emphasised the problem of illegal abortions, the 'hard cases' in terms of women who were raped, and the attempts of the Church to impose its theological beliefs.

The personal problems associated with lack of availability of abortions were particularly emotive, and an effective leaflet entitled 'In Desperation' contained 'a small selection from many such letters received by the Abortion Law Reform Association each week'. One of these read as follows:

I went to the hospital to terminate my pregnancy. I was only a few weeks and I had to wait to see one doctor and then another, and so on till I got into such a state I thought it would be done, but they said 'No'. I begged them as this is my tenth child. My husband has a bad heart and is off work a lot. My children's ages run from 16 years to my youngest who is 13 months and it's just too much for me. I go mad sometimes with worry, also I get so upset I sit and cry for hours. If I could have had £15 I could have got it done from a woman, but who would have that amount of money with all my children. I can tell you sometimes I wish I had the nerve to end it all, that is how I get, so I think if a woman wants it done she is entitled to it.

Using cases such as this ALRA was able to show the suffering of women faced with poor social conditions or the illegal abortionist, and mobilise public support. Overall, ALRA was thus a highly effective pressure group.

Opposition

The opposition to abortion was at first sporadic and unorganised. It faced the problem that the law was on its side, which made it difficult to generate enthusiasm. Diane Munday set out their problem as follows: 'If you are a fighter you fight against something. There is no glory or pleasure or satisfaction in fighting for something that exists' (personal interview, 22 June 1979). So the opponents of the Act had to attempt to overcome the feelings of apathy of their potential supporters, especially in the early part of the campaign. Norman St John Stevas, Britain's leading Catholic layperson, noted the lack of opposition from Catholics at the time of the second reading of the Abortion Bill: 'Last Friday was a bad day for public morality in Britain . . . The response of Catholic M.P.'s was all the more disappointing because of the very considerable effort made by the Catholic Union to rally opposition to the Bill. An excellent brief was provided and a number of meetings were held in the House to inform members on the issues involved' (*Catholic Herald*, 29 July 1966). Only fourteen out of the thirty-two Catholic MPs turned up to vote at the Second Reading and it seems that the Catholic Church was caught off guard. Lord Craigmyle, leader of the Catholic Union, said that the vote 'was a shock to us' and talked of 'the appalling weight of the abortion lobby'.

The Church, therefore, was not ready for this particular battle and the fact that it was opposed to contraception diminished its credibility. It was easy to understand Lord Craigmyle's complaint: 'If a Catholic makes a speech on abortion, his views are dismissed, he is not heard with respect . . . we are, as it were, being persecuted for Christ's sake' (*New Society*, 9 March 1967). The Church was in a weak position and, furthermore, prominent Anglican clergymen were willing to attack its stance. An article in the *Evening News* (15 November 1966) by Nicholas Stacey, the Rector of Woolwich, entitled 'Why Rome Is Wrong', blamed the Church for being responsible for a large number of illegal abortions because of its attitude to birth control. It also outlined one of the problems for the Pope: 'If he now sanctions the use of mechanical methods of contraception, he has to admit that his church has been wrong in the past. This would cut at the roots of its authority.'

This kind of attack raised questions about the Catholic Church's position and its leadership was not particularly astute in putting forward its views. One particularly clumsy attempt was made at the Annual Conference of the Institute of Directors on 10 November 1966 when Cardinal Heenan attacked the Abortion Bill and then astonished his audience by saying: 'You directors, if you stand off men, may be responsible for the death of countless unborn children' (*New Society*, 9 March 1967). The supporters of the Bill were quick to point out that unemployment was not a criterion for abortion and the attack was counterproductive. The feelings against Catholic intervention therefore grew, and when the Society for the Protection of Unborn Children was formed in January 1967 it excluded Catholics from its committee. But although the Catholic hierarchy was not involved in the organisation of the major pressure group, it was Catholics who became one of the main sources of opposition. By December 1966, Peter McDonald, a wealthy Manchester lawyer, had distributed over 300,000 copies of a pamphlet entitled 'To Be or Not to Be . . .', possibly the first of the emotional leaflets from the anti-abortionists. It drew comparisons with Dachau and Belsen, and said 'if the Abortion Bill goes through, Herod will laugh in Hell. There will be perpetuated in our name a massacre of the Innocents more dreadful than any Herod could have imagined.' It also opposed abortion for rape and so implied the need to tighten the British law.

Eventually there was a growth in the Catholic grass roots movement. One group based in Manchester duplicated 1,500 copies of a petition against the Bill. The Union of Catholic Mothers urged its 30,000 members to write to their MPs opposing change, and several leagues representing 6,000 Catholic doctors announced that their members would perform no abortions. This pressure built up through the latter part of 1966 as an extensive article in the *Scotsman* (3 December 1966) described:

> In the last few days, an immensively powerful Roman Catholic lobby against the Private Member's Bill to reform the antiquated abortion law has been gathering momentum throughout Britain. Suddenly the country is flooded by anti abortion petitions, M.P.'s are inundated with letters, huge meetings of Catholics express passionate opposition to the principles of the Bill . . . In Scotland M.P.'s who might have been expected to support David Steel's reform are taking a different line: in Paisley last Sunday, John Robertson, Protestant Labour M.P. for a constituency with 9,000 Catholics in it pledged a mass meeting of 1,000 Catholic anti abortionists that he would vote against the Bill. Other Glasgow M.P.'s are known to be swithering.

But though pressure was being brought to bear against the Bill it was already too late, and in some senses could be dismissed. For example, the reason for quoting the *Scotsman* above is not just the information it gave but because it located the pressure as coming from the Catholic Church. This made it much more easy to discount.

Society for the Protection of Unborn Children

SPUC had its beginnings in the correspondence columns of the *Church Times* in the autumn of 1966. One of its proponents was Elspeth Rhys-Williams, whose mother had been a member of the Birkett Committee in the 1930s. Other members were Lord Barrington, who had fought against Silkin's abortion bills in the Lords, and the Bishop of Bath and Wells, who became the most prominent churchman on its governing body (*New Society*, 9 March 1967). Possibly its biggest coup was gaining the support of Aleck Bourne, the credit for which is taken by Phyllis Bowman, SPUC's press secretary at the time. She heard Bourne speak and say that if he could have saved both the raped girl from suffering and also the foetus he would have done so. He was against any extension of the grounds as he felt his case had made the law sufficiently liberal and so became a willing supporter who was able to provide a great deal of credibility to the SPUC campaign. His presence also prevented SPUC from making the absolutist position the official policy of the organisation. Two other prominent supporters were Professor Peter Huntingford, a gynaecologist, who was later to change his mind on the issue, and C. B. Goodhart, a Cambridge-based academic who wrote extensively on the subject of illegal abortions.

The ploy of not having any Catholics on the executive took into account some of the factors mentioned above, and SPUC used the usual techniques to attempt to sway Parliament. A petition it devised calling upon the government to set up a Royal Commission to consider all the relevant facts was distributed in April 1967 and all the 10,000 Anglican vicars were asked to collect signatures. However, it seems that most were not sympathetic, one pointing out in a circular letter that the petition was launched by two Roman Catholic MPs, Norman St John Stevas and James Dunn. Furthermore, the British Council of Churches met and concluded that Christian compassion in the face of human suffering did require a measure of reform (Hindell and Simms, 1971, p. 100). The aim of a million signatures on the petition was not reached but, on 1 July, 530,000 names were taken to 10 Downing Street in the company of the two main sponsors together with Jill Knight, MP, Gordon Oakes, MP, and various medical personnel including six uniformed nurses.

As well as organising various activities such as lobbies and letter writing campaigns, SPUC commissioned a Gallup Poll. The questions were directly related to the Bill and phrased in such a way as to show support for the SPUC campaign. One rather tortuous one asked: If a Lords amendment was rejected should the government set up a Royal Commission? SPUC took heart from the fact that a majority of the population said they would support a Commission in these circumstances, a ploy which would have postponed a change in the law indefinitely. In fact SPUC became quite skilled in a short time; it was, the overall social conditions that were against its success.

Medical Bodies

The leaders of the major medical groups were opposed to much change in the law. A short time before the Second Reading the Royal College of Gynaecologists produced a report which suggested that major change was not necessary since no gynaecologist would hesitate to induce an abortion under the existing law whenever 'the continuation of the pregnancy would be detrimental to the physical or mental welfare of the woman'. It set out its misgivings as to the dangers of the operation and stated categorically: 'the majority of gynaecologists in this country can see no urgent need for reform of the law governing abortion' (Hindell and Simms, 1971, p. 168). However, it recognised that some change was inevitable and took the view that the following restraints should be imposed:

1 The grounds should be strictly limited.
2 They should be authorised by a consultant gynaecologist.
3 They should only be carried out where there was 'substantial risk that the child if born would suffer from such physical or mental abnormalities as to deprive it of any prospect of reasonable enjoyment of life'.
4 No abortions should be carried out on the grounds that

conception took place under the age of consent as this might lead to promiscuity and to pressure being placed on doctors.

The preservation of the freedom of the gynaecologist was a recurring theme in the report and it warned that legislators should be reasonably sure of their co-operation before changing the law.

The BMA report published in July 1966 was similar to that of the Royal College of Gynaecologists. The major difference between the two organisations was that the BMA did not agree that abortions should be restricted to consultant gynaecologists. One of the reasons for the opposition of the medical profession was its belief that too much change could result in women telling their doctors what to do. The profession therefore strongly concurred with the suggestion of the Church of England that nobody other than the doctor could make the assessment of whether or not the pregnancy should be terminated.

Tactics of the Anti-Abortionists

The necessity for those who disagree with an issue on ethical or moral grounds to formulate their argument in a way that is acceptable to the rest of the population has already been discussed. The main argument of the advocates of reform was that there were many illegal abortions each year often performed in dangerous circumstances with great risk to the woman. The main effect of legalisation would be to transfer these from the illegal to the legal sector. Furthermore, the reformers stated that rich women have always been able to gain access to doctors willing to perform abortions if the fee is right, and so reform would give poor women what rich women had always been able to afford. This was a powerful argument for legalisation, for it suggested that there would be little change in the overall number of abortions.

The opponents of the Bill had, therefore, to try to promote an alternative scenario. They argued that the number of illegal abortions was relatively low and that the advocates of reform were inflating the number for political reasons. Furthermore, they suggested, a change in the law would not lead to a reduction in illegal abortions but would just make people more 'abortion minded' and both legal and illegal abortions would increase. They also argued that it would fundamentally alter the moral values of society and lead to a lack of respect for life in general.

It is interesting to contrast the statements of two Conservative MPs in the Committee on David Steel's Bill (*Hansard*, 8 and 22 March 1967):

Pro Choice.   Sir George Sinclair (Dorking): 'The object of this Bill, as I see it is not to encourage abortion on demand, but to help women in cases which it defines, as clearly as is practicable, to obtain abortions legally and not to be driven, as many of them are today, to seek illegal operations. As it now stands, the Bill seeks to transfer as many of these defined cases as possible from the illegal to the legal list. If it is successful it will considerably increase the number of legal operations and reduce the number of illegal ones.'

Anti Choice.   Norman St John Stevas (Chelmsford): 'It is essential, therefore, that we should have the maximum amount of information available so that action will be taken if necessary. My belief is that action will be necessary, because not only will it be found that the illegal rate of abortion will rise but that the legal rate will bound up as well, and there will be a general increase in demand for abortion throughout the country.'

This argument that the number of illegal abortions would increase was used by virtually all those opposed to liberalisation.

The findings of the academics also reflected their side of the debate. Glass's (1940) suggestion that there were 100,000 illegal abortions a year was given widespread publicity. However, SPUC academics were proposing a much lower figure. For example C. B. Goodhart (1973) claimed that 100,000 was much too high and that 'the true figure could not have exceeded 20,000, and was probably nearer 15,000 criminal abortions a year in Britain before 1967'. He also raised the spectre of the abortion rate continuing to rise to enormous levels rather than tapering off as the abortions in the illegal sector were transferred. So even at the academic level there was serious dispute. It is interesting to note that in a report the Royal College of Gynaecologists suggested a figure of 14,600 criminal abortions each year rather than 100,000, and asserted that liberalisation might not eliminate illegal abortion but rather make the population 'abortion minded' as it claimed had happened in Japan, Hungary and Czechoslovakia (*BMJ*, 2 April 1966). The anti-abortionists also emphasised the dangers of abortion. In particular they often said that it was more dangerous than childbirth. SPUC claimed this in its literature calling for signatures for a Royal Commission, and we shall see that this claim was an important factor in the final shaping of the law.

Action in Parliament

The fact that abortion was considered an issue of conscience meant that the law could only be changed if one of the top six MPs in the Private Members ballot chose to introduce it and if the conditions in the Commons were suitable for its passage.

There were a number of early attempts to introduce legislation. In 1952 Joseph Reeves drew a place in the ballot and decided to introduce a Bill. He was, however, not high enough in the order and had only one and a half minutes in which to speak. Soon after Lord Amulree, a liberal peer, attempted to introduce a Bill into the Lords which he subsequently withdrew. In 1961 the Second Reading of a liberalising Bill in the Commons, introduced by Kenneth Robinson was talked out without a vote. In 1965 Renee Short attempted to introduce a Bill under the ten-minute rule, a device for airing the subject, but this was also talked out, as was a Bill introduced by the Conservative MP Simon Wingfield Digby. Lord Silkin introduced two Bills into the House of Lords, one of which fell at the end of the session, but it was not until David Steel drew third place in the Ballot that a change in the law looked likely.

There were a number of factors that had changed in terms of the parliamentary situation. First of all Labour had a large majority and its MPs were more sympathetic to abortion reform than the Conservatives. Secondly, there were people in key positions who could be relied upon to help its passage. Roy Jenkins, the Home Secretary, was known to be a supporter of change and the Minister of Health was Kenneth Robinson who, as has been shown, had introduced his own Bill. Douglas Houghton was in the Cabinet and ALRA had in him an impeccable contact in the government. There was also the advantage of a long parliamentary session due to the timing of the election, which would make it easier for the Bill to pass through all its stages. There was no attempt from the opposition to talk out the Bill and it passed its Second Reading on 22 July 1966 by 223 votes to 29. The vote showed clearly the left-wing nature of the support. Fifty-one Conservatives voted for the Bill, which was about a fifth of their total strength, whereas 161 Labour members were in support which was more than two-fifths of their total. The Liberals supported the Bill by ten to one.

Steel's Bill thus had the overwhelming support of the House, and the problem of its passage was largely a technical one, although there was also the danger that the medical profession might become too alienated and refuse to co-operate with the Act. A further problem was that it could be amended in committee, and it was the 'social clause' that was particularly under attack. In fact in November 1966, after pressure from the British Medical Association, the Royal College of Gynaecologists and the Church of England, David Steel issued a statement that he intended to withdraw the social clause which had provided for abortion where the woman's capacity as a mother might be overstrained. This action was regarded as a betrayal by ALRA who had to face the fact that they did not have control over the Bill. This point was made to me by Vera Houghton: 'There comes a time when your Bill becomes their Bill'. Members of Parliament are not the puppets of the pressure groups.

It was not until 18 January 1967 that the Bill went into committee, which contained twenty-two people who had voted for it, three who had opposed it and five who had abstained. The opponents did what they could to slow its progress by introducing as many amendments as possible, and the Bill's supporters did their best to oil the passage. The unofficial whip of the supporters was Peter Jackson and he told me (private communication, 1977) that for the most part the policy of those on his side was to keep quiet. After the committee the Bill returned to the House for the Report Stage, where there were a number of attempts to prevent its progress. But after an all-night sitting, the Bill passed its Third Reading on 13 July 1967 by 167 votes to 83. This was a much smaller victory than the Second Reading, but reflected the fact that some, like Leo Abse, had voted for the Bill at an earlier stage even though they were basically anti-abortion.

The Bill then moved to the Lords. Lord Silkin seemed the obvious person to pilot it through because of his previous interest in the subject but at first he was doubtful, feeling that the Bill was too weak now the social clause had been 'given away by the sponsor to pacify the opposition'. He felt it might be better to introduce a stronger Bill at a later time, but eventually changed his mind. In the Lords a number of amendments were introduced. A clause specifying that only consultants should carry out abortions was introduced at one stage but then voted out again, and various other changes were suggested. But by far the most important alteration came at the end of the debate. One of the problems was to define the degree of risk to the pregnant woman necessary for a legal abortion. Lord Parker, the Lord Chief Justice, who was generally opposed to the Bill, noted that all the suggestions such as 'grave risk' or 'serious risk' would cause problems of definition in the courts. He therefore proposed a much simpler criterion – that abortion should be legal if the risk to life or the risk of injury to health was greater by continuing the pregnancy than by terminating it. This amendment seems to have been accepted with little thought – even the Home Office said that it was not a profound change. However, Norman St John Stevas pointed out that if abortion were really as safe as Renee Short and the other reformers claimed, then abortion would always be legal. The anti-abortionists were in a difficult position on this matter for, as we have seen, they had been claiming that abortion was more dangerous than childbirth. Now they were caught out by their own arguments and the amendment was included as the Act received the Royal Assent on 27 October 1967.

The British Abortion Act has its weaknesses as we can all recognise. It does not give women the right to choose an abortion, so women still have to plead with their medical practitioners. Furthermore, there was no obligation placed on the NHS to provide free abortions, so overall 50 per cent, and in some areas over 90 per cent, of women still have to pay for their operations. It has been argued that it is possible that if the leaders in the 1960s had planned abortion on request they would have had more support. The women's movement might well have mobilised and developed around the issue, as happened in New York. However these US agitators were working after the British success, with different laws, and a more developed women's movement. All in all, therefore, despite its acknowledged weaknesses, the 1967 Act must be seen as a great advance.

5
Legalisation of Abortion in America

The abortion laws in the United States were overthrown in a campaign that lasted only twelve years. During this relatively short time the laws for all states changed from being restrictive to being amongst the most liberal in the world. This change was much more marked than the more gradual liberalisation in Britain and was due to a combination of social, medical, political and legal factors.

The discussion on the background to the British 1967 Act has shown that one of the important influences was the liberalisation of sexual attitudes. This occurred also in the United States, and for largely the same reasons. There was a similar growth in the power of the radical middle classes with the expansion of education and decline in the conservative forces. The number of young people had increased as it had in Britain. In fact Coleman (1966) has pointed out that the baby boom beginning in 1946 would cause a 50 per cent increase in the age group 14–24 by the end of the decade 1960–70. With an increasing proportion of students in higher education, as in Britain, the increase in this highly visible group was much greater (Francome, 1976a).

There was also growth in the availability of contraception. The Supreme Court decision of 1965 overthrew restrictions on married people using birth control on the grounds of the right to privacy, and other decisions in the courts were important in a move towards liberalisation. The legalisation of *Lady Chatterley's Lover* was discussed earlier, and these kinds of changes paralleled those in Britain. However, there were a number of social differences, of which three are particularly important. First of all, due to the greater heterogeneity of the society and the greater number of religious conservatives, the acceptance of 'permissiveness' was much less universal than in Britain. Secondly, the sexual divisions in the United States were stronger. Betty Friedan (1963) put this kind of difference down to what she called 'The Feminine Mystique', the belief that women should have a totally different role in society to men. This concept seems to have been much more prevalent in the United States and to have frustrated women's attempts to gain equality. In Britain the grants system promoted equality, at least for some, amongst the sexes. In the United States many of the male students had jobs and were wealthier which meant it was much easier to keep up traditional patterns of relationship with the men paying for evenings out and women playing the more passive role. The fact that these traditional sex differences are more deeply delineated in the United States has meant that the women's movement has had far more problems in obtaining a revaluation of roles. In terms of sexual behaviour the double standard is stronger there and, although liberalisation of attitudes occurred, it was more because sexuality began at an earlier period of the relationship rather than that the sexist nature of the relationship ended (Francome, 1980d).

Thirdly, the change in attitude towards radicalism was much stronger in the USA. Student radicalism developed from issues which deeply affected their lifestyle. The civil rights movement grew from activists involved in the summer project of 1962 and concerned itself with manifest and institutionalised racism at home. The war in Vietnam was not just an ideological issue but affected those who were threatened with the draft. The direct relevance of these issues led to a much more fundamental revaluation of the basic values of society than occurred in Britain (Francome, 1976a).

These important differences in radicalism between the two societies, with other factors, led to the United States abortion campaign ending in a very different way from that of British liberalisation. In fact in the USA there was not really one campaign but two separate ones – first a campaign for liberalisation, and then a demand for repeal.

Revival of the Reform Movement

In the United States during the 1930s the demands for legal abortion had faded away, and after the Second World War there was at first no pressure to get it restarted. Planned Parenthood (1945) took the view that it should push for contraception as an alternative. A pamphlet entitled *Planned Parenthood's Campaign for 1945* argued that one reason for birth control was the high number of abortions which were 'the second largest cause of maternal mortality and, for every woman who dies, three are made sterile or invalid'.

This argument that abortion was dangerous and that the numbers could be reduced by contraception meant that Planned Parenthood continued to take an anti-abortion stance up until the 1960s. In fact as late as 1963 a pamphlet could state: 'Abortion requires an operation. It kills the life of a baby it has begun. It is dangerous to your life and health' (Planned Parenthood, 1963). Despite such comments, Planned Parenthood was the source of the first major event to consider abortion. In 1957 it held a conference of various specialists to discuss it (Lader, 1967, p. 2) at which the participants proposed the establishment of consultation centres for women seeking termination along the lines of those in Scandinavia. It also called for a study of the various abortion laws by authoritative bodies such as the Council of State Governments and the American Law Institute (ALI) in order to frame a model law that could be presented to the states to replace existing statutes.

ALI responded to the call in December 1959 when its model Bill was revealed (Lader, 1967, p. 145). It recommended that a doctor be permitted to terminate a pregnancy:

1   If continuation of pregnancy 'would gravely impair the physical or mental health of the mother'.
2   If the doctor believed 'that the child would be born with grave physical or mental defects', or
3   If the pregnancy resulted from rape or incest.

This proposed Bill was revealed to the public in 1962 as part of the Model Legal Code approved by ALI. Its presentation aroused a great deal of interest and Alan Guttmacher, President of Planned Parenthood, commented: 'Its mere promulgation opened the medical profession's eyes to the preservation of health as being a justification for abortion' (Walbert and Butler, 1973, p. 68). In the following year the American Medical Association 'took note' of the ALI Bill. However, until 1967 there was little interest from the states. From 1962 to 1966 only five legislatures considered an ALI-type Bill, and in no case was the law changed.

The biggest pressure during this period was in California. An attempt at reform failed in 1961. Two years later Assemblyman Alan Beilenson believed he had a better opportunity for success when he had a clear majority in committee for a 'do pass' recommendation (Lader, 1967, p. 146). However, pressure against the Bill grew and in this and subsequent years until 1967 it was unsuccessful. Furthermore there was organised opposition to the Beilenson Bill within the pro-choice movement. The first organisation to concentrate solely on abortion was set up in California by Patricia Maginnis and called the Society for Humane Abortion (Lader, 1967). Maginnis was the first woman to call for outright repeal of the law, but she felt that the Beilenson Bill was inadequate since it would not cover all the women in need. The second abortion organisation to be set up was the Association for the Study of Abortion, founded in 1964. One of its aims was to educate the public by providing speakers for civic gatherings, radio and television shows (Lader, 1967, p. 148). However, it would not carry out any political activities because of its tax exempt status which limited its sphere of influence. Thus in the mid-1960s there was still no national organisation pressing for abortion reform, and the early changes in the law in 1967 were the result of local activity.

Reform v. Repeal

At this stage the situation in the United States seemed to be moving in the same direction as in Britain with a limited liberalisation of the laws and an extension of rights to some categories of women. One of the most important campaigners during this period was Alan Guttmacher, and he consistently argued the case for reform rather than repeal. In 1959 (p. 237) he said, 'I do not want blanket permission to abort any woman who is unhappily pregnant; I do not think our civilization is ready for this or that it ever should be'.

Eight years later he reiterated his view that the path of reform was preferable. He pointed to the ALI Bill and the British law and commented:

> I believe with stubborn conviction that our archaic abortion laws should be overhauled. They should be made more lenient so as at least to grant legal sanctions for all women to be legally aborted for those indications which many doctors now recognize for their individual private patients. In addition certain social, humanitarian indications should be added which even today's more liberal doctors deem untouchable. What would such a revision accomplish? It would not eradicate the

legal, social and medical blight of illegal abortion. This can only be done by legalizing abortion on demand, as has been done in Japan and Eastern Europe. I am opposed to this for the U.S. in 1967. I believe that social progress is better made by evolution than revolution. Today, complete abortion license would do great violence to the beliefs and sentiments of most Americans. Therefore I doubt that the U.S. is as yet ready to legalize abortion on demand, and I am therefore reluctant to advocate it in the face of all the bitter dissension such a proposal would create. (Guttmacher, 1967, p. 12)

So Guttmacher at this stage still placed himself fully within the reformist camp, and it seems that the medical groups were of the same opinion.

At its meeting in Atlantic City in June 1967 the American Medical Association (AMA) House of Delegates considered a policy recommendation on abortion. It suggested that the AMA should adopt a policy which was a modification of the Model Penal Code of the American Law Institute. This proposed that abortion should be allowed for threats to the life or health of the woman, where the infant might be born with incapacitating physical or mental deformity, and where there was evidence of rape or incest. The policy also recommended that three doctors should examine the patient and the operation should be performed in a hospital. The statement with minor changes was accepted as AMA policy. Thus there were reform Bills with institutional support, and a number of states passed them. Colorado was the first in 1967 and California and North Carolina followed shortly afterwards. In 1968 Georgia and Maryland liberalised their laws and in 1969 they were followed by Arkansas, Kansas, Delaware, Oregon and New Mexico. It seemed at first that New York was also going to have a reform Bill. In 1968 Governor Rockefeller set up an eleven-member commission to examine the law and to make recommendations for change. This commission proposed a Bill on the ALI model plus an additional clause allowing abortion on request for any mother of four children. The Bill was, however, rejected by the New York State legislature in 1969 and it must have seemed to many at that time that a repeal Bill would have no chance of success. Yet in July 1970 the New York legislature passed a law giving abortion on request in the first twenty-four weeks of pregnancy – an unlikely sequence of events in the context of theories of gradualism in the process of social change. However, as is discussed fully below, the overall victory of the repeal forces was due to a number of factors specific to the situation in the United States (Lader, 1973).

First of all, there was the lack of a recognised national reform organisation that had the allegiance of most of the activists. The Association for the Study of Abortion, the nearest group to this was not political. So when the National Association for the Repeal of Abortion Laws was formed it did not compete with anyone. Lader (1973, p. 88) tells how he, Lonny Myers and Ruth Smith met in his apartment in late 1968 to discuss a national conference on abortion laws at which the aim would be to set up an organisation for repeal. That this was a possibility reflected the fact that there was a substantial body of support amongst the radical groups. The involvement of the feminists around the complete right to choose was one important factor and, further- more, they were supported by those who had been organising the referral services. Parts of the New York clergy had set up a consultation service and they noted that the reforms being proposed would leave many women without access to legal operations: 'Our day to day work taught us how few women wanted abortions for the reasons most liberals conceded were justifiable. When we started, most of us favoured some liberalisa- tion of the law, but within a six month period every clergy believed passionately not in liberalisation but in repeal of the law' (Carmen and Moody, 1973, p. 102). Other radicals argued a similar case, and by the time of the NARAL conference in February 1969 there was a solid base in the formation of New Yorkers for Abortion Law Repeal.

There was also a change of mind amongst some of the older advocates of reform. Alan Guttmacher described his conversion thus:

The more I studied early results from the five states which had been the first to liberalize their laws, the more I began to espouse the opinion that abortion statutes should be entirely removed from the criminal code. The number of legal abortions being undertaken under the new liberalized laws, when contrasted with the figures for the previously undertaken illegal abortions, were far too low. (Walbert and Butler, 1973, p. 60)

Guttmacher went on to discuss the fact that in 1968 California had only 5,000 abortions under its new law, and told of a visit to Colorado where there were many bureaucratic obstacles. He concluded that

> Abortion on request – necessitating the removal of 'abortion' from the penal codes – was the only way to democratic legal abortion and to sufficiently increase the numbers performed so as to decrease the incidence of illegal abortions. I came to this conclusion in 1969, forty seven years after abortion first came to my medical attention when I was a third year medical student. (Walbert and Butler, 1973, p. 60)

Thus with the additional support of the older generation of radicals, repeal won out over the reform position. However, the question remains as to what were the social and political conditions that allowed it to succeed.

Role of the Constitution

If the legislators in the United States pass a law, it can be challenged on the grounds that it infringes guaranteed rights. The courts have a great amount of formal power and can decide that a law is completely invalid. In Britain courts do have some power of interpretation, as witnessed in the Bourne judgement, but the courts' role is within narrow limits. They are not allowed to declare a law passed by Parliament unconstitutional. In contrast it is possible within the United States system to try to have a law totally annulled by a declaration of unconstitutionality. This is illustrated by two important court decisions in 1969 which changed the nature of the abortion debate. On 5 September 1969 the California Supreme Court declared the state law unconstitutional after the trial of Dr Leon Belous. In its decision the Court defined the rights of a woman over her own procreation for the first time. The ruling was also the first State Supreme Court decision in United States history to declare an abortion statute unconstitutional (Lader, 1973, p. 110), and it set a precedent for other pending cases. Belous had been tried under the pre-1967 law, not the one that was in operation by the time the case came to court. However, a similar decision was taken two months later in the trial of Dr Milan Vuitch who had been accused of breaking the abortion law of Washington DC. On 10 November 1969 the law was declared unconstitutional and Washington became the first area of the country where abortion was completely legalised (Francome, 1980e, p. 615). According to the decision there was no necessity for hospital treatment and any licensed physician could perform abortion if his equipment met the required standards. It was thus in the courts that the advocates of repeal had their first success.

The Medical Profession

A second factor, and one that was again different from Britain, was the attitude of the medical profession. In Britain the social researchers had found doctors largely opposed to change. A survey conducted in 1967–8 found that only 22 per cent thought that a woman with several children should be able to have an abortion (Cartwright, 1970). It was only after the Act had been in operation for two years that a liberalisation of medical attitudes was noted. In the United States it seems that there was much greater support for change. A survey by the journal *Modern Medicine* in 1969 showed that 51 per cent of US physicians wanted abortion available to any woman upon her request to a competent physician (Lader, 1973). This contrasts markedly with the attitudes of British doctors. It reflects both a more liberal view and the different roles played by doctors in the two societies. In Britain there is quite strict control of medical practice, especially in hospitals where a consultant is in charge of the medical care and other doctors are regarded as being in training. In the USA professional independence is much more guarded and individual doctors act more freely. They are allowed to enter hospitals and carry out operations based on their professional judgement, and the general practitioner has much greater freedom than a British doctor (Bunker, 1970). Thus the belief in non-intervention of the law could in part be due to a general belief in the right to freedom from interference. Furthermore, doctors in the USA stood to gain financially by legalisation, whereas the British surgeons were concerned that a large increase in abortion patients would draw resources from other services.

The Women's Movement

A third difference between the societies was the role of the women's movement which was much more active in the United

States. Paradoxically it was a man, Lawrence Lader, who was the catalyst in this direction. He told me (personal interview, 1978) that he first came to the conclusion that abortion should be a woman's right after discussions with Margaret Sanger, and in his book *Abortion* (1966) he called the complete legalisation of abortion 'the one just and inevitable answer to the quest for feminine freedom' (p. 169). Lader had known Betty Friedan for a number of years, and when she became the first president of the National Organisation for Women (NOW) he persuaded her that abortion should be one of its main aims. This became NOW policy at its convention in 1967, and from that time on the abortion movement in the United States had the backing of a strong and articulate women's movement.

It is possible that if the British movement had adopted a more militant position it might have received more support from the women. Lucinda Cisler, talking of the USA, said in 1970: 'Part of the reason that the reform movement was very small was that it appealed mostly to altruism and very little to people's self interest: the circumstances covered by "reform" are tragic but they affect very few women's lives, whereas repeal is compelling because most women know the fear of unwanted pregnancy and in fact get abortions for that reason.' This comment was echoed by Assemblywoman Constance Cook, the sponsor of the New York repeal Bill: 'I knew that women did not want reform, at least not enough to go out and work for it, whereas I suspected they would work for repeal, and they did' (Lader, 1973, p. 125). In Britain the women's movement did not become involved with the abortion campaign until the Act had been passed.

Confrontation Tactics

A fourth difference between the two societies was the much greater appeal of confrontation tactics in the United States. I have already shown how the movement towards radicalism was more relevant to the immediate position of those involved. They were also much more likely to engage in direct action, as could be seen from the invasion of the segregated Woolworths shop in 1960. Black students waited in vain for a white waitress to serve them, and later returned with many of their colleagues (Lauter and Howe, 1970, p. 27). This kind of approach to political activism had direct relevance to the abortion campaign. Members of the movement not only worked for changes in the law but also set out to provide abortions and to effect a direct challenge.

One of the earliest exponents of this tactic was Pat Maginnis, and in 1966 the *New York Times* (4 December) carried the headline 'Abortion Classes Offered on Coast'. The article reported that she was touring California giving advice on abortion methods and information on countries where they could be obtained. At the time Maginnis was 38 years old and had had three pregnancies and three abortions, two of these self-induced. Her organisation, the Society for Humane Abortion, had a mailing list of 2,000 and her lectures on abortion techniques were usually attended by 30–60 people. She was arrested in the summer of 1966 by the San Francisco police who charged her with violating the city's anti-abortion ordinance by distributing handbills calling for a change in the law. But the court dismissed the charges as a violation of her rights of free speech. It seems clear that her lectures were in breach of the Californian law, for this stated: 'Every person who solicits any woman to submit to any operation or to use any means whatever to procure a miscarriage, unless the same is necessary to preserve her life, is punishable by imprisonment'. The law also carried a prohibition on the passing of abortion information but the police refused to prosecute her a second time. A spokesperson for the San Francisco Police Department said: 'All we'd do is give her publicity. We believe the courts would turn her loose' (*New York Times*, 4 December 1966). The District Attorney made a similar point and said he believed she had a constitutional right to state her position. So Maginnis continued her lectures, and her actions suggested that the laws were unenforceable.

On the East Coast there were similar challenges to the legal system, one of the most important being the formation of the Clergy Consultation Service. Lader proposed that the clergy should take action, and the fact that twenty-one Protestant and Jewish clergymen were going to refer women for abortion was revealed in a front page article in the *New York Times* on 27 May 1967. Women who rang up were counselled and referred to sympathetic doctors. The leader of the movement was the Reverend Howard Moody of New York's Judson Memorial Church, and a woman's committee headed by Arlene Carmen set out to evaluate potential doctors' 'medical training, professional experience and quality of their offices'. The clergy kept accurate records and so were able to afford the women increased protection.

Their actions were illegal within the letter of the law but they decided to be open about their referral system in the belief that it would be better to let everyone know what they were doing: 'The legal advice which gave us the most assurance was Mr. London's recommendation that we never assume or admit that were were breaking the law. At all times we were to behave as though we were acting within the laws of New York State and that as clergy we were bound to follow a higher moral law' (Carmen and Moody, 1973, p. 25). The fact that the clergy were able to set up such a service is very surprising, and it is difficult to imagine a British group performing such a role. In part it reflects the fact that they had much greater freedom of action than their British counterparts. However, it seems that another crucial factor was the radicalising effect of other social movements. At the first meeting it was the clergy who had been involved in both the school integration battle in New York and in other areas of civil liberties who were willing to be most active in the abortion campaign (Carmen and Moody, 1973, p. 21).

The counselling service was in demand right from the start, and in 1968 6,500 women were passed through the referral system in New York City. Moody wanted to prevent women from having to travel far and so he encouraged the setting up of consultation services in other major cities. These clergy services decreased much of the mystique surrounding abortion and led to increased acceptance. The organisers tried to take a conciliatory attitude towards the Catholic Church in order to reduce its opposition.

There was also recognition of their predecessors' role. Carmen and Moody state that on some occasions they were accused of being too conservative in terms of challenging the law, but they believed that they should not jeopardise their work unnecessarily and leave women without a source of help. Their agency lasted until the New York law came into operation in 1970.

Another referral service on the East Coast and the only one with its own clinic was that of Bill Baird in Hempstead, which also opened for abortions in 1967. Baird took a much more aggressive approach in his campaign for birth control and abortion rights and over a period of years was imprisoned eight times in five different states. It was he who organised the first abortion march from Times Square to St Patrick's and over the years became the person the opponents of abortion most regarded as their enemy. In August 1974 the *Boston Globe* reported that a church had refused to allow a mother to have her daughter baptised there because she had publicly supported him. Baird was not, however, just opposed to the Church, but also attacked those on his own side who he felt were not active enough. At one point he organised a 'sit-in' at the headquarters of Planned Parenthood and also picketed certain women's groups whom he accused of sexism because they discriminated against him. His personality did not lead him to compromise and this led to him being a controversial figure. Lader points out that many in Planned Parenthood were outraged by his inflammatory tactics, but 'Still, after each Baird hurricane, the movement made considerable progress. Each of his arrests affected the law in questions. Each innovation – the mobile van, for instance, with which he brought contraceptive and abortion information directly into ghetto areas – set a pattern that was finally followed elsewhere' (Lader, 1973, p. 51). In the struggle for legalisation Baird scored some important victories. Possibly the most notable was the Supreme Court decision of 1972 which overthrew the laws against contraception for single people. His activism did not cease with the Supreme Court decision and he has continued to be involved in fighting restrictions. Those like Pat Maginnis and Bill Baird who were willing to risk prison for their beliefs helped to bring the campaign into the open.

The Nature of the Opposition

A fifth and final difference between the two societies was the nature of the opposition. In Britain the dominant opposition was not publicly opposed to abortion in all circumstances and in its early days remained separate from the Catholic Church. However, in the USA the 'Right of Life' movement was more overtly linked to Catholicism and less willing to compromise. This meant that some of the right wing who might have been opposed to abortion on extended grounds were alienated from the movement. The uncompromising nature of the opposition was due to the same cultural factors that led to the dominance of the repeal groups and also the much greater involvement of the Catholic Church. As was mentioned in the British context, there is a tendency for pressure groups to take an extreme position, since the activists are always those who are most strongly committed. In Britain, however, while both sides managed as far as possible to contain this tendency, in the USA this did not happen. In fact the whole nature of the debate was far more acrimonious. When the first reform Bill was being considered in New York the opposition forces became so rowdy that two members of the Catholic Lawyers Guild left the hearing to draft a formal apology (Lader, 1973, p. 64). With both sides entrenched in stances so widely divergent further confrontations were inevitable and have continued at a high level of intensity.

Two of the key anti-abortion activists, Dr and Mrs Willke, used their *Handbook on Abortion*, first published in 1971, as a basis for their campaign, and also pictures of aborted foetuses. They had some success in changing public attitudes, possibly the most notable from their point of view being a referendum campaign in Michigan. A referendum on the abortion law was due to take place in November 1972 and on 15 October it looked as if the reform, which would allow abortion on request up to twenty weeks of pregnancy, were going to be passed. An opinion poll in the *Detroit News* showed support from 59 per cent of the electorate with only 37 per cent in opposition. However, in the later stages the Willkes visited Michigan and ran an aggressive campaign. They appeared on television, radio and in debates and helped to organise the distribution of the 'foetus brochure' to nearly all the 2 million homes in Michigan. There was also a massive amount of television advertising with one being repeated as much as thirteen times a day in the two weeks before the election. This intense activity resulted in the referendum being defeated by 62 per cent to 38 per cent, an extraordinary turn-around. A referendum on abortion in North Dakota was also defeated and by a larger margin (Willke and Willke, 1975, p. 36). If the anti-abortion forces could have mounted this kind of campaign all over the USA the law might have never been overthrown in the Supreme Court. However, they did not have the resources to carry out this task. Furthermore, the opponents of abortion were not even guaranteed the support of all Catholics.

In this respect a key role was played by Robert Drinan, a Catholic priest who was Dean at the Boston Law College. At first Drinan was opposed to the abortion law changes. In 1965 he argued:

> Any change of a substantial kind in America's abortion laws would be a notable departure from that body of Anglo-American law which regulates conduct deemed to constitute a crime against society ... However convenient, convincing or

compelling the arguments in favour of abortion may be, the fact remains that the taking of a life, even though it is unborn, cuts out the very heart of the principle that *no one's* life however unwanted and useless it may be, may be terminated in order to promote the health or happiness of another human being. (Drinan, 1967, p. 122)

At first Drinan was one of the major debating opponents of those in the Clergy Consultation Service. However, once the argument moved away from abortion on specific grounds towards removal of all the laws Drinan found it much easier to give his support. In a paper at the International Conference on Abortion in Washington DC in September 1967 entitled 'The Right of The Foetus to be Born', he criticised the fact that certain states were considering passing reforming laws:

The right of the fetus to be born, now protected in Anglo-American law may be seriously compromised within the near future by changes in the laws of England, Canada and several states in America. In eliminating the right of *some* fetuses to be born the law enters an area which it has never entered before – an area where it will be required to decide by what norms and by whose judgements what persons are to be born and what persons are to 'die' before their birth. (Buck, 1968, p. 57: italics in original)

Although Drinan opposed reform, paradoxically he continued to accept the case for total repeal:

One way to avoid the necessity of making these choices would be for the law to withdraw its protection from *all* fetuses during the first twenty six weeks of their existence. Under this arrangement the law would not be required to approve or disapprove the choices of parents and physicians as to who may be born or not born. (Buck, 1968, p. 57: italics in original)

This argument put at a conference sponsored by the Joseph P. Kennedy Foundation, where there was a general anti-abortion feeling, led to some urgent rethinking amongst many who had opposed any changes. Drinan's views effectively split the Catholic opposition and gave respectability to the argument that, while abortion was wrong, the law should not be imposed on those who did not accept this view.

These, then, were some of the social and political forces that led to the possibility of repeal laws, and in 1970 the states of Hawaii and New York both gave a woman the right to choose an abortion during the early part of her pregnancy.

Repeal in Hawaii

At first Hawaii, like many other states, seemed to be moving towards a reform Bill along the lines of the ALI proposal. In 1967 Senator George Loo introduced a reforming Bill, and in the following year the Republican Party introduced a pro-abortion reform plank into its platform. In 1969 four ALI-type Bills were introduced into State House and, as they were signed by a total of thirty-three legislators out of fifty-one, there was already majority support for change. However, there was also support for a repeal law. Senator Yoshinaga had introduced a repeal Bill in 1967 and similar ones were introduced in both the House and Senate in 1969 (Steinhoff and Diamond, 1977, p. 14). So the choice facing the legislators was whether to pursue repeal or reform.

A number of factors led to the repeal path being chosen. Steinhoff and Diamond (1977) suggest that one factor was the British expansion of legal abortions: 'The British experience made it more and more apparent that great numbers of women sought abortion for reasons outside the scope of the ALI provisions' (p. 13). Again, the ALI Bill was regarded as being too restrictive. A second factor was the views of Robert Drinan, and in Hawaii they seemed to be particularly influential. Father Dever, the Superintendent of Catholic Schools, argued against abortion but nevertheless indicated that if some change in the law were inevitable, then like Drinan he would favour full repeal rather than reform (Steinhoff and Diamond, 1977, p. 32). Even more important was the conversion to the Drinan position of Senator Yano. Yano appreciated the fact that the Drinan argument allowed him to work for change in the abortion law while still maintaining his personal opposition at the level of individual choice. In September 1969 he announced his support for repeal and that he intended to introduce a Bill in the next legislative session. So one of the two major leaders in the fight for abortion repeal in Hawaii was a Catholic legislator with ten children who had been honoured as a Knight of the Pope (Steinhoff and Diamond, 1977, p. 26). The support for the repeal over the reform position therefore began to increase, and Steinhoff and Diamond report that by the autumn of 1969 partial reform 'was rapidly being swept aside in the mounting enthusiasm for total repeal' (1977, p. 29).

In their campaign the advocates of repeal followed the typical pressure group tactics. They began to enlist the support of sympathetic organisations, and by the time of Senate Committee hearings on the subject in February 1970 had the endorsement of twenty-three different groups. Secondly, they organised polls. A questionnaire was distributed to members of the Hawaii Medical Association and it showed that: 96 per cent wanted some changes in the law; a third supported total repeal, and amongst obstetricians 56 per cent supported total repeal. Advocates of change gave publicity to these results as they did to opinion polls of the general public which showed a similar strong desire for a new law. A third technique used by the abortion rights activists was to organise petitions – Zero Population Growth (ZPG) collected 5,000 signatures from registered voters in a month. Fourthly, activists developed contacts with legislators by telephone calls, letters and visits and each one was provided with a copy of Guttmacher's book *The Case for Legalised Abortion Now* (Steinhoff and Diamond, 1977, p. 61).

The major arguments used in the debate were similar to those in other campaigns. The repealers stressed the high number of illegal abortions, the fact that poor women were being discriminated against, the need for abortion where contraception had failed, the fact that unwanted pregnancies led to social problems, and the need for population control. This latter argument seems to have been more prominent in Hawaii than elsewhere, and ZPG organised a number of activities. Apart from the petition, it sponsored a tactical symposium on how to change the abortion law, canvassed virtually the whole of the legislature in person and provided support at various other events. The arguments of the opposition also followed the usual pattern. They stated that abortion was murder of innocent life, that it would lead to promiscuity, that illegal abortions would not decline, that euthanasia would follow and that abortion would lead to moral decay. Even the views of Norman St John Stevas were reprinted in the *Hawaii Catholic Herald* (Steinhoff and Diamond, 1977, p. 73). They also argued that a change in the law would lead to Hawaii becoming an abortion Mecca and drew attention to the situation in Britain. This latter accusation led to a residency restriction being imposed.

The repealers were not surprisingly concerned that at the last moment the Catholic Governor would veto the Bill. However, in a statement in which he expressed his personal abhorrence of abortion, he drew attention to the traffic in illegal abortions suggesting that it was 'best at this point in time, our laws remain totally silent on the question of abortion'. In supporting his statement he also drew attention to the necessity of separating the roles of Church and state authority (Steinhoff and Diamond, 1977, p. 172). With his decision in 1970 the United States had its first repeal law.

New York State Law

Although Hawaii was the first state to repeal its law, the New York law had no residency requirement and with its passage legal abortion became possible for all American women who could afford it. The passing of the Act was, however, a complicated process and its success was due to a number of seemingly contradictory social forces.

At first, as we have already seen, it seemed likely that New York would have a reform act. In 1964 the New York Medical Academy had urged that the state law should be amended to permit abortions where there was danger to the physical or mental health of the woman or her prospective child. In the following year state obstetricians showed their support for change when a survey of 1,200 showed that 87 per cent wanted the law liberalised (*New York Times*, 31 January 1965). But in addition to the local medical support for a liberal law, political support was also growing. At the end of 1966 Governor Rockefeller had called for liberalisation, and in 1967 an ALI-type Bill had been introduced, although it did not get out of committee into the Assembly. In 1968 Senator Albert Blumenthal re-introduced an ALI-type Bill and it appeared possible that it would be successful. Blumenthal was confident: 'I am delighted at the seeming willingness of the Governor to act at this session of the legislature and to do so in a fashion which is consistent with the actions in three other states and in Great Britain' (*New York Times*, 10 January 1968). His feelings seemed to be supported by public opinion. A poll of New York State residents showed that 75 per cent were for liberalisation, 17 per cent were opposed to it and 8 per cent were undecided. The poll also included a religious breakdown and showed that there was strong support in each of the three major religious groups: 98 per cent of Jews, 83 per cent of Protestants and 72 per cent of Catholics were in favour of an extension of the law. However, despite the popularity of the proposed measure, it failed to get the necessary support. Blumenthal commented on the failure: 'The pressure was just too great in an election year. We had the four votes we needed and they backed out'. When he was asked the reason for the withdrawal he pointed to Charles Tobin, Secretary of the New York State Catholic Committee representing the state's eight Roman Catholic dioceses (*New York Times*, 4 April 1968).

In 1969 the prospects looked even better. Having canvassed the Assembly, Blumenthal was pledged 82 votes and only 76 were needed for passage. Furthermore, the Senate majority leader Earl Brydges, a Catholic opponent, had stated that, while he personally opposed the change and could keep it locked in committee, he would not use his power in this way. Nevertheless, again the Bill failed, and this time in dramatic fashion. Assemblyman Martin Ginsberg, who had been considered pledged to the Bill, gave a strongly emotional speech which led to 14 votes being lost. Ginsberg had been crippled by polio in infancy and was dependent on heavy braces and a cane. In his speech he drew attention to his infirmity and argued that a law permitting abortion on the grounds of deformity could set a terrible precedent: 'If we are prepared to say that a life should not come into this world malformed or abnormal then tomorrow we should be prepared to say that a life already in this world which becomes malformed or abnormal should not be permitted to live'. In an emotional ending to his speech, he postulated: 'God saw fit to let me live in this form and condition . . . so that I could be here on April 17th to speak on this specific bill' (Lader, 1973, p. 123). He sat down to loud applause – and that was the end of the attempt at liberalisation for another year.

These two later defeats made the supporters of a change in the law somewhat wary in predicting their chances for 1970. The *New York Times* (26 January 1970) reflected this feeling, commenting that there were various alternatives but that there was 'a mood of uncertainty over whether to act on the controversial issue or to leave the decision to the courts'. Despite these defeats, however, the pressure for repeal had steadily built up. As Lader reports:

> Starting with the New York Civil Liberties Union and the Unitarian–Universalists in 1965, repeal gained the backing of most protestant denominations in the State Council of Churches, many Jewish groups like the National Council of Jewish Women and the American Jewish Congress, the Liberal Party, Americans for Democratic Action, National Organization for Women, American Public Health Association, American Medical Women's Association, Physicians Forum, National Association of Social Workers, Citizens Committee for Children, and the New York Women's Bar Association among others. By January 1970 over fifty such organizations with millions of members supported repeal. (1973, p. 125)

Also by this time the pressure from the women's groups had begun to be effective. Margaret Mead was quoted in the *New York Times* (27 February 1970) as saying that she would 'repeal all abortion laws and give the responsibility to the church and the medical profession'. She argued that all the states should take action at once so that none of them would be swamped with abortion requests, and this statement by the best known American anthropologist gave weight to the stance being taken by NOW. The women's groups were also making a serious attempt to have the state laws overthrown in the courts in 1969–70. During the course of four linked cases much evidence of the problems of women in terms of illegal abortion and other factors were revealed. In the event the decision was not delivered because of the subsequent change in the law, but the fact that such a trial was taking place was important in terms of the overall debate. The women's groups also put direct pressure on the politicians. Of particular interest was the hesitant statement of Rockefeller to the Women's Legislative Forum on 13 January 1970 that he would probably approve a repeal Bill.

Mayor Lindsay was much less circumspect and in March 1970 added his voice to those calling for repeal. His statement echoed the comments of others who had been converted to the repeal position (*New York Times*, 8 March 1970). He drew attention to the fact that in 1967 he had favoured an ALI-type Bill, but since that time the evidence from the states which had passed such a Bill showed that still a large number of poor women had found abortions difficult to obtain. He commented that decisions in Washington DC and California had 'cast considerable doubt not only on the constitutionality of New York's law but on the right of the State to over regulate this area of medical needs on the grounds that it constitutes an invasion of privacy' (*New York Times*, 8 March 1970). Mayor Lindsay supported his position by a similar argument to that put forward by Drinan:

I realize that many people hold religious and philosophical convictions which find abortion to be an unacceptable solution to this problem. By removing this question from the penal law altogether, the state avoids making any moral judgement on this subject . . . I hope the New York State Legislature will now move forward and repeal the present law, leaving the decision to be made by the pregnant woman and her physician. (*New York Times*, 8 March 1970)

The effect of Drinan's thinking on this statement is quite clear, and two of the key workers behind the Clergy Consultation Service also drew attention to his influence. Carmen and Moody (1973, p. 38) commented: '[Drinan] never knew the influential role he played in developing the theological and legal position the Clergy Consultation Service finally took on the abortion issue . . . to have a Roman Catholic theologian of Drinan's stature writing an incredibly convincing argument for repeal as over against reform was a real boost in the battle ahead.'

But possibly Drinan's biggest single influence was on the views of Assemblyman Ginsberg. Although he had been the key agency in stopping the Bill in 1969, in January 1970 the *New York Times* reported that he would find a total repeal Bill acceptable as it would not discriminate against those with physical abnormality. It can be seen therefore that a seemingly more radical Bill might have more support. However, the actual passage of the Act was not simply the product of the prevailing social forces but also the result of a number of tactical errors on the part of the opposition and dramatic last-minute decisions.

Possibly the most important blunder was the introduction of a radical Bill into the Senate by the majority party leader, Earl

Brydges. Brydges, a Catholic anti-abortionist, had the power to keep an abortion bill locked up in committee. He had also announced his distaste for the radical Bill of Constance Cooke on the grounds that it 'could allow an abortion of a foetus a day before normal birth'. He therefore set some of his staff members to prepare his own Bill, and when he introduced it into the Senate it aimed to make abortion simply a question for the woman and her physician without any other qualifications. In the light of Brydges's known feelings and his past comment on the Cooke Bill it is not surprising that the advocates of abortion were more than suspicious of his motives. Senator Thaler, for example, said that a more moderate reform measure could pass the Senate but that Brydges would not let such a Bill reach the floor. He predicted that the Bill would fail and that the issue would be put off. However, the Brydges plan misfired. When the 57 men in the Senate passed the Bill by 31 to 26 votes it simply read, 'An abortion act is justifiable when committed upon a female by a licensed physician' (*New York Times*, 19 March 1970). The voting patterns mirrored those occurring in Britain with the opposition made up largely of the right wing plus the Catholics. The split according to party can be seen in Table 5.1.

Table 5.1   *Senate Vote in New York State, 1970*

	Democrats	Republicans	Total
For Bill	18	13	31
Against Bill	6	20	26
	24	33	57

Source: New York Times, 11 April 1970.

The vote shows that three-quarters of the Democrats in the Senate supported the Bill while over 60 per cent of the Republicans opposed it. In terms of race it does not seem that the 'black genocide' argument held much sway and the *New York Times* reported that as well as pressure from the women's groups there was strong influence in favour of the Act from minority groups whose 'members most often became statistics in the grim catalogue of women killed by crude illegal abortions'.

Religion was important and the overall opposition of the Catholics was clear from the vote, with 18 of 22 opposing the Bill. However, the Catholic opposition was more muted than it might have been. As has been argued, Brydges could have bottled up any bill in committee, but it appears that an informal arrangement was made. The Church schools were sorely in need of funds from public sources yet these were banned by the Blaine amendment. This set out the separation of Church and state more clearly than did the United States First Amendment, and Lader (1973, p. 128) suggests that the real Catholic target for 1970 was to abolish Blaine. He speculated that 'Rockefeller may have assured the Senate Majority leader Brydges of his opposition to Blaine while giving lip service to the Cook Bill', The *New York Times* (22 March 1970) also noted that Catholic opposition was muted, and suggested that the Church was more concerned with parochial school support: 'Recently, Catholics from Long Island jammed the lobby of the Senate to cheer Senator Edward Speno, a Long Island Republican, and a Catholic, who is pushing for more State money for Parochial Schools.' The article continued by saying that, as he had such support, Speno felt free to vote for the abortion Bill. Thus it seems that at this time abortion was not regarded as the key issue for Catholics.

When the Bill was passed down to the Assembly there were again anxious moments. In order for it to succeed 76 votes were needed out of the membership of 150, and in committee two changes were proposed to the Brydges Bill. First, a time limit of twenty-four weeks from the moment of conception was imposed (except to save the woman's life) and, secondly, abortion was to be carried out on a woman only 'with her consent'. The former was introduced to quieten fears about late abortions, and the latter was suggested to allay concern about pressure on teenagers and poor members of minority groups. Those pushing for the change were confident that they had the necessary votes. But the first time round two members recorded their 'yes' position and left the chamber, and in a confusing decision their votes were discounted and the Bill failed. The members, nevetheless, raised it again and this time it looked as if the supporters were going to fail to meet the mark by one vote. However, in the last moments there was a change of mind. The *New York Times* (10 April 1970) reported:

Assemblyman George M. Michaels of Auburn, his hands trembling and tears welling in his eyes, stopped the roll call only seconds before the clerk was to announce that the reform bill had been defeated by a single vote. He said 'I realise Mr. Speaker that I am terminating my political career, but I cannot in good conscience sit here and allow my vote to be the one that defeats the bill. I ask that my vote be changed from "no" to "yes".'

Michaels's prediction was correct and at the next election he was defeated on this issue. However, with his change the 76 votes were reached. The party background is shown in Table 5.2.

Table 5.2   *Assembly Vote in New York State, 1970*

	Democrats	Republicans	Total
For Bill	46	30	76
Against Bill	24	49	73
	70	79	149

Source: New York Times, 10 April 1970.

The pattern was similar to that of the Senate. Two-thirds of the Democrats were supporters compared to just over a third of the Republicans.

The Bill, as amended, had then to return to the Senate for the fourth and final vote. In an emotional speech Brydges read from the *Diary of an Unborn Child* from the day of conception when 'it is already determined that I will love flowers'. He didn't read it all, but it ended 'Today my parents killed me' (*New York Times*, 11 April 1970). He was opposed by Senator Laverne, a Catholic, who pointed out that 60 per cent of Catholics did not uphold the Church's view on the issue. However, by this stage the debate was simply the restating of known positions and the vote was identical to the first taken. The next day Rockefeller signed the Bill into law and the advocates of legal abortion had achieved what to them had seemed an impossible victory. In subsequent years there were challenges to the Act, which were vetoed by Rockefeller. These, however, came to an end with the Supreme Court decision in January 1973.

Supreme Court Decision

The Supreme Court of the United States consists of nine judges who are appointed by the President for life. The fact that they do not have to fight elections and thus respond to political pressure distinguishes them from many other American judges. In theory they should just interpret validity of laws in terms of the constitution. In practice, of course, they are influenced by the climate of opinion.

Views on abortion continued to liberalise after the passage of the New York Act, and in August 1972 a Gallup Poll showed that 64 per cent of the public including a majority (56 per cent) of the Catholics believed that the decision to have an abortion should be left solely to the woman and her doctor. An article discussing the results in the *New York Times* (25 August 1972) suggested that there had been a continuous movement towards liberalisation. It stated that in 1968 less than 15 per cent wanted liberal laws, but this percentage had risen to 40 per cent in 1969 and 50 per cent in 1971. So the final rise was the culmination of a series of steadily changing attitudes.

By 1972 medical opinion had moved towards a repeal position. In March 1971, a survey of specialists in obstetrics and gynaecology in New York found that two-thirds of them favoured the new abortion law. A couple of months later liberal laws were endorsed nationally when the American College of Obstetrics and Gynecology urged that the decision on abortion should be left to doctors and their patients. It seems that the working of the New York Act was one factor which led to the liberalisation of views. In October 1972, the New York City Health Services Administrator stated that the experience of two years' legal abortion on a mass scale had cut the maternal death rate, reduced infant mortality and had reduced illegitimate births for the first time since the keeping of statistics had started in 1954 (*New York Times*, 7 October 1970).

A further reason for the change in the climate of opinion was the general movement to the left in response to the war in Vietnam. It is probable that the liberalisation of attitudes amongst students and anti-war protesters was concentrated on the coasts rather than the Mid-West or the South. However, in terms of political importance the liberal areas carried more weight. Thus effective public opinion was to the left of overall opinion in the country. These changes all worked together. The challenge to the law came from two cases. One woman was assigned the pseudonym Jane Roe to protect her privacy. She instigated an action against Henry Wade, the district attorney of Dallas County, Texas, where she lived. She claimed the Texas anti-abortion statute violated the

United States Constitution (Mohr, 1978, p. 247). Sarah Waddington, the lawyer who argued the Texas case before the Supreme Court, told me in an interview in 1978 that the decision they finally took would not have occurred in the climate of opinion even two years earlier. She also said that the Court's prior decisions were important, and also the fact that the advocates of legal abortion had largely won the academic debate about the genesis and maintenance of the abortion laws. There were two major issues involved. First was the question of privacy, and second was that of the background to the laws and the question of the origins of life.

The right to privacy had already been decided in particular reference to the question of birth control. In 1965, in Griswold v. Connecticut, the Supreme Court had recognised the existence of a constitutional right of privacy within marriage. In this case it was decided that the states could not prohibit a couple from using contraceptives within their marital relationship. This decision had of course wider connotations as Barnett (1973, p. 52) points out:

> Despite the emphasis in the Griswold opinion upon protecting bedroom activities from the prying eyes of the state, it is possible to see in the decision a rather differing import. Instead of cloaking in privacy bedroom activities in general, the decision can be read as establishing the right of a married couple to decide if and when they wish to have children, that decision being an integral part of the marital relationship.

This decision for married people was extended to single persons. In Eisenstadt v. Baird, 1972, it was argued that the marital couple were not an entity but were two individuals who both had the right to ensure that the government did not interfere in matters so fundamental as the decision whether or not to have children. It was on this right of privacy that the Supreme Court struck down the Texas law in Roe v. Wade.

This development of a concept of privacy was therefore one key factor in the legalisation. A second was related to the concept of the foetus as an unborn child, and the academic work of NARAL's legal adviser Cyril Means was particularly important on this point. Means (1968) wrote on the background of the abortion laws and his work was quoted in the Supreme Court decision seven times.

Furthermore, even when he was not quoted his ideas seemed to have been important in guiding the thinking of the judges. In his first article he made a detailed analysis of the major historical factors underlying the abortion laws. He pointed out the fact that, under English common law, abortion had been legal until quickening and further argued that from the moment of conception until quickening there was no protection under common law: 'The pre-quickened foetus is not now, and has never been, itself an object of protection by our criminal law; the common assumption that it is will be dispelled by a study of legislative history, herein revealed for the first time' (Means, 1968). He produced various pieces of evidence to support his contention and suggested that in terms of the constitution birth was a precondition for personhood.

In explaining the reasons for the abortion enactments Means stated that it had been an unsafe operation in the nineteenth century (p. 211). He argued that the main purpose of the laws was to protect the life and health of women with unwanted pregnancies. He continued by quoting the evidence of Christopher Tietze that some time in the early twentieth century abortion became a safe operation and, indeed, safer than childbirth. It followed that the previous reasons for abortion restrictions were no longer valid (Means, 1968, p. 512). He drew attention to the fact that the British 1967 Abortion Act had reasoned in terms of safety, and commented:

As a matter of meaning it uncannily recaptures the intentions of all the British and American legislators on this subject in the nineteenth century . . . the new British clause would not have looked 'radical' at all to the nineteenth century parliamentarians and legislators. It looks radical now only because it has so widely been forgotten what the real purpose of the abortion statutes was. (Means, 1968, p. 514)

Means went on to question whether the legislators had the right to insist that a woman must risk the hazards of childbirth rather than be allowed a relatively safe legal abortion.

In Means's second paper (1971) he produced further evidence to support his contention about the right to abortion under common law in the early months of pregnancy. But in fact he went further and argued that under common law women had the right to abortion throughout pregnancy. One of the arguments with which he took issue was that of John Noonan and David Louisell who asserted that according to Coke, late abortion was murder. Means claimed that they had made a mistake and misquoted Coke as calling a post-quickening abortion 'a great misprison and so murder' when in fact he had not written 'so' but 'no' (Means, 1971, p. 359). He further stated that Coke did not quote the common law correctly and that even after quickening abortion was not even a misprison (misdemeanour). This finding obviously had important constitutional implications:

> Were the American Medical Profession now suddenly to remember the reason for the passage of these laws, they would grant an abortion to every woman in the first or second trimester who requested one; for, today, abortion is always safer than childbirth, as the New York figures now show, not only through the first trimester but during the first 24 weeks of pregnancy. (Means, 1971, p. 396)

Mr Justice Blackman considered the relevant documents and recognised the importance of Means's research in delivering the opinion of the court. He accepted Means's claim that Coke had been misinterpreted. The Judge also noted Means's later point that even post-quickening abortion was not established as a crime and agreed that the major reason for the introduction of the laws was to protect the health of the woman. In his ruling Judge Blackman outlined three major areas of interest. First, the right of privacy, secondly the interest of the state in protecting the health of the woman involved, and thirdly the interest of the state in protecting potential life. He noted that some were arguing that the woman's right of privacy was absolute throughout pregnancy but he rejected this contention. He took the view that it applied during the first three months of pregnancy and that within this period the decision on abortion should be left to the woman and her attending physician. After this time, however, the interests of the state in promoting the health of the woman became of increased importance, and so the states could regulate abortion procedures in ways that were reasonably related to maternal health. Once viability had been reached the states could proscribe abortion in pursuit of its interest in the potential human life except when it was necessary to preserve the life or health of the woman (Osofsky and Osofsky, 1973).

This decision was won with a 7–2 vote and the only Catholic Justice was included in the majority. With it all the state laws were overthrown, and even the New York law was unconstitutional because it did not allow abortion for 'health' after viability. At the time of the decision four states had abortion on request – Alaska, Washington, Hawaii and New York; fifteen states had relatively new laws based on ALI-type conditions – Alabama, Arkansas, California, Colorado, Delaware, Florida, Georgia, Kansas, Maryland, Mississippi, New Mexico, North Carolina, Oregon, South Carolina and Virginia. Some other states such as Wisconsin and New Jersey had liberalised their laws by means of court decisions but many still had their traditional nineteenth-century laws.

Not all advocates of legal abortion were fully happy with the Supreme Court's decision. For example, Congresswoman Bella Abzug said she would introduce a Bill that would go further and 'eliminate any state laws of any nature concerning the regulation of abortion' (*New York Times*, 23 January 1973). However, a more serious problem in terms of the working of the future law was that it was imposed from outside. Although the polls showed that most people were in support, there were various areas of the country which were very conservative and had strong opposition to abortion. This meant that the ruling was necessarily going to introduce a great deal of conflict.

6
Worldwide Change

In this chapter the post-war changes in Eastern European countries and China are reviewed, followed by the legalisation in Nordic countries and Europe. Finally the changes in the British Commonwealth are discussed.

It is instructive to first look at the estimated number of abortions performed in various countries as shown in Table 6.1. This shows that Western Europe generally has lower abortion rates than Eastern Europe, reflecting the much greater tradition of contraceptive usage. The Nordic countries have rates somewhat above those of the rest of Western Europe. Tietze (personal communication, 10 September 1982) estimates that only a quarter of Japanese abortions are reported, but that there has been a decline of 60 to 75 per cent since 1960 when over 3 million abortions were carried out. This reflects a move towards methods of contraception. The level in West Germany is low, partly because many women travel to Holland for their abortions. The rates in the Netherlands, and to a lesser extent in Britain, show that even with freely available abortion the incidence can be low with good contraceptive usage. Overall there are wide variations in rates. The following discussion will also show that legalisation in various countries occurred in very different ways, but that there is a basic similarity in the social forces in operation.

Eastern Europe

The first substantial liberalisation of abortion laws occurred in the Socialist countries of Central and Eastern Europe during the period 1955–7. The Soviet Union liberalised its law in December 1955 with twin aims – first to reduce the harm done to the health of women by abortions carried on outside hospitals, and secondly to give 'women the possibility of deciding themselves the question of motherhood' (Field, 1956). Following this lead all the Socialist

Table 6.1   *Abortion Rates in Selected Countries*

Area and country	Year	Number of abortions	Rate per 1,000 women, 15–44	Rate per 1,000 pregnancies
Eastern Europe				
Poland	1978	145,600[1]	18.3	17.8 (1977)
Czechoslovakia	1980	100,200	31.1	29.7
Hungary	1980	80,900	36.3	35.6
German Democratic Republic	1977	80,100	22.5	26.0
Yugoslavia	1975	288,100	58.5	42.5
Soviet Union	1970	10,000,000[4]	180.0	70.0[4]
Bulgaria	1978	127,800	68.3	48.5
Nordic countries				
Greenland	79/80	460	39.8	32.4
Denmark	1980	23,300	21.4	28.4[2]
Finland	1980	15,000	13.9	19.3
Norway	1980	13,500	16.3	21.0
Sweden	1980	34,900	20.7	26.9
Iceland	79/80	530	10.2	9.2 (1976–8)
Western Europe				
Italy	1980	220,300[1]	18.5	22.4[2]
Netherlands	1980	19,700	6.2	9.8
Scotland	1980	9,100[3]	8.4	11.6
Switzerland	1966	21,800	8.4	8.3
France	1979	156,800	14.1	16.8
German Federal Republic	1980	87,700	6.6	12.4[1]
England and Wales	1980	128,900	12.8	16.7
Elsewhere				
Canada	1980	65,800	11.5	15.1[2]
USA	1980	1,533,900	29.3	30.0
Hong Kong	1980	9,400	8.6	9.8[3]
Singapore	1980	18,200	28.4	29.5
India	1980	358,000[1]	2.5	1.7
Japan	1980	598,100[1]	22.5	27.4
Tunisia	1979	19,200	14.6	9.4 (1977)
Cuba	1980	104,000	47.1	43.2
New Zealand	1980	5,900	8.6	10.5
Australia	1975	60,000[4]	21.7	20.0

Source: Prepared for Tietze, 1983.
Notes: [1] Reporting incomplete.
[2] Preceding year.
[3] Includes residents of Scotland obtaining abortions in England.
[4] Estimate.

countries except Albania extended their laws (David, 1982). By 1960 Poland, Czechoslovakia, Bulgaria, Hungary, Romania and Yugoslavia allowed abortion on broad social grounds or on request in the first twelve weeks (Potts *et al.*, 1977, p. 388). The Hungarian law had an unusual feature in that it made a special extension to eighteen weeks for minors. The GDR had changed the draconian regulations of the Third Reich in 1947 and 1950 to allow abortion on request for those under the age of 16, over the age of 40 or with five children, but full liberalisation was delayed until 1972 (David, 1982). Others could have an abortion if this was agreed by a commission which took into account the 'total life situation of the pregnant woman'.

The changes contributed to the decline in birthrates, as is shown in Table 6.2. The figures show that the birthrates in Bulgaria, Czechoslovakia and Hungary halved during the forty-year period 1920–60. By 1962 Hungary had a population growth rate that was the lowest in Europe (Wulf, 1980).

Table 6.2   *Birthrates in Eastern European Regions*

	(per 1,000 population)		
	1920	*1960*	*1980*
USSR	n.a.	24.9	18.3
Bulgaria	39.6	17.8	14.3
Hungary	30.2	14.7	13.9
Czechoslovakia	26.7	15.9	16.2
Romania	37.6	19.1	18.6
Poland	37.6	22.3	19.5
GDR	23.1	17.2	14.6

Source: New York Times, 4 March 1962; David, 1983.

Eastern European countries tended to have very high rates of abortion. In Hungary they exceeded the number of deliveries and in 1964 had 1.4 abortions for every birth (Tietze and Dawson, 1973, p. 10). Romania announced even higher figures of 4 abortions per live birth in 1965 (Tietze and Dawson, 1973, p. 12). By 1971 Bulgaria had almost as many abortions as births. It seems that the rate for the Soviet Unions was also high, although there has been a dearth of official data. An article in *The Times* (11 May 1981) suggested that there were between 2.5 and 4 abortions to every birth and that each woman had an average of six to eight abortions in her lifetime.

The very high rates of abortion and the fears of a declining population were factors behind the attempts to cut down the abortion rates. Romania was the first to do this in 1966, after which the births almost doubled, but then fell back to almost the original level as illegal abortions increased (Francome, 1976b). The other two Eastern Bloc countries – Bulgaria and Hungary – to remove the right to choose an abortion created many more exceptions, as discussed in Chapter 1 (p. 2). Bulgaria, two years after tightening the law in 1974, still had more abortions than it had had in any year in the 1960s. In Hungary there was a reduction in the number of abortions from 169,000 in 1973 when the law was changed to 89,000 in 1977. The rate is still high and in 1977 was nearly four times that of England and Wales. In fact evidence from the 1977 Hungarian Fertility Survey suggests that there has been a strong movement towards birth control (Wulf, 1980). Only 11 per cent of women at risk of an unplanned pregnancy were reported as not practising any form of contraception. Furthermore, 36 per cent of married women were on the pill, a higher figure than France (28 per cent), the USA (22 per cent) and Britain (26 per cent). So it may seem surprising that the abortion rate is not lower (Wulf, 1980).

In Czechoslovakia in 1973 committees were set up of three people to approve abortion. The decision was made on the woman's request and on specific grounds such as that she was over the age of 40, had three living children, or a 'disturbed family life'. The committees approved 93 per cent of requests in 1979 (David and McIntyre, 1981, p. 225). In 1980 the Czech authorities stated that decisions by abortion committees 'must be in harmony with the interests of the entire society in quantitively and qualitatively improving the development of the birth rate, while (at the same time) the interests of the woman and those of her family must (also) not be overlooked' (United Nations, 1980a, p. 55). So here again there are references to population planning often characteristic of Eastern European states.

There has been a suggestion that the Socialist countries of Eastern Europe do not want women to use birth control because abortion can more easily be controlled to increase the birthrate when necessary. With the possible exception of Romania, however, this does not seem to be borne out. The Soviet Union, for example, has started giving sex education classes and advice on contraception (*The Times*, 11 May 1981), and the East Germans began producing the birth control pill to reduce the number of abortions as early as 1965 (*New York Times*, 13 July 1965).

China

Abortion was legalised by a directive from the minister of health in 1957. Peiping University president Ma Ying-Chu was quoted in the *New York Times* (28 July 1957) as saying that China must attempt to limit its population or face defeat in efforts to industrialise and raise living standards.

In a special article Chen Muhua, a Vice-President of the People's Republic, reported that China's population had risen from 540 million in 1949 to 975 million in 1978 (Muhua, 1979). However, he drew attention to its success in reducing the crude birthrate from 40 per 1,000 population in the 1960s to 18.4 in 1978. The rate of natural increase had dropped from 23.4 to 12.1 per 1,000 between 1971 and 1978. He said that the aim was to get zero population growth by the end of the century. Of 17.4 million births, 5.2 million were third or higher order, and if these could be eliminated the rate of natural increase would be reduced to only 7 per 1,000. He also drew attention to incentives to persuade people to have just one child. These included a stipend until the child was 14 years old and priority in schools and jobs. He commented that Marxist states had been over-critical of Malthus and stressed the role of people as producers rather than consumers. He argued that a rapidly expanding population was detrimental to capital accumulation, hindered attempts to raise culture and affected the standard of living. In an oblique reference to abortion he suggested that it would be better to improve birth control use: 'We still have to strive to reduce the incidence of remedial measures'. Later reports (*Wolverhampton Express and Star*, 28 February 1980) talked of some provinces reducing the wages of those with more than one child by 10 per cent. Thus it seems that China is making the most determined effort to control population size, even though such measures could lead to poverty amongst large families.

The Nordic Countries

We have seen that Iceland, Sweden and Denmark all liberalised their laws in the inter-war period (see p. 73). This process continued in the post-war years with a further liberalisation leading eventually to demands for repeal of the laws.

In Sweden in 1946 a further indication was added to the three earlier ones. This was to allow abortion if there were reasons to assume that childbirth and care would seriously undermine the woman's physical and psychic strength with reference to her living conditions and other special circumstances (Linner, 1968, p. 76). The Thalidomide tragedy led to a further liberalisation in 1963 when the law was changed to allow abortion for expected handicap or severe disease. However, at this time there was no abortion for social reasons and the method of gaining approval was time-consuming. In the period 1963–4 the patients at one hospital had an average of 25.8 days' investigation and spent an average of 10.1 days in hospital (Potts *et al.*, 1977, p. 386). However, it seems that from that time practice changed, and by 1967 the hospital had halved the period of investigation and length of stay. Nowadays most abortions are carried out on an out-patient basis.

Finland liberalised its law in 1951 and Norway in 1965. By this time the laws in each of the five countries were broadly similar and included medical and social/medical grounds and eugenic considerations such as the hereditary transmission of mental disease.

Pressure to change the laws came from women tired of the bureaucratic delays. Swedish women began to travel to Poland for abortions and in the winter of 1964–5 twenty of them were threatened with prosecution. Swedish law stated that it was illegal to do abroad what it was illegal to do in Sweden (*New York Times*, 14 February 1965). The opposition to the proposed prosecution was so strong that it was dropped, and a result of the furore was the setting up of an eight-member commission to review the situation and to propose changes in the law. This recommended in 1971 that abortion should be removed from the Penal Code, although abortions by lay persons should be illegal.

In Denmark the law was changed in 1970 to allow abortion on request to all women living in Denmark and over the age of 38 years, and for those with four or more children (Tietze, 1979). Finland passed a similar measure in the same year and allowed abortion on request for women aged under 17 and over 40 years (Potts *et al.*, 1977, p. 393).

In 1973 Denmark became the first of the Nordic countries to introduce abortion on request in the first trimester. It was followed by Sweden in 1975. This law allowed abortion on request in the first eighteen weeks of pregnancy. The law insisted, however, that between twelve and eighteen weeks there must be a discussion with a social worker. Iceland and Norway also liberalised their laws in 1975 but stopped short of abortion on request.

In Norway the issue has been very controversial. An attempt to introduce abortion on request failed by one vote in 1974, although it had the support of a majority of the population. It was opposed by the Campaign Against Abortion on Demand which arranged for a petition of 610,000 signatures to be presented to the parliamentary body (*Manchester Evening News*, 8 November 1974). Opposition also came from the State Evangelical Lutheran Church. However, the deciding vote was from a labour member who voted with the opposition. In 1975, *The Times* (26 April) reported that about thirty women singing and brandishing placards had invaded the Norwegian Parliament. The demonstration was organised by the Association of Fertile Women and was ended when police removed the participants. In 1977 King Olav announced in Parliament that a woman should have the opportunity to decide on an abortion when she could see no other way out of her problem. The law was passed in 1978 and gave abortion on request in the first trimester (*The Star*, 13 October 1977; *The Times*, 3 February 1982).

After the Labour Party lost the election in 1981, problems arose in forming a coalition. The Christian Democratic Party wanted the right to choose an abortion removed from the law and a much more restrictive Bill introduced (*Guardian*, 18 September 1981). The Conservatives, who had progressed in the election, wanted their MPs to make up their own minds on the subject. Other action against the law had been occurring in the courts and Boerre Knudsen, a vicar, refused to perform his state duties in protest against abortion on demand. On 3 February 1982 *The Times* reported that the court supported him and stated that it felt abortion was the killing of a small human being: 'It is impossible to fix any point on the road from conception to birth where an acceptable limit can be set for performing an abortion'. Thus the issue is still very much a live one in Norway.

Finland has reduced the usual time limit for abortion from sixteen weeks to twelve weeks. After this time an abortion can only be given if the board of medicine agrees. Like Iceland it still has not introduced abortion on request (*Guardian*, 21 June 1978).

In 1979 the seven bishops representing the 130,000 Catholics in the five Nordic countries met in Germany to consider the implications of the new laws. They concluded that Catholic doctors and nurses must decide for themselves whether to assist with abortions.

Holland

The great difference between developments in Holland and those in other countries is that the big increase in quasi-legal abortions preceded any change in the law. A Dutch abortion law of 1836 had proved to be ineffective as it had been necessary to prove that the foetus was alive at the time of the operation. In 1911 the law was amended so that abortion was also considered a crime against public morality (Ketting and Schnabel, 1980). From this time onwards there were abortions only on 'medical grounds', and in the 1950s an estimated 10,000–15,000 illegal abortions (Treffers, 1965, p. 58).

Although the Dutch were amongst the pioneers of birth control in the nineteenth century, it appears that progress in this area was slow. One strong belief reported during this period was that birth control mentality was a major cause of induced abortion, and this was to be discouraged. However, with the introduction of the pill in 1964 it became accepted that birth control could prevent abortion, and in a small country such as Holland the pill spread rapidly amongst the population. In 1969 the ban on birth control advertisement was lifted, and by 1971 the cost of the female-oriented methods were covered by the country's public health insurance and so free of charge. By 1977 41 per cent of Dutch women aged 15–44 were on the pill – by far the highest usage rate in the world. This change in the use of birth control obviously affected attitudes, for when it failed physicians felt responsible, and women began to expect the right to control their own fertility. Thus the views on abortion were necessarily going to change.

When the British law came into operation in 1968 it meant that Dutch women were able to obtain safe legal abortions in the new private clinics. This further underlined the use of the threat of an unwanted pregnancy as a method of social control. These two facts, together with an overall increase in 'permissive' attitudes, led to a totally different climate of opinion. In Britain the change in interpretation of the law with the Bourne case was rather traumatic. However, in Holland it was much less dramatic. In 1966 a famous Dutch Law Professor Ch. J. Enschedé concluded that the concept of what was 'medical' had become much broader amongst physicians and that this should apply to abortion as well. He suggested that physicians were within their rights under the law if they carried out abortions on a wide range of social grounds, such as if the woman were single or had completed her family. This statement seemed to take the medical profession by surprise. However in 1967 it was approved in Parliament by the Secretary of Justice, and it became increasingly accepted that any abortion carried out in proper conditions by a doctor was legal (de Bruijn, 1979, p. 192). The Dutch Psychiatric Association proposed that the woman was the best equipped to decide whether she wanted an abortion and the doctor's role should be to ensure that the operation was not dangerous for her health and that she genuinely wanted it (Ketting and Schnabel, 1980).

In the late 1960s there was, however, a shortage of capacity which was alleviated by the setting up of specialist clinics from 1971 onwards. In 1970, 816 Dutch women had their abortions in England, but by 1973 the number had dwindled to 101, and foreign women even began to travel to Holland for their abortions (OPCS, 1974). Although the abortion rate for resident women was low – only an average of 5.2 abortions per 1,000 women of child-bearing age from 1975–9 – the influx of foreigners was estimated by Stimezo, the Dutch National Abortion Federation, to be as high as 61,000 from Germany (Federal Republic), 12,000 from Belgium and 9,000 from France in 1975 (Ketting and Schnabel, 1980).

It might be thought that with this relatively uncontentious change in legal practice the political developments would not be too problematical. However, Dutch politicians were in a peculiar situation. The Socialists wanted a change in the law to legitimate the de facto situation and to give women the right to choose. Their main allies in this approach were the liberals, a group otherwise identified with right-wing economic policies. Other right-wing groups, the GPV and SGP, said that they would only accept abortion when the woman's life was critically endangered (*Guardian*, 16 June 1979). The Christian Democrats (CDA) headed by a Catholic, Dries Van Agt, wanted a restrictive law, but they were politically more identified as central within the Dutch political spectrum. It was Van Agt who for a number of years tried to close the Bloemenhove (Flower Farm), a non-profit-making clinic for mid-trimester abortions (*The Times*, 25 May 1976). In 1974 the High Court rejected his arguments, and in 1978 the women's movement occupied the Bloemenhove and successfully prevented police attempts to close it down (*Morning Star*, 15 September 1976). Van Agt wrote to Parliament and threatened to resign unless the clinic was closed. Dramatic development followed:

> Van Agt's most recent move has been to inform the clinic's medical staff that further use of the medical equipment will be considered a criminal offence. Despite this the clinic continues to operate normally. Hundreds of women demonstrators working in shifts guard the clinic against an eventual raid. They have said they can rally the support of a thousand or more within minutes. (*Sheffield Morning Telegraph*, 11 June 1976)

The clinic stayed open, Van Agt did not resign, and as Justice minister he was able to prevent any Bill reaching the statute book. He emerged as Prime Minister in 1978 after disagreement over abortion had been a key factor in the failure of the Labour Party and Christian Democrats to agree a coalition (Van Os, *Financial Times*, 5 September 1977).

Van Agt managed to get a Bill through Parliament in April 1981 – the eighth in eleven years (*Guardian*, 30 April 1981) – which allowed for abortion on request up to twenty weeks in specially-licensed clinics but called for a five day 'meditation' period between the request and the operation. It was opposed by two members of Van Agt's party who felt it was too liberal, and by the Labour opposition who felt that the decision should be left to the woman and not part of the criminal law.

France

The legalisation of abortion on request in the first ten weeks of pregnancy occurred on 17 January 1975. It overthrew the 1920 Abortion Law which together with the ban on birth control resulted from concern over the size of the population after the carnage of the First World War.

The change in law had many similarities to that of the United

States. In both cases the debate was concerned with repeal, with abortion on request up to a specific time being actually won, and with the role of state financing, the position of minors, and the gestation period. There had been a liberalisation of attitudes in France since the Second World War, as is indicated by the fact that in 1950 there were 2,885 people sentenced for abortion but in 1969 only 471 (*The Times*, 15 November 1974). The sentences were also reduced. One case which gained much publicity and brought the issue to great prominence was the Bobigny affair, which concerned a girl aged 17 who had been aborted after rape, whose trial took place in November 1972 at Bobigny, near Paris. She was acquitted, her mother received a fine, and the abortionist a suspended sentence.

There was some early attempt at reform, such as a Bill put forward by a Gaulist Deputy in 1970. But when this fell the advocates of free abortion decided to demand repeal by an aggressive campaign. In April 1971 343 women signed a manifesto published in the left-wing magazine *Le Nouvel Observateur*, stating that they had had abortions and calling for repeal. The list included well known writers and actresses such as Jeanne Moreau, Catherine Deneuve and Simone De Beauvoir, and none could be prosecuted because the offences were out of time (*The Times*, 15 November 1974). This direct challenge by the growing women's movement supported by the left wing was a crucial factor in producing change. In calling for freedom the radicals were able to point to the support they had from public opinion and to the fact that the law was unworkable. The report of one poll said that almost 60 per cent of the population was in favour of abortion on demand in the first ten weeks of pregnancy (*Catholic Herald*, 27 December 1974). Mme Simone Veil, the Minister of Health responsible for the preparation of the Bill, claimed that 300,000 French women had abortions each year despite its illegality, an estimate which appears to be a little high in terms of later figures. However, the enormity of the problem of law enforcement was encapsulated by the Minister of the Interior, M. Poniatowski, who showed that it would have been necessary to send more than 15,000,000 women to prison in the previous half century (*The Times*, 15 November 1974).

It might seem surprising that France, a nominally Catholic country, should legalise abortion. However, there is also a strong tradition of atheism and the French Catholic Church, unlike its

British counterpart, finds most of its strength in the rural areas, which makes campaigning more difficult in terms of easy access by the national mass media and central government. The head of the Church in France announced on television that 'Abortion is an act of death, a failure and certainly an evil' (*New Humanist*, February 1975), and anti-abortion organisations spent an estimated 3 million francs opposing change. The Church also produced a ten-page papal statement, approved five months previously, on the eve of the debate in the National Assembly, but in the face of the other pressures this was not effective (*New Humanist*, February 1975).

One of the confusing aspects was French medical opinion. In 1973, after 500 doctors had said they had performed abortions (*The Times*, 15 November 1974), 10,000 doctors came out against a liberal bill. They formed an organisation led by Professor Lejeune called Association of Doctors Respecting Human Life (*Yorkshire Post*, 30 August 1973) and represented one in six of those practising medicine. The French Medical Council was also opposed. It once called abortion 'a work of death' and said that if liberal abortion were allowed it would necessitate the recruitment of volunteer doctors to undertake the work as 'one cannot ask the medical body both to save life by every means and to kill' (*The Times*, 22 November 1974). However, a sampling of medical opinion three months before the launching of Professor Lejeune's group found that four out of five wanted the law reformed (*The Times*, 17 May 1973). So it seems that the medical profession was divided.

The voting in the French Assembly followed predictable patterns, but support from the left was more solid that in Britain or the United States. On a free vote, 105 Socialists and Radicals out of 106 voted in favour. Similarly 73 out of 74 Communists were in support. But only 99 out of the 291 members of the three parties forming the government voted for the Bill. The final version gave abortion on request until the tenth week of pregnancy or after that if there were serious risk to the woman's health or foetal deformity. The government set fees of between £40 and £70 for abortion and insisted that those under the age of 18 should get parental approval (*Observer*, 23 March 1975). In addition, the law tried to prevent hospitals from specialising in abortion by insisting that terminations must not form more than a quarter of a hospital's total operations. The new law was initially on five years' trial.

The Act took some time to take effect, but the number of French women coming to England for abortion dropped rapidly, a good index of its effectiveness at the early stages of pregnancy. In 1979 the law was made permanent. It was opposed by 20,000 feminists complaining that it was too restrictive, with the major focus of attention on the failure of hospitals to provide services, restrictions on minors, and the restrictive time limit. In 1982 the government promised to cover the costs of abortion on the national health service (*The Times*, 5 March 1982).

West Germany

The situation here contrasted markedly with events in the United States. There we saw that the legal situation and the role of the Supreme Court led to a 'repeal' as against a 'reform' law and the courts acted for radical change. In Germany the situation was just the opposite. The Supreme Court declared a 'repeal' law unconstitutional and set out guidelines for a 'reform' Bill.

We saw that in April 1971 famous French women publicised their abortions. Inspired by this, less than two months later (2 June), twenty-four well known actresses, journalists, singers and film stars had their photos on the front page of *Stern* news magazine. All had signed a declaration to say that they had broken German law. In all, a total of 374 women had signed, the eldest being 77 and the youngest 14. The supporters of liberal abortion used the incident to argue that the law was unworkable. One of the organisers, Ingrid Huebner, was quoted as saying: 'If all the women who have had an abortion had the courage to take out a summons against themselves the law would be swamped by a flood of 5 million trials'. In theory, under German law, state attorneys have no choice but to prosecute in cases even where a person is self-accused. Actress Romy Schneider, despite having a warrant threatening to prosecute her, flew to Bonn to a party given by Chancellor Willy Brandt. This act contravened the terms of the warrant and gave further publicity to the case (*New York Times*, 24 June 1971).

The 1871 Penal Code, which was being opposed, in paragraph 218 provided for up to five years' imprisonment. In campaigning for the Bill the divisions in society between left and right, and particularly between the women's movement and the Catholic hierarchy, became accentuated. Estimates were that 44 per cent of West Germans were Catholic (*New York Times*, 27 April) and the Church was linked to the right-wing Christian Democratic Party. So to the women's movement the Church was not only a patriarchal institution trying to control their lives with a religious doctrine to which they did not subscribe, but it was also the backbone of their right-wing political opponents. The acrimony led to churches being daubed with slogans like 'ban 218', and invaded by large groups of women. On Easter day 1974 the Primate, Cardinal Dopfner, had his service at Munich Cathedral interrupted by a tape-recorded attack on him being released from a confessional booth (*New York Times*, 22 April 1974). So the degree of conflict was very great and the direct action against the Church highlighted the divisions in the society.

International changes obviously affected the debate. The number of German women coming to Britain for an abortion rose from 3,621 in 1970 to 13,560 in 1971 and 17,531 in 1972 (OPCS, 1972, 1973, 1974). Even more began going to Holland, where estimates for 1975 were for 61,000 German women having their abortions, while the number coming to Britain had fallen to 3,400 (OPCS, 1978). Furthermore the legalisation in East Germany in 1972 meant that women there had rights to control their own fertility not available in the West (*New York Times*, 10 March 1972). These pressures, together with a sympathetic coalition government made up of the Free Democrats and the Social Democrats, meant that the law could be changed. The Bill provided for abortion on request up to twelve weeks and under stricter conditions for late in the pregnancy. The vote in April 1974 was 274, including Chancellor Brandt, in support of the change and 233 opposed. The Christian Democrats, however, referred the law to the Constitutional Court and the law was not implemented in the interim.

It was nearly a year later (April 1975) that the Court ruled by 6 votes to 2 that the Constitution guaranteed the right to life to everyone (*New York Times*, 26 February 1975). The Court said that the state had a duty to protect the human being from the beginning of its existence, which the ruling placed at the fourteenth day after conception. The ruling also asserted that the 'bitter experience' of the Nazi period in Germany provided historical grounds for determining that protection of life should receive absolute priority. Tietze told me (10 September 1982) that the German Supreme Court has two parallel panels and it was 'bad luck' that the more conservative one decided the case, ruling that abortion could only take place in the first three months of pregnancy for rape, danger to the woman's health, foetal deformity or when a birth would cause 'grave hardship'. The decision delivered in Karlruhe inevitably brought a wave of protests. A thousand people marched through the town in one of several demonstrations organised by the West German Trade Union Federation (*Guardian*, 26 February 1975). In Bonn the ruling Social Democratic Party organised a silent march of protest. A lower court judge, Erich Weidler of Hannover, was quoted as saying: 'If a poor woman is convicted of abortion before me because the law is the way it is, I will seek the least possible punishment, let's say 100 marks [£40] and I would pay it from my own pocket' (*New York Times*, 23 March 1975). Overall, a poll showed that 59 per cent of German voters had been in favour of the repeal law.

The law was amended by the Bundestag in line with the Court's guideline on 18 May 1976, and it prescribed a very bureaucratic procedure. Abortion was allowed for risk to the woman's health and up to twelve weeks for rape. It was allowed up to twenty-two weeks for genetic or other unusual indications. The controversial 'social indicators' allowed abortion for unbearable psychological stress. Each woman had to receive counselling which would include discussion of alternatives and the abortion had to be performed in a hospital or authorised premises by a physician other than the certifying physician. After the Act there were many problems with facilities. In 1977 Elke Keinath Vogel, a health official, said that in the South there were difficulties in getting abortions even for valid reasons, whereas in Hamburg the situation was easier (*New York Times*, 18 June 1977). However, even in Hamburg the bureaucracy was such that many women preferred to travel to Holland where in 1976 they could get abortions for £60 including lunch and coach fare (Neville, 1976). There is some controversy about the official German figures, and Dr Ulrich Wolff, writing in the medical journal *Der Deutsche Arzt* (German Doctor), stated that the official statistics showing a negligible increase in legal abortion between mid-1976 and mid-1977 were nonsense. Dr Wolff claimed that many doctors were failing to report the true figure (*General Practitioner*, 21 October 1977) and the abortions can be carried out in the office of a gynaecologist. A good index of availability is the decline in women travelling abroad. The number going to Holland fell to 32,000 in 1979, half the figure five years earlier, and the number going to Britain fell to 726, a decline to a quarter of the previous level over the same period (Office of Population Censuses and Surveys, 1981).

Italy

The abortion law in Italy was slightly liberalised by a Supreme Court Decision in 1976, but was changed to give women abortion on request on 28 May 1978. The legalisation owed much of its impulse to developments in France. As *The Times* stated: 'France's decision to legalise abortion has left many Italians with a feeling of bitter isolation . . . All Italy's northern neighbours have now given their women the right to terminate pregnancies under decent and controlled conditions' (6 December 1974). In fact the many similarities with the political structure in France – the Catholic Church being linked to the right-wing Christian Democratic Party and the radicals being anti-clerical – led to great similarities in the kind of campaign fought. It was much more aggressive than that of the British legalisation and with much more use of confrontation tactics. In Britain and America radicals are used to co-operating with liberal religious groups, which is not the case in France and Italy. Italians would have to wait a long time for a Clergy Consultation Service such as occurred in New York.

Some incidents show clearly the differences in campaign style. We have seen how in Britain and the United States the organisations for free abortions argued that liberalisation would help family life by ensuring that every child was wanted, and thus tried to keep a 'respectable' image. In contrast, Italian feminist groups began to refer women for abortions. The Centro Informazione Sterilizzazione e Aborto (CISA) aimed to help women directly and make the country face up to the issue (*The Times*, 15 April 1976). It was headed by a 55-year-old single woman, Adele Faccio, who at the age of 36 deliberately bore a son. CISA introduced suction abortion in Italy and accompanied women to cheap doctors or, if their pregnancies had passed three months, to London. When the inevitable arrests came Faccio went to Paris to carry out a speaking engagement. She then gained maximum publicity by announcing that she would give herself up at a large abortion rally in Rome. She returned to Italy with the help of borrowed documents and a wig to force the arrest to take place in front of the press, television, and hundreds of supporters. *The Times* commented: 'The episode had the desired effect of turning Adele Faccio into a heroine and martyr and making the embarrassed carabinieri officer appear the stooge of an obtuse regime bent on imposing its crude fascist laws' (15 April 1976).

In a second incident a gynaecologist, Dr Conciani, a member of the Radical Party, was imprisoned for two months without trial for performing abortions. Three MPs, two of them women, exercising their rights as parliamentarians to visit any prison in Italy, saw him and then refused to leave, saying they wished to be charged as 'accomplices' of the gynaecologist. These kinds of incidents kept the issue in the news and challenged the legitimacy of the law (*Guardian*, 6 November 1976). As they show, the attack on the abortion law was led by the women's liberation movement and the Radical Party, this latter being more a pressure group for civil rights which played a crucial role in the legalisation of divorce in 1970 and its confirmation in 1974. It was these two groups which forced open the issue of abortion by obtaining the half million signatures to call for a referendum.

One of the crucial points abortion activists made was that there was a high level of illegal abortions and that doctors were making large profits out of the suffering of women. There were three estimates of the number of illegal abortions. The World Health Organisation reportedly estimated 1,500,000 abortions in 1975, the Italian health authorities estimated 800,000, and the women's movement 3 million a year (*Economist*, 25 January 1975). A poll found that 93 per cent of Italians believed it was easy for a rich woman to have an abortion performed by a physician and that 63 per cent of Italians wanted a new law (*People*, vol. 2, no. 3, 1975). By 1975 it had become clear that the law had to change. The decision in February of the Constitutional Court meant that abortions could be performed if the woman's physical or psychological health was in danger. However, the change could not stop there (Willey, 1975). The Christian Democratic Party, having lost in the 1974 divorce referendum, desperately wanted to avoid another failure. It therefore proposed a Bill which would stop abortion being referred to as 'a crime against race' and would reduce the sentence for abortion after rape. It was not the kind of solution that would address itself to the size of the problem (*ALRA News*, March 1975).

The Communists made a series of proposals including the development of maternity and child welfare services. They called for abortion to be allowed for social and economic reasons in addition to cases of harm to the woman's physical and mental well being. However, they were not agreeable to abortion on request (*Scotsman*, 17 December 1975). The Socialist Party was the one with the aim of lifting all sanctions against abortion during the first three months of pregnancy (*Morning Star*, 12 June 1975). The threat of the referendum was a major one in encouraging the other parties to accede to its view. More than the necessary half million signatures were obtained in six weeks in 1975 to make the threat a real possibility. But the necessary compromise could not be agreed and in 1976 the government fell, as it was the only way to stop the referendum from taking place. Italian law only allows a referendum to occur between 15 April and 15 June and not within one year of an election.

One of the crucial issues in the debate was the relationship between Church and state. This problem became accentuated with the 'Seveso' case when an explosion led to women being exposed to a chemical known to cause foetal malformation. The Christian Democrats agreed to thirty-eight women having abortions which caused a rift between it and the Vatican (*Catholic Herald*, 20 August 1976; *Universe*, 7 July 1978). The Communists increased their support during the election. However, the Christian Democrats continued to oppose radical change. At the beginning of 1977 the Chamber of Deputies voted by 319 to 277 to reject the view that abortion on demand would violate the constitutional right to life (*Birmingham Evening Mail*, 19 January 1977). However, in the Senate the Christian Democrats had more success when by 156 votes to 154 they managed to defeat a Bill which would have given abortion on request to 16-year-olds. The Communists had by this time come round to support a 'repeal' Bill, and in subsequent discussions insisted that it should be left to the woman to make the final decision at the early stages (*Morning Star*, 9 June 1972). The compromises were obviously going to be on such issues as parental permission for minors, extent of bureaucratic obstacles, and the degree of exclusion for conscience. Less than a month before a referendum would have been mandatory, the Act was passed. The final draft allowed abortion on request during the first ninety days of pregnancy at the expense of the state; those under 18 needed parental approval or that of a magistrate. A doctor could also make the woman wait seven days (*The Tablet*, 6 June 1981). The law gave doctors the right to conscientious objection, and estimates were that over 70 per cent were taking this option (Watson, 1979).

There were various protests against the law's non-implementation. In November 1978 Italian feminists occupied a Turin hospital for a week. However, the Italian Medical Association ordered doctors to 'obey the law and carry out abortions' and soon the number of women travelling to England began to drop, so that in 1979 188,000 legal abortions occurred. This level is well below the estimated level of illegal abortions and suggests that there was still unmet demand. However, it is three times the number performed by the British National Health Service.

The Church opposition to the Act had increased. In 1978 the bishops ruled that women having abortions would face automatic excommunication (*The Universe*, 22 December 1978), and when a referendum on the issue was called the *Observer* commented that 'The Pope has virtually entered the hustings' (3 May 1981). In the referendum on 17 and 18 May 1981 voters had three alternatives: they could vote for a restrictive law put forward by the pro-life movement; they could leave the law as it was; or they could vote for the Radical Party's proposal to decriminalise abortion even for minors and to remove time limits. Both proposals for change were heavily defeated as the major parties apart from the Christian Democrats called for a 'double no'. Even before the voting Joan Lewis in Rome for the *Catholic Herald* predicted the final result:

> There is a silent majority in this predominantly Catholic country which admits that abortion, however heart rending and agonising the problem, is here to stay. The more vocal of this majority argue that it would be better to search deeper and find the causes of this 'social plague' as they call it. They say that abrogating the current law would not eliminate abortions and indeed, could encourage clandestine abortions, which have a high mortality rate. (Lewis, 1981)

The pro-life amendment was opposed by 67.9 per cent of the voters. The Radical Party's was opposed by 88.5 per cent. So the law remained as it was and the extent of the support suggested that further change in the near future was very unlikely.

Israel

One of the surprising things about the situation in Israel is that the law became so contentious. It might be thought, given the role of Jews in liberalising the law throughout the world, that their country would have moved quickly to abortion on request. This is particularly so because we know that as long ago as 1952 the District Court of Haifa ruled that abortion openly performed on bona fide medical grounds was permissible. From that time onwards doctors were not prosecuted and in practice abortion was freely available from medical practitioners.

Pressure to change the law came from feminists who wanted the right to choose an abortion. They were supported by those on the left but opposed by the orthodox religious groups, the right wing and the Israeli Society of Gynaecologists. The *Jewish Chronical* (19 March 1976) reported that a meeting of 500 rabbis proclaimed a worldwide day of prayer to prevent the law coming into being as it could 'spell suicide for the nation'. This kind of argument has a long history, as we have seen, and a variant was later used by the British Chief Rabbi (*Jewish Chronicle*, 29 January 1982) when he argued that without abortion there would have been 4 million Jewish Israelis rather than 3 million. He drew comparisons with the murder of Jews by the Nazis. The weakness of this argument is that many women who have abortions when they are young nevertheless go on to have children at a later date. The right-wing nationalist Knesset members opposed the Bill and pointed to the need to increase the Jewish birthrate. Geula Cohen of Herut said, 'The only Bill needed is one to encourage the birth rate not decrease it' (*Jewish Chronicle*, 28 January 1977). She was opposed by the civil rights leader Ms Shulamit Aloni: 'A woman's body is her own. It is not there to service the State, the Army or the nation.' The opposition of the gynaecologists seems to be largely due to the fact that they objected to women feeling that they had the right to make them carry out an abortion (*Daily Telegraph*, 27 February 1976). When in June 1976 they were meeting at the Tel Aviv Hilton Hotel their meeting was invaded by fifteen women calling, 'We want abortions legalised'.

The arguments of the proponents of the Bill were similar to those used elsewhere. They drew attention to the high number of 'illegal' abortions and said that the change in law would help poor women who could not afford the high cost, and would ensure good medical conditions (*Jewish Echo*, 6 February 1976).

The law was passed in February 1977, despite some misgivings from the feminists that it did not go far enough. It stipulated that permission for the abortion would be needed from a three-member committee consisting of two doctors, one of whom must be a gynaecologist, and a social worker. The grounds for abortion were:

1 That the woman is below 18 years or over 40.
2 That the pregnancy is the result of incestuous or other illegal sexual relations.
3 The foetus is likely to be born with a physical or mental defect.
4 The pregnancy is likely to endanger the life of the woman or cause her physical or mental injury.
5 The family or social circumstances of the woman are such that for her to have another baby would be seriously injurious to her or her children.

The Act appeared to work as expected. Dr Yehoshua Weisbrot was reported in the *Jewish Echo* (17 February 1978) as saying that he did not expect the number of abortions to rise above the 15,000–20,000 annual average before the law came into effect. This level appears to have been maintained with one estimate putting the number of abortions at 18,000 a year. However, in 1976 the law came under pressure after the election had left Prime Minister Begin with difficulties in forming a coalition. The religious party Agudat Israel, which had four members in the Knesset, refused to support the Begin government unless the fifth 'social' ground for abortion were removed. About 43 per cent of abortions were carried out under this condition (*Glasgow Herald*, 13 November 1979). It was a government measure and so subject to the whips. At the first vote it was 58–58 and the removal of this ground was defeated as nearly a dozen coalition members, including the Justice Minister, opposed the change. The matter was brought up again, and this time Begin made it a vote of confidence and invoked a law requiring ministers to vote with the government or resign. The vote this time was 55–50 for the government, despite the fact that many members were unhappy about the way they had to vote. A woman member was quoted as saying: 'I feel very bad and I hope to see a time when it will be changed. I didn't change my views. I only changed my vote because it was put as a confidence vote in this government' (*New York Times*, 26 December 1979).

Many thought that the legal change would not be likely to make a great deal of difference. A leading Jerusalem gynaecologist asserted (*Jewish Chronicle*, 19 March 1982) that 'any woman who really wants to terminate her pregnancy will find a way to get it done'. His prediction was substantiated, for subsequent reports showed that the number of abortions was not reduced. Indeed the Minister of Health, Dr Sadan, calculated that through abortion six potential divisions of Jewish soldiers had been murdered (*Spare Rib*, February 1983).

Changes in the Commonwealth

Most of the countries in the Commonwealth inherited the 1861 Offences Against the Person Act. So when Britain amended its law as with the Bourne decision or the 1967 Abortion Act it was bound to have a ripple effect throughout the rest of the Commonwealth. Zambia became the first of the African Commonwealth countries to reform its restrictive law in 1972 and permitted abortion along the lines of the British 1967 Act (Cook, 1976).

Two other countries to change their law were Zimbabwe in 1977 and the Seychelles in 1981. The Seychelles law almost follows the British Act and permits abortion where 'continuance of pregnancy would involve risk to the pregnant woman's life, or risk of injury to her physical or mental health greater than if the pregnancy were terminated' (Cook and Dickens, 1983, p. 21).

A second group of nine African Commonwealth countries have liberalised their law along the lines of the Bourne judgement and allow abortions to protect the woman's physical or mental health. The Southern States of Nigeria incorporated Bourne in 1938, as did Kenya in 1959 and Ghana in 1960. Tanzania, Gambia, Uganda and Sierra Leone also applied Bourne. In Sierra Leone, Lesotho and Swaziland English common law still applies and although these countries allow abortions for maternal health it is not clear how far they proscribe abortion before quickening (about fourteen weeks) as termination was allowed up until this time in common law.

The third group of countries – Botswana, Malawi, Mauritius and Nigeria (Northern States) – just allow abortion if there is a risk to the life of the woman (Cook and Dickens, 1983). There is evidence of widespread illegal abortion in Africa. In Tanzania at the main medical centre in Dar es Salaam in 1978 over 4,000 of a total of 6,000 admissions were diagnosed as either spontaneous or illegal abortion cases (Cook and Dickens, 1983, p. 121). Complications were common and there were nine deaths – a mortality rate of over 2 per 1,000. There is also evidence of much illegal abortion in Nigeria (Akingbar and Gbajumo, 1970). It can be argued that restrictions on legal abortion are against the African charter of human rights which provides in Article 16.1 that 'every individual shall have the right to enjoy the best attainable state of physical and mental health' (Cook and Dickens, 1983, p. 58).

In an analysis of a total of sixty Commonwealth countries and dependent territories Cook and Dickens found that eighteen only allowed abortion to save the life of the woman, thirty allowed abortions to protect the woman's physical or mental health and twelve allowed abortion on wider grounds than this. A meeting of the health and justice ministries of thirteen Commonwealth countries in Barbados in June 1979 proposed that abortion should be available on request during the first trimester. However, the 1974 Singapore law is still the only Commonwealth one providing abortion on request and its law allows this until the twenty-fourth week (Cook and Dickens, 1983; Paxman, 1980; *Financial Times*, 1 November 1983). We will now consider some of the Commonwealth countries in more detail.

Australia

Like the USA, Australia has a Federal structure. However, because there is no Supreme Court each of the seven states can decide its own law. The situation with regard to abortion was similar to that in the United States in that before legalisation there was widespread performance by doctors for financial gain and with the agreement of the local police. This matter came to a head in Victoria in 1969 when four members of the force were convicted after abortionists were offered protection against prosecution for 10 per cent of their fees. (Wainer, 1972).

Australian activists, like those elsewhere, could work for liberalisation either through the courts or through the legislature. The first state to pass a liberal law was South Australia in 1969. Commenting on the legalisation Yusuf and Briggs (1979) stated that interest in the issue had been aroused by the passing of the 1967 British Act. The major pressure group was the Abortion Law Reform Association of South Australia, which was an offshoot of the Humanist Society. Support was also gained from the Methodist and Presbyterian churches. Opposition came not only from Catholics but also from the Lutherans. The influence of the British Act can be clearly seen in the wording of the South Australian Act, which was to allow abortion when two doctors took the view that 'continuance of the pregnancy would involve greater risk to the life of the pregnant woman or greater risk of injury to the physical or mental health of the pregnant woman than if the pregnancy were terminated'. This was, of course, the wording that had been used by Professor Huntingford to justify abortion on request in Britain.

In Victoria the law was broadened by the case R. v. Davidson, 1969, where a State Supreme Court Judge had to give direction on the use of the word 'unlawfully' as placed in the British 1861 Act and copied into the legislation. The British Infant Life Preservation Act (1929) did not apply, so the Judge did not have the recourse to this as Macnaghten had had in the Bourne trial. Instead he tried to specify what was meant by 'unlawfully'. He pointed to the fact that the word was nowhere statutorily defined and said that, for abortion to be lawful, 'I think that the accused must have honestly believed on reasonable grounds that the act done by him was necessary to preserve the woman from some serious danger. As to this element of danger, it appears to be in principle that it should not be confined to danger to life but should apply equally to danger to physical or mental health' (Royal Commission, 1977, p. 141). This liberalisation of interpretation applied not only to Victoria but also to Capital Territory.

Northern Territory passed a liberalising law in 1973 (Paxman, 1980). According to Treloar et al. (1977), in New South Wales the law in operation from 1900 allowed abortion if the woman's life or health, mental or physical, was judged to be endangered by the pregnancy. In a trial in 1971 five people, including two doctors, were acquitted on charges of unlawfully terminating pregnancies. Mr Justice Levine expanded the term 'mental health' to include social and economic stress. In 1974 they set up a 'pre term' clinic modelled on the free-standing clinics in the United States.

Elsewhere there was also liberalisation of practice though Queensland, a state considered by many to be the most reactionary in Australia – in 1977 it banned street assemblies (*Sunday Times*, 4 May 1980) – came under threat of great restrictions. A Bill would have allowed abortion for rape and incest only after police investigations, and rubella in the early months would not have been sufficient grounds. A doctor who advised a patient to go to Sydney (NSW) for an abortion would be regarded as 'frustrating the objects of the Act' (Section 19) and could be struck off the medical register. The pressure for this Bill came after 'Right to Life' groups had been unsuccessful in their attempts to enforce existing laws against a clinic in Brisbane. The state Premier, Bjelke-Petersen, sought the advice of a New Zealand anti-abortion lawyer, J. D. Dalgerty, and a primary aim was to close the only 'fertility control clinic in the Northern half of Australia' (*Sunday Times*, 4 May 1980). The Bill was opposed by the Australian Medical Association, by the rank and file of the political parties, and by a demonstration of 3,000 women who defied the street assembly ban. In the event the Bill was defeated at the Second Reading as 19 members of the government crossed the floor to vote against it. Only a late technical move to make it a Private Member's Bill prevented the government from being defeated.

This was, of course, a great victory for the advocates of abortion rights. However, there is still a very strong anti-abortion movement in Australia and battles are likely to continue, especially over such issues as funding.

New Zealand

The abortion law in New Zealand was also modelled on the British Offences Against the Person Act. The statute in operation in the 1960s had been passed in 1961, and from the late 1960s there was a gradual liberalisation. For example, the number of therapeutic abortions in public hospitals more than quadrupled during the period 1969–73 (Potts *et al.*, 1977).

A crucial development was the setting up of the Auckland Medical Aid Centre in May 1974. This aimed to provide cheap abortions, and though 80 per cent of GPs had referred patients to it (*Guardian*, 24 October 1978), there were several attempts to close it. The Royal Commission (1977) drew attention to the fact that it carried out more abortions than all other public and private hospitals together. In 1975 one of its doctors, James Woolnough, was tried in the Supreme Court on twelve counts of using an instrument to procure abortion. Mr Justice Speight employed the same argument on the use of 'unlawfully' as had been employed in the earlier trial in South Australia. Woolnough was acquitted in a second trial after a hung jury and thus the law was effectively extended.

The Royal Commission, established in 1975 as a result of the furore caused by the setting up of the Auckland Centre, had a strong anti-abortion flavour. For example it talked of a seven-week foetus as being an 'unborn child', and was therefore not surprisingly critical of the work of the Auckland Centre. It pointed out that the Centre had turned down only 4.6 per cent of applicants for abortion for legal reasons in 1974–5, and 2 per cent in 1975–6. It noted the Centre's argument that doctors had become aware of the legal requirements but commented: 'It could be argued that the reduced percentage of refusals is consistent with the Centre taking an even more relaxed view of the law than it did in the first year of its existence' (Royal Commission, 1977, p. 169). When the Royal Commission reported in 1977 it proposed that abortion should only be allowed for 'serious danger to the physical or mental health of the woman', and that a bureaucratic committee system should decide areas. However, it did suggest that abortion should be allowed for foetal abnormalities.

When the law came to be changed later that year it had been hardened somewhat, and the influence of the anti-abortionists could be seen. In New Zealand this opposition group was relatively strong. The Society for the Protection of the Unborn Child (SPUC) was formed in 1970, and by May 1975 was able to organise an 8,000-strong march on Parliament. It seems more extreme than the corresponding British group, and in its literature makes great use of the Willkes' book and reproduces its photographs. The anti-abortionists persuaded the government to drop the 'fetal handicap' exception in the law which was passed on 14 December 1977, though there were allegations that the law had been passed unfairly since seventeen MPs, fourteen of whom opposed the legislation, were out of the country. The new law was also unpopular with the medical profession and the general population. Facer (1978) reports a poll that showed only 15 per cent approving the Act and 66 per cent disapproving. One in six voters signed a petition of protest, and in fact pressure was so great that there were slight modifications in 1978 to allow, amongst other changes, abortion for foetal abnormality.

The Auckland Centre closed immediately after the Act came into effect and the number of abortions was reduced in the following year. The Sisters Overseas Service (SOS) arranged for women to fly to Australia, but then the Auckland Centre re-opened and by 1980 the rates of abortion were back to the level of 1976.

Canada

The debate in Canada has centred on the trials of Dr Morgentaler, a campaigner for abortion rights since 1967.

The law was liberalised somewhat in 1969, but like the later New Zealand statute was very cumbersome. It allowed abortions only in hospitals which had appointed a committee of not fewer than three physicians, and specified that abortion should only be given where continuation of the pregnancy 'would or would be likely to' endanger the life or health of the pregnant woman. Although the law was restrictive, the number of abortions increased from 11,000 a year in 1970 to 43,000 in 1973.

The law might have continued with a gradual liberalisation had it not been for the prosecution of Dr Henry Morgentaler in Quebec, a province where it was very difficult to obtain a legal abortion. He was first prosecuted in 1970, but these proceedings came to nothing and he was able to continue. Between 1969 and 1973 he carried out over 6,000 abortions, but in August of that year a police raid led to him being prosecuted again. Morgentaler relied on the 'Good Samaritan' provision of the Criminal Code (Dickens, 1976) which protects a person carrying out surgery for another's benefit if 'it is reasonable to perform the operation, having regard to the state of health of the person at the time the operation is performed and to all the circumstances of the case'. He was acquitted by the jury, but in a clear breach of common law rights the Quebec Court of Appeal ordered a conviction. This was upheld by the Canadian Supreme Court, and in March 1975 Morgentaler went to gaol to serve ten months of an eighteen-month sentence. This he continued to serve even after the government in Ottawa undertook in July 1975 to change the law to prevent any further appeal court ordering convictions after a jury trial. When I met Morgentaler in Washington DC in 1978 he told me that he had been responsible for a change in the law called the 'Morgentaler Amendment'. As he sat in prison after his 'not guilty' verdict, at least he could take comfort from the fact it would not happen to anyone else. Morgentaler was acquitted on another abortion charge in May 1975. His only defence was the concept of necessity, which the Judge warned the jury not to consider. This time the Quebec Court of Appeal upheld the acquittal and, according to Rene Domingue, the Crown Prosecutor, its decision 'opens the door to abortion on demand' (Illman, 1976).

The Morgentaler cases had obviously thrown the law into great confusion. The government tried to respond in October 1974 when Otto Lancy, Federal Minister of Justice, advised the appropriate authorities that 'social and economic considerations were not to be taken into account in determining whether a pregnancy lawfully could be terminated'. However, in the following year he back pedalled and in a statement to the Canadian press denied saying that economic factors could not be taken into account (Illman, 1976). The government also set up the Badgley Committee to consider the working of the Act and whether it was 'operating equitably across Canada'. This Committee reported in 1977 that only 20 per cent of hospitals had set up abortion committees and that after the first visit to the physician it took an average of eight weeks to obtain the abortion. It also found that two-thirds of the hospital committees required the consent of the woman's spouse. In the case of single women some committees even required the consent of the male responsible. Not surprisingly, an estimated 10,000 Canadian women (about one in six having abortions) had their terminations in the United States.

The anti-abortionists have attempted to restrict rights by a variety of methods. The *Catholic Herald* (31 October 1980) for example, reported that 'Pro life victories at two British Columbian public hospital society meetings have led to the abolition of the committee which approves abortion at one hospital and a probable abolition of the committee of another'. They have also worked through the courts, and had a notable success when the Ontario Supreme Court ruled that foetuses and natural fathers had rights. The *Scottish Catholic Observer* (6 March 1981) reported that lawyer Paddy Smith had filed an injunction 'on the grounds that the unborn baby is an individual entitled to all the legal rights of a Canadian citizen'. The Court accepted the crux of the argument based on English case law on estates whereby a conceived child can inherit from a deceased parent who died prior to its birth. The Court's decision seems strange in the light of the fact that the law is quite clear that any rights are contingent on birth. The evidence, therefore, suggests that access to abortion in Canada is going to remain problematical with restrictions according to area, partner's rights and bureaucratic obstacles.

India

India in some ways mirrors China in terms of government concern with over-population. In 1951 it sponsored a birth control programme and since that time has continued to push various measures. One was sterilisation, which was particularly encouraged in the nineteen months of the Emergency until March 1977, by which time over 10 million people had undergone vasectomy or tubal ligation. Many of these operations were compulsory for parents of three or more children, a programme which contributed to Mrs Ghandi's defeat and was subsequently drastically cut back. Since she has returned to power there has been much greater emphasis on freedom of choice.

The 1971 laws allowing abortion came into operation in 1972 and permitted abortion on a wide variety of grounds. There were problems with implementation and in 1973 only 24,000 abortions were recorded. These increased to 98,000 in 1975, 214,000 in 1976 and 278,000 in 1977. However, in 1982 Professor S. M. Dasgupta told a population control conference that nearly 4 million illegal abortions were carried out each year. He called for a liberalisation of the law to allow abortion on request and said (*Guardian*, 17 February 1982) that the reasons for the huge number of illegal abortions were the ignorance of many people about the Act, the lack of facilities and personnel, and the ambiguous wording of the Act. One of the problems is that 80 per cent of people live in the villages, many of them without electricity or running water, and are outside the coverage of the health service.

Conclusion

As has been shown, the British change in the abortion law had an important influence on the rest of the Commonwealth. But changes in other former colonial powers may also prove to be important. French colonies often have very restrictive laws, for example, in Chad a 1965 law shows its inspiration from the French law of 1920 and makes it a criminal offence to disseminate 'contraceptive or anti-nationalist propaganda'. The change in French law makes this clearly an anachronism, and so amendments can be expected.

This survey of developments in the Commonwealth has shown how the progress towards abortion freedom has followed many different paths and advanced at widely differing paces according to the different countries.

7
British Debate After 1967

After the Abortion Act of 1967 many people felt that the issue was over. There was a confidence about the changes. Suicide had ceased to be a criminal offence, the death penalty had been abolished, homosexuality legalised, and birth control had become openly available to single people. It seemed that the legalisation of abortion was just part of an overall change in attitude towards 'crimes without victims' (Schur, 1965). However, in subsequent years there was a great deal of controversy and by the end of 1982 there had been ten Bills concerned with abortion – eight of which were intended to restrict the working of the Act.

There does appear to have been further liberalisation in behaviour. For example, calculations which I made reworking the data of two sex surveys to make them comparable, showed a large increase in teenagers having non-marital sex (Francome, 1979). Furthermore, the changes of the 1960s in terms of greater freedom of sexual morality seem to have been consolidated. Living together before marriage is now generally acceptable behaviour, and the continued movement towards sexual equality has enabled women to have greater control over their lives. The class differences have been reversed since the nineteenth century, with surveys showing that the middle class are now more likely to agree with pre-marital sex (*Evening Standard*, 11 May 1970).

Attitudes to abortion amongst the general public have also liberalised, and the medical profession now supports legal abortion. A survey of members of the Royal College of Obstetricians and Gynaecologists, which had originally been very opposed to the Act, showed that 22 per cent thought the Abortion Act was a major advance, 60 per cent felt that it was a reasonable compromise, and only 14 per cent thought it was a mistake (*British Medical Journal*, 10 May 1975). The pressure against the Act has not come from disquiet amongst the general population, nor from those performing the operations. Rather there have been other factors involved. In fact the opposition can be divided into two separate periods, the first up to the James White Bill in 1975 was marked by a decline in pressure from advocates of a liberal law. The second was the galvanising of pro-choice opinion in response to this threat to the Act.

Decline in Pressure from ALRA

Once the 1967 abortion law had been passed, many of the activists believed that the issue had been decided and so moved on to other campaigns. For example, some prominent ALRA members wanted to spread birth control information in order to help reduce the number of abortions. A passage from ALRA's Annual Report for 1969–70 read as follows:

> The executive committee believes that the abortion problem will assume a proper perspective in the eyes of many members of the public only when it is seen as part of an overall campaign to avoid unwanted pregnancies. This suggests that the best course for ALRA, both from the point of view of reducing the need for abortion and of defending, and perhaps later extending, the Abortion Act, lies in a campaign for better facilities in the whole field.

At the AGM in 1970 it was decided to vote over a large part of ALRA's reserves to the Birth Control Campaign. This move displayed a confidence that the Act could be maintained fairly easily and it was passed despite the opposition of a few key workers. One of the activists particularly against the decision told me, 'I was out on a limb. You see I was the one that was going to these anti-abortion meetings and getting the feel of the audiences; seeing how unscrupulous they were in putting their case, and I've never underrated the Catholic Church and I think so many of our people do ... It is the oldest pressure group in business. It is wealthy and powerful and one should never underrate its power.' In retrospect it can be seen that many misjudged the opposition. However, it is in some degree understandable that the change which had been worked for for so long should be regarded as safe while its effects were being evaluated.

Anti-Abortion Pressure

While the pressure from the supporters of the Act declined, pressure from the anti-abortionists increased. When abortion was illegal those fighting the law had had a number of advantages. The presence of an underground network providing abortions made a mockery of the provisions of the law, and those with access to the services of a Harley Street doctor often felt an obligation to others who were having to make do with unqualified and possibly unskilled operators. However, after legalisation these advantages diminished and the opponents of the law were able to capitalise on the changes. First of all abortion became visible for the first time, and statistics showed abortion to be relatively common. Furthermore, the number of recorded abortions kept rising in the years until 1973 and seemed to give credence to the theories about people becoming 'abortion-minded' and using abortion as a contraceptive. There were also problems due to the fact that Britain was the first major Western European country to liberalise and so large numbers of foreign women began to come over, giving rise to comments about Britain being the 'abortion capital of the world'. Those arriving at the airports would not know where to go and so newspaper reports talked about 'taxi touts'. Attempts were made to create a moral panic, and while these were not totally successful the fears helped recruitment amongst those inclined towards an anti-abortion position.

LIFE

At the time of the 1967 Act SPUC was the only anti-abortion pressure group, but in August 1970 it was joined in battle by a second group, LIFE. LIFE had its origins in the correspondence columns of the religious press and takes a position much closer to that held by the Catholic Church. When it was first formed Norman St John Stevas, MP, spent half his weekly column in the *Catholic Herald* attacking it for 'dividing the forces of righteousness'. There is certainly the potential for conflict, for LIFE has the aim of outlawing all abortions. In 1976 Professor Scarisbrick, LIFE's most eminent supporter, was asked under what conditions he felt abortion was justified. He replied that it was acceptable in the remote situation where both the woman and child were going to be dead 'before the baby is viable' (Select Committee, 1976b).

This answer implies that if only the woman were going to die, abortion should not be tolerated. This is spelt out a little more clearly in Scarisbrick's booklet (1971) where he argued that 'the unborn child has as much right to life as his mother has . . . It must be wrong deliberately and directly to kill either; even for the sake of the other.'

In a pamphlet entitled 'Fifteen Errors of the Abortionist' (no date) LIFE disagreed with abortion in rape cases, arguing that it 'won't undo the horrible fact of rape and will add a new horror'. The differences in position sometimes lead to disputes with SPUC, in the midst of one of which Scarisbrick wrote to *The Universe*:

> It would be a pity indeed if there were a lack of harmony between members of LIFE and SPUC. May I, on behalf of LIFE say that we have always supported SPUC and, as the huge LIFE turnout at the recent SPUC rallies showed, we do so more than ever! There is a difference of function and aim between us, but we can and do work together. We will not be content with merely returning to the pre-1967 situation, when thousands of legal abortions were performed. (10 December 1976)

However, despite this confidence displayed by Professor Scarisbrick for achieving totally prohibitive legislation, it is SPUC which has carried greater credibility with the politicians. Those MPs introducing restrictive Bills such as James White and Bill Benyon have been careful to point out that they are not totally anti-abortion, and LIFE has continued to appear too extreme within the British context. Since 1976, when Scarisbrick made that conciliatory statement, LIFE has become less convinced of the case for gradualism and seems to be looking towards a much tougher line. An article in *LIFE News* (Autumn 1978) declared:

> We have tried gradualism and found it does not work. We must be bold and go the whole 'hog'. We must fight on principles and openly tell the world that there can no more be a halfway house on this issue than there can on, say, piracy, blackmail, racism or torture. In the short run absolutism may seem absurd. In the long run it is the only thing that will succeed.

This is obviously a direct challenge to the gradualist stance taken by SPUC, and this debate of course mirrors the earlier ones that appeared in the pro-choice movement in Britain. As in that case, it seems that the gradualists have kept the predominant position. But LIFE is hoping for a change:

> We must take courage from America. After a debate similar to ours, the absolutists are in charge there. The Right to Life movement has rejected gradualism and makes no bones about going for total victory, an Amendment to the Constitution to override the fateful decision of the Supreme Court on 22 January 1973 which opened the floodgates of American abortion. (*LIFE News*, Autumn 1978)

There is pressure to move towards this absolutist position because most of the key activists are absolutists. When in 1979 it was clear that John Corrie was about to introduce a Bill restricting abortion rights, I asked Professor Scarisbrick under what conditions LIFE would support it. He said that he would withhold support if it only reduced the time limit to twenty weeks without altering the grounds. He explained that in his view, although it would save about 15,500 babies who had passed twenty weeks, 'day care would be stepped up and the amount of killing would increase'. In the event Corrie's Bill as first published was relatively restrictive, and the *Guardian* (11 July 1979) reported that Scarisbrick welcomed it as reducing the number of abortions by two-thirds.

The Society for the Protection of Unborn Children

After the Abortion Act came into force, SPUC needed to rethink its tactics. One rule it changed was that which did not allow Catholics on to the executive. Phyllis Bowman, the SPUC Press Secretary, became converted to Catholicism and in 1975 took over as Director. In an interview with her I suggested that SPUC had been more willing to compromise than LIFE (14 May 1979). She disagreed with me and set out her organisation's position as follows:

> With SPUC we have always stated categorically that we have people who accept abortion for general medical indications and those who take an absolute stand and these have come together to fight against the Abortion Act 1967. That is not compromising; it is an agreed stand. The other thing is from my

own point of view. I personally take an absolute stand on abortion. This is what I teach a child. On the other hand I have never fought for an absolute law. I do not think, in certain circumstances, if a woman were dying, you could force her to make a martyr of herself by law.

Thus she would like all abortions made illegal except to save the life of the woman. However, she continued:

I feel on this with the doctors who carry out abortions for genuine medical reasons. Aleck Bourne put this in a nutshell. He once said to me that had he been able to save the baby of the girl who had been raped and saved the mother from her trauma, he'd have saved both. But with the abortionist it is a deliberate act of killing to make sure certain humans don't survive.

It seems from these comments that SPUC is taking a more moderate line than LIFE or the American organisations. So I questioned her further as to whether she felt that by going for minor changes such as a reduction of the time limits it could weaken the pressure for a stronger Bill later. I drew attention to the opposition to piecemeal changes in the United States on these grounds from Michael Schwartz. She replied that she felt that LIFE might take that view but: 'It's rather like saying in Nazi Germany that you wouldn't save certain Jews because you couldn't save the lot. I find that argument arrogant.'

There is thus a tactical difference between SPUC and other major groups. However, as long as it can maintain the support of LIFE on various amending Bills, SPUC's position is strengthened by appearing moderate. It spearheaded the major attempts at restriction in Parliament. It organised its first mass lobby of the House of Commons on 28 November 1973 and people attended from 450 constituencies. Its literature claims: 'In all over 10,000 people attended. M.P.'s described it as the biggest mass lobby on a moral issue in the history of Parliament and the majority of M.P.'s considered our deputation to be extremely well informed. As a result most of the M.P.'s agreed to support amendments to the law.' By the early 1970s SPUC had become a highly efficient pressure group. When in November 1974 James White drew a high place in the Private Members ballot, the whole issue of abortion was once again brought into great prominence.

Early Attempts at Restriction

In July 1969 Norman St John Stevas tried to introduce an amending Bill into the House under the ten-minute rule. His measure claimed to be merely rectifying certain abuses with the support of the medical profession. He was defeated by 11 votes, and in the following year a similar Bill was introduced by Bryant Godman Irvine. This Bill was, however, also facing defeat, so its supporters talked it out to prevent a vote being taken. This defeat led to the view that the Abortion Act was safe so long as a Labour government was in power. When the Tories won in 1970 Norman St John Stevas began to seek out support for a change in the law. He explained in his column in the *Catholic Herald*, however: 'There is little chance of getting amending legislation without a preceding full scale enquiry . . . I have worked for it for more than three years' (Hindell and Simms, 1971, p. 221).

The Lane Committee formed in June 1971 set out to investigate the way the Act was working, not its underlying principles. Evidence was received from 194 organisations and 529 individuals, and overall the Committee seems to have carried out its research thoroughly. The Report published in April 1974 largely supported the way that the Act was being operated (Lane Report, 1974, p. 184):

> We have no doubt that the gains facilitated by the Act have much outweighed any disadvantages for which it has been criticised. The problems which we have identified in its working, and they are admittedly considerable, are problems for which solutions should be sought by administrative and professional action, and by better education of the public. They are not, we believe, indications that the grounds set out in the Act should be amended in a restrictive way. To do so . . . would be to increase the sum of human suffering and ill health, and probably drive more women to seek the squalid and dangerous help of the back-street abortionist.

The Lane Committee continued by noting that its generally tolerant attitude might well have disappointed those who regarded the Abortion Act as a party of the general decline in sexual morality. However, it stated that abuse of freedom by a minority must be lived through for the sake of the greater advantages to the society.

The Report did propose some restrictions, such as a reduction of the time limit to twenty-four weeks, but it was obviously a great blow to the anti-abortionists. The Lane Committee had effectively stalled any parliamentary action for three years and not come out with the kinds of conclusion they would have liked. In response SPUC produced a detailed report by C. B. Goodhart (1974) which attacked the major findings and criticised the evidence. It argued that the Committee membership was not representative of the population as a whole, 'Since a large majority of electors are opposed to abortion on request which as the report frankly admits, is in practice permitted by the provisions of the Act'. Goodhart also said that the Committee would have produced a better report if it had contained people with known views both for and against free abortion. He was unhappy that some of SPUC's suggestions had not been accepted, and did his best to cast doubt on the evidence. However, Goodhart's academic style would probably have had little effect and the controversy over the Act might have died down if the anti-abortionists had not had the good fortune of the publication of the book *Babies for Burning*.

Babies for Burning

After the Lane Committee had completed its research but before publication of the report, a series of articles appeared in the Sunday paper *News of the World* written by freelance journalists Susan Kentish and Michael Litchfield. The story was first announced in the paper on 24 February 1974, and the following three weeks contained the 'full shocking facts'. Included in the allegations were that seven pregnancy testing agencies had declared Susan Kentish pregnant when she was not, and four doctors had, after examining her, agreed with this finding. When later asked about the findings of the Lane Committee, Litchfield commented: 'Investigate! They could not have uncovered the gravy in a steak and kidney pie'. While he was a Conservative Candidate in the 1974 General Election he extended his allegation – 'Dear Sir, we regret you are pregnant' was the headline in the *Daily Express* (2 October 1975). Litchfield and Kentish then wrote a book based on the *News of the World* material and this was published as *Babies for Burning* in December 1974. At this time

Litchfield appeared to be credible, having not only been a candidate in a General Election but also because he claimed to have won the Pulitzer prize for articles written about the Mafia and published in *Life* magazine. Furthermore he claimed that he had taped all the interviews on which the articles and book were based.

The allegations he made included the following:

1 Not only did the pregnancy testing agencies declare Kentish pregnant, but samples of his own urine also received positive tests. He claimed that his urine was passed and sealed in front of an independent witness, Dr Peter McCormick, a GP in Litchfield's home town of Kettering (*News of the World*, 24 February 1974).
2 There were strong Nazi sympathies amongst abortion doctors. Litchfield claimed that a chemist running a pregnancy testing agency had told him, 'My business is all to do with selective killing. That was the great dream and immense philosophy of Hitler . . . Euthanasia is next of the Agenda . . . so that life will terminate for everyone on their sixtieth birthday . . . Most of the doctors involved in abortion whom I deal with are disciples of this cause.'
3 That an unnamed gynaecologist committed murder, and when Litchfield posed as a manufacturer the man agreed to sell him foetuses to be processed into soap. The murder charges were alleged to refer to the doctor carrying out abortion so late that the foetuses were viable. An alleged quote from the doctor was 'One morning I had four of them lined up crying their heads off. I hadn't the time to kill them then and there.'

These and other allegations shocked and influenced Parliament. All members were sent the book, and a proof copy was sent to James White who later explained he had read it before drafting his 1975 Abortion Bill (*Guardian*, 19 January 1978). It was also read by Leo Abse, White's mentor, who said that the book corroborated the 'urgent' need for changes in the law (Gillie *et al.*, 1975). On 30 January 1975 Ronald Butt made allegations based on the book in *The Times*, and by the Second Reading of James White's Bill on 7 February it was at its maximum impact.

Those in the abortion agencies knew that the allegations did not ring true and Diane Munday, Press Secretary of the British Pregnancy Advisory Service (BPAS), contacted the *Sunday Times*. Its report was published on 30 March 1975 under the headline 'Abortion Horror Tales Revealed As Fantasies', and it attacked a number of the book's major allegations. The article pointed out that the administrator of the Pulitzer prize said that there had been no award to Michael Litchfield and that in any case it was not given for articles in *Life*. The authors agreed that a general practitioner did witness Litchfield passing urine and that all the testing agencies did receive samples from a Mrs Duffy, the pseudonym Litchfield said he used, and all except one that arrived in a contaminated bottle (and not the type of bottle Dr McCormick said he used) were positive. But, the *Sunday Times* report continued,

> Could Litchfield have sent two sets of samples in his chosen name of Duffy. The agencies can only trace one set of that name. So did Litchfield by accident use another name on the set witnessed by Dr. McCormick ... on the same day that the 'Duffy' samples arrived. February 13th, three of the agencies also received urine samples from an A. Price, of 17 Haynes Road, Kettering. All were negative. There are two interesting points about A. Price. One is that the only A. Price who then lived at that address was Arthur Price, an 87 year old widower at the time of his death on Boxing day last year. Yet the letter accompanying the samples said: 'I think I must be pregnant because I have missed two periods and I am not on the pill'. The other interesting feature is that Arthur Price was the grandfather of Michael Litchfield.

The assertions about Nazi sympathies were also challenged. One doctor whom Litchfield claimed had made favourable references to Hitler was Jewish, had lost his wife and son in Auschwitz and was himself imprisoned in Dachau and Buchenwald. The chemist Litchfield claimed to have quoted was also said by him to have books the titles of which did not seem to exist. Thirdly, Litchfield claimed to have on tape the interview with the doctor in which he agreed to sell foetuses for soap. However, nobody heard the tape except for the anti-abortion MP Leo Abse, and he only managed to hear Litchfield making the appointment and was told: 'With the proper equipment it would be possible to hear the rest of the tape which it was too indistinct for me to make out'. The unnamed doctor concerned was quoted as telling *The Times*: 'I would have thrown him out of the window if any such thing had been mentioned'.

This article discredited the book in the eyes of most people, but Litchfield continued to maintain that it was genuine. He and Kentish gave evidence before the Select Committee set up to consider the Bill, and in September 1975 he wrote a letter to the *Church Times* saying that they had forty hours' playing time to support the allegations that they had tapes of a doctor talking of 'Hitler's progressive thinking'. David Steel, however, pointed out that this tape did not exist and commented 'I have never seen such a pair of charlatans before a Select Committee' (*Hansard*, 9 February 1976, col. 116). By Feburary 1976 James White and Leo Abse were trying to dissociate themselves from the book although Jill Knight, Conservative MP for Edgbaston, was still claiming that 'None of the allegations in the book has ever been disproved' (*Hansard*, 9 February 1976, col. 109). Litchfield continued to defend it even after a 1978 libel action when he and Kentish had to apologise to British Pregnancy Advisory Service in the High Court. Of course, the victory for BPAS in the libel suit did not get anywhere near the original publicity.

James White's Bill

This had its Second Reading on 7 February 1975 and was passed by 203 votes to 88, although it did not proceed to attempt to become law but went by agreement to a Select Committee. It set out to restrict the grounds for abortion, in particular to exclude abortions performed on social grounds, although James White, the MP for Glasgow, Pollock, said that he did not take a 'hard line on abortion' and that abortion should be available for women with problems (*Hansard*, 7 February 1975). However, White argued that the Act was being interpreted too liberally, that a group of doctors would perform abortion on request for cash and that this was against the wishes of the sponsors of the original Act. He stated that he and his supporters 'want to make the 1967 Act work as it was intended to work' (*Hansard*, 7 February 1975).

Leo Abse drew attention to the statistical argument and stated 'we have unwittingly given abortion on demand' (*Hansard*, 7 February 1975). Those defending the Act of Parliament tried to argue that this was not true. However, as early as 1971 Professor Huntingford had said that he practised abortion on demand, and so this was difficult to maintain, although in many areas of the country it was still very difficult to get an abortion (*Daily Telegraph*, 21 July 1971). SPUC gave great publicity to Huntingford's statement (Select Committee, 1976b, p. 25) and also claimed that the activities of ALRA were counterproductive. Paul Cavadino, a member of the SPUC executive, stated at the SPUC Annual General Meeting on 1 March 1975 that

> The ALRA campaign was an excellent campaign from our point of view in that again and again M.P.'s who were pressing to restrict the law pointed out that Abortion on Demand was being practised very widely. Peter Huntingford, who is carrying out abortion on demand policies stated this and he also stated that he thought they did not contravene in any way the working of the Act. The M.P.'s kept saying again and again, that abortion on demand was not the intention of Parliament. ALRA then proceeded to launch a campaign for Abortion on Demand but played very much into the hands of the M.P.'s proposing the Bill. Secondly, they had a Press conference at which they produced Huntingford who stood up and said he was doing abortion on demand, they underlined what they were doing was not the wish of Parliament, and had their own man prove their point for them. At this stage I would like to welcome the spies from ALRA who are in the audience and thank them all for the work on our behalf.

SPUC claimed ALRA's activities were working to its advantage and some believers in liberal laws opposed ALRA's tactics. A new group of workers had taken over and they believed in a much more aggressive policy. Those who had been behind the organisation during the passage of the Act were critical of this development, and the old issue of reform against repeal was revived. However, this time it was those who were aiming for the 'Right to Choose' who gained the ascendancy in the abortion movement. In this respect an important factor was the catalysing effect of the Bill on the women's movement, and from 1975 support for abortion rights grew. Demonstrations against the James White Bill led to the formation of the National Abortion Campaign (NAC) a grass roots organisation in favour of free choice. On 21 June 1975 20,000 people demonstrated against the Bill and in October the group had its first national conference. It called for:

1   Free abortion on demand on the National Health Service.
2   Incorporation of private clinics within the National Health Service.
3   No forced sterilisation with abortion.
4   Increased research and training.
5   The removal of anti-abortion doctors from positions where they can obstruct women.

The Bill also jolted the labour movement into action and in 1975 the Trades Union Congress (TUC) Women's Advisory Council, the TUC, and the Labour Conference all opposed the Bill and called for abortion on request. With these developments the abortion rights movement took a new turning and for the first time the advocates of free choice began to develop mass support of a kind that could match the opposition. There was, however, by no means total support for abortion on request. Many of those in the agencies felt that the existing position should simply be defended. The doctors' organisations that opposed restrictions reflected this divide. Doctors in Defence of the 1967 Act took the view that it would work to keep the Act as it was, but a second group, 'Doctors for a Woman's Choice', aimed to give women the right to choose especially in the early months of pregnancy. In later years this group has increased in importance.

Select Committee

This Committee, which was seen by the anti-abortionists as a second delaying tactic, aimed to examine Mr White's proposals in some detail. It fell at the end of the parliamentary session but was reappointed following a debate in the House on 9 February 1976. The Committee was viewed by pro-choice groups as simply a device for forcing restrictions. They believed that the talk of abuses of the Act was just a tactical ploy in order to cut back services, and there is no doubt that in this they were at least partially correct. The Lane Committee had already sifted the evidence, so at best the Select Committee could only repeat the analysis of the same material. Faced with sitting through what they felt to be a charade, the six pro-choice members on the Select Committee resigned

(19 March 1976) and ALRA and NAC refused to give evidence.

Partially as a result of this, when the Select Committee produced its 'Minutes of Evidence' in 1976 it concentrated almost exclusively on information from the anti-abortionists. Pride of place was given to the evidence of SPUC and LIFE, while that of the major medical bodies was excluded. In some respects the emphasis of the report resembles the anti-abortion books used by the campaigners, so ALRA produced a pamphlet pointing out some of the shortcomings (Francome, 1977a). Amongst the points made were:

1 The Committee only published the result of one opinion poll, whereas the results from four major organisations were available.
2 It spoke of the only doctors' poll discussed as 'a completely false poll', whereas there had been seven polls of doctors' opinion by recognised bodies and all of these pointed in the same direction – that doctors supported the provisions of the Act.
3 The Committee consistently argued that illegal abortions had not fallen and might have increased. In support it printed a discredited article from the *British Journal of Criminology* (discussed more fully on pp. 173–4).

The level of debate in the Committee also left something to be desired, for in the published evidence virtually all the old arguments against contraception were revised and used against abortion. Professor Scarisbrick of LIFE talked of abortion as 'national suicide', the Rev. John Stevenson of the Church of Scotland said abortion undermined the family unit (Select Committee, 1976, p. 160), Margaret White of SPUC said it increased mental disturbance, and LIFE quoted the suggestion of the Wynns (1973) that abortion in a high percentage of cases led to sterility (Select Committee, 1976b, p. 22). However, the most bizarre point came when Leo Abse used the argument that 'great men would not be born' against the Methodists, who were the most liberal of the religious groups giving evidence. As this was one of the favourite arguments against contraception early this century, it was strange that a champion of birth control should use it now (Select Committee, 1976b, p. 176). If it is a reason for not supporting abortion, it must also be an argument for not supporting contraception.

An uninitiated observer reading the evidence would have believed that the Abortion Act had been an unmitigated disaster. However, the recommendations coming from the Committee were relatively mild. It proposed that there should be a reduction in the time limit to twenty weeks with certain exceptions for foetal or maternal health; that in private practice there should be restrictions on the signing of the forms between partners; that the police should have access to certain records when investigating offences; and that all referral agencies which charge fees should be licensed. There was, however, no advocacy of a change of grounds. On this issue the report stated: 'Your committee ... make no recommendation: a decision must be left to the individual consciences of Members' (Select Committee, 1976a, p. 5). These proposals were so mild that one of the pro-choice campaigners toyed with welcoming the report as a justification that the Act was working well. However, others suspected that the proposals were designed to obtain a large majority on a mild Bill which could then be stiffened at the committee stage. And indeed the proponents of later restrictive Bills said they were following the recommendations of the Select Committee.

Illegal Abortions

In Chapter 4 it was shown that the anti-abortionists argued that with legalisation the number of illegal abortions would not decrease but would in fact increase. Their belief that this was a good tactic was confirmed in 1967 when Gallup found that if liberalisation led to an increase in illegal abortion most people would oppose it. The question and the result are shown in Table 7.1

Table 7.1 *Would You Approve or Disapprove of Increasing the Number of Illegal Abortions by Passing the Abortion Bill If It Were Shown That:*

	Approve (per cent)	Disapprove (per cent)	Don't know (per cent)
a) it leads to a decrease in back-street abortions	62	9	28
b) it leads to an increase in back-street abortions	8	54	38

This result was republished in the minutes of the Annual General Meeting of the Society for the Protection of Unborn Children on 13 March 1976 and it shows clearly that public support for legal abortion would be very much lower if it led to an increase in back-street operations.

The anti-abortionists were therefore pleased when an article appeared in the *British Journal of Criminology* in January 1976 written by Paul Cavadino, one of the members of the SPUC executive. This drew attention to the fact that David Steel had said that his Act would 'stamp out the backstreet abortions' and considered various possible indexes. The article criticised the use of the decline in material deaths, the decline in the number of women admitted with incomplete abortions through the 'emergency bed service', and the decline in prosecutions. It asserted that 'The only index of illegal abortion which is even remotely reliable is the number of hospital discharges after treatment for incomplete abortions, and even the interpretation of these figures is fraught with difficulties' (Cavadino, 1976, p. 63). Cavadino gave figures from the Hospital In-Patient Enquiry (HIPE) that the number of women discharged from hospitals in England and Wales after incomplete 'illegal abortions' rose from 220 in 1966 and 360 in 1967 to 1,110 in 1972 and 670 in 1973, and concluded that there had been no significant reduction in illegal abortions and that there might even have been an increase (Cavadino, 1976, p. 67).

My interpretation of his article was that he had tried to discredit all the possible indices except the one that served to support his case. The series of figures do not in any way ring true as they have such great fluctuations, and in October 1976 I published my reply in the same journal. I pointed out that Cavadino had made a mistake in double counting some of the figures, that HIPE was based on a 10 per cent sample and so the number of cases was small and, most important, that there must have been an error in the government figures. 'There are sixteen different regions plus Greater London from which information is gathered, yet in 1972 70% of the illegal abortion cases came from two of these areas neither of them London. It is impossible that illegal abortions could be so distributed. The series of figures which Cavadino suggested are the nearest to a "reliable index" are shown to be the most unreliable.' I also reported figures for Romania where the making of abortion illegal had led to an increase in maternal deaths, suggesting a rise in illegal operations. I concluded that there had been a significant fall in the number of illegal abortions (Francome, 1976b).

At the request of Cavadino, Mr Biggs Davison asked questions in the House of Commons on two occasions to discover if my analysis was correct, and in both cases the minister confirmed the findings (*Hansard*, 16 February and 28 March 1977). In fact the British Government then produced new lower figures for the number of discharges, although even these showed such wide variations that they were of no use as an index (Francome, 1977b). While working on a reply to Cavadino I noted that the main problem was with the 'dark number', the amount of secret abortions, and that once legalisation has occurred it is possible to make a good estimate of the number of operations if you know the number of legal abortions occurring after the Act, the increase in abortions due to the Act and the proportionate change in illegal operations. I therefore set out to calculate these and suggested that the estimates of 100,000 abortions a year (80,000 illegal and 20,000 quasi-legal) before the Act were largely correct and that by 1973 the number of illegal abortions was down to about 8,000 a year (Francome, 1977c).

However, despite the fact that use of the Hospital In-Patient figures has been discredited, the anti-abortionists have continued to use them. The Conservative anti-abortionist William Benyon, MP, used Cavadino's figures in support of his anti-abortion Bill in April 1977 in a letter to a Birmingham doctor. This was well over a year after they had been refuted. Diane Munday wrote to him and set out his error (26 April 1977):

> These figures were quoted extensively by SPUC and in letters from you prior to the Second Reading of your Abortion (Amendment) Bill. At the time it may have been reasonable for you to accept them as accurate, as you may not have seen the Francome paper 'How Many Illegal Abortions' in the British Journal of Criminology which detailed the false interpretations and basis of these statistics. However, on 16th February in a written answer replying to a Parliamentary question by your anti abortion colleague, Mr. Biggs Davison, the minister of State at the DHSS made it quite clear that these figures are in error as they include the number of 'septic and illegal' abortions twice. After seeing that answer I hoped you would no longer quote false figures. Will you give an undertaking not to use them again?

Benyon did not reply, and the anti-abortionists have continued to use the false data. As late as September 1979 Bowles and Bell quoted the Cavadino article in the *New Law Journal* with no discussion of the criticisms. There is thus reason to expect that some anti-abortionists will continue to argue that illegal abortion has increased despite the fact that the usual indicators all show that this is not the case.

Bills After the Select Committee

Since the Select Committee reported in July 1976 there have been several Bills which have attempted to legislate its recommendations or some variant of them. The first two introduced by William Benyon, Conservative MP for Buckingham in 1977, and Sir Bernard Braine (Conservative MP for Essex South East) in 1978, both had little chance of success. One of the crucial arguments was that the time limit for abortion should be reduced from twenty-eight weeks to at least twenty-four weeks as recommended by the Lane Committee, or twenty weeks as suggested by the Select Committee. In arguing for a reduction there was support in Parliament and the general public. However, the anti-abortionists did not just want this change. Their aim was to gain as many restrictions as possible. One of the divisions was over whether to accept a mild change which could then prevent others at a later date.

The issue of compromise was also one for the pro-choice groups. For example, at the time of the Benyon Bill in 1977 secret approaches were made to those on the Parliamentary Committee for a very mildly restrictive Bill. There was support for this amongst some pressure group operators because they saw it as a way of getting the abortion issue out of the way without having any real affect on availability. However Jo Richardson, MP, told me that she and the other women on the Committee believed in fighting all along the line. The Benyon Bill therefore fell when it ran out of time at the end of the parliamentary session. Braine's Bill was a ten-minute rule Bill – a device for raising issues – so it did not progress.

John Corrie Bill

Once the Conservatives had won the election by a substantial majority in 1979 it became clear that an anti-abortion Bill was a distinct possibility and that it would have a good chance of becoming law. The Scottish Conservative MP John Corrie, Member for Bute and North Ayrshire, drew number one in the ballot and announced his intention to introduce a Bill which would among other things reduce the time limit of abortion to sixteen weeks.

Strangely, the parliamentary conditions mirrored many of those present at the time of the passage of the original Act in 1967. First of all there was a government with a substantial majority, secondly the timing of the election meant that there would be a long parliamentary session and thirdly there were people in positions of power who would favour the Bill. Norman St John Stevas, for example, was leader of the House and in charge of the parliamentary timetable. Furthermore, the Prime Minister was known to be in favour of some change. The Bill was also aided by a well orchestrated publicity campaign. In the run up to the General Election there were three stories of abortions resulting in live births. Two of these were known earlier but released at the time of maximum impact. The anti-abortionists were clearly attempting to strike at the most sensitive area of legal abortion just as in the past advocates of legalisation had concentrated on cases of rape. The tactics worked in that a great many Members of Parliament felt that they should back Corrie's Bill to reduce the time limit. They contributed to the high support at the Second Reading on 13 June 1979 (Marsh and Chambers, 1981, p. 105). There was a great deal of confusion, but the official voting breakdown is shown in Table 7.2.

Table 7.2   *Vote on the Second Reading of the Corrie Bill*

	For	Against	Total
Conservatives	176	14	190
Labour	54	82	136
Liberals	4	1	5
SNP	2	0	2
Plaid Cymru	1	1	2
Irish MPs	5	0	5
Total	242	98	340

Source: Hansard, 13 June 1979.

The results show that the Labour Party was the only one which did not have a majority in support of the Bill. The Conservative support was overwhelming and more than 9 out of 10 voted for it. This wide difference between Labour and Conservative members in voting patterns is a continuation of the situation since the 1960s, and also compares with the experience in the United States. The voting patterns in 1979 also confirm my earlier finding (Francome, 1978b) that Members who supported abortion rights were opposed to capital punishment. So 101 out of the 102 Members who voted, or intended to vote, against Corrie also opposed the death penalty. Supporters of Corrie voted for capital punishment by a majority of 128 to 97.

At the Second Reading the Bill tried to bring changes in three main areas:

1   A reduction in the time limit for an abortion from twenty-eight to twenty weeks, with an exception if there were a high possibility that the resulting child would be severely handicapped.
2   A restriction of the ground for abortion. The statistical argument was to be removed and abortion allowed only 'where there was substantial risk of serious injury to the physical or mental health of the pregnant woman'.
3   The referring part of the work of the charities would be hived off from the facility which carried out the abortions.

The likely effect of these changes was open to debate. Although Professor Scarisbrick had said that the number of abortions would be reduced by about two-thirds. Corrie denied this and at a later date said he wanted to reduce the number of abortions by 20 per cent (*Guardian*, 13 July 1979; BPAS Newsletter, December 1979).

Committee Stage   The role of the Parliamentary Committee is to consider the Bill in some detail and to report back to the House of Commons for a Third Reading. As the composition of the Committee represented the vote at the Second Reading Corrie and his supporters had almost total control of what changes were to be introduced. However, supporters of the Bill were divided. The two representatives of the government took one view. A group containing Michael Ancram, Conservative MP for Edinburgh South, wanted the Bill to remain very restrictive while Benyon and Corrie were more willing to make concessions.

The tactics of the opposition were clear. There was no opportunity to filibuster the Bill, for Corrie would just pass a sittings motion as had been done at the time of the Benyon Bill. Nor could they expect to get any changes at this stage. They had therefore to wait to introduce any substantial amendments on the floor of the House of Commons where they felt that the Bill could be watered down. Parliament's procedure is that the Committee discusses the Bill and that at Report Stage the whole House can consider anything the Committee has missed. If any amendment has been called in Committee it cannot be discussed again at Report. So the tactics of the opponents of restriction were, therefore, to change the Bill as far as possible by force of logic but not to introduce any amendment they felt could pass at Third Reading.

Report Stage   In the weeks leading to the Report Stage of the Bill, which was due to start on 8 February 1980, it was clear that both sides would aim to organise as many events as possible to influence parliamentary opinion. The anti-abortionists arranged their Mass Lobby of the House of Commons on 30 January 1980 and the pro-choice groups organised theirs for the following Tuesday (5 February). Estimates suggested at least 10,000 were present on each occasion, and the opponents of the Bill were pleased that they were able to match the anti-abortionists in organising this kind of event.

Table 7.3   *Public Opinion on Abortion in Britain, November 1979*

	Men *(per cent)*	Women *(per cent)*	All *(per cent)*	
Should	71	81	76	
Should not	18	11	14	
Don't know	11	8	10	(sample 1,004)

Source: Francome, 1980b.

It was also necessary to monitor public opinion, and three polls were published between 1 February and 6 February 1980. Having made some preliminary investigations with Gallup I contacted *Woman's Own*, and the magazine agreed to pay for a survey that would contain more questions than any previous poll. Gill Cox, the *Woman's Own* researcher, agreed the final wording of the questions with Gallup. We were anxious that the questions should reflect the abortion decision as closely as it could be arranged. The final wording of the crucial question on the right to choose was therefore: 'Do you think that the choice as to whether or not to continue a pregnancy should or should not be left to the woman in consultation with her doctor?'

The result (Table 7.3) shows that more than four out of five women and seven out of ten men agreed with the right to choose when the question was asked in this way. This result gained wide publicity and was carried in all the national newspapers. The opinion of the women in the survey was considered particularly important. The *Observer* editorial read, for example:

MR. CORRIE'S BAD BILL

Mr. John Corrie's Abortion (Amendment) Bill, which goes back to the floor of the House of Commons this week, is a partisan measure. Its supporters are many and various, but the backbone of the 'restrictive' movement is Roman Catholic. The Church abhors the destruction of the foetus as a 'crime' against a 'person'; it is a matter of conscience. The Corrie Bill floats on a powerful tide.

Fortunately, it is not too late for Parliament to recognise that the right to exercise one's own conscience is not the same as to ram that conscience down the throats of others. The right of a woman to take responsibility for what happens to her own body is also a crucial part of the debate.

Four out of five women, according to a survey conducted last week for 'Woman's Own', think the choice should be left to the woman concerned in consultation with her family doctor. A majority of all adults believe the law should be left as it is or made more liberal. Members of Parliament, who are predominantly male and in that sense unrepresentative in an issue of this kind, should take serious note of the fact that this proposed reform is not wanted by the public at large, and most definitely not wanted by women. (*Observer*, 3 February 1980)

These results were broadly confirmed by a survey in the *Sunday Times* (3 February 1980) which also showed that most people were in favour of a reduction in the time limit. However, another poll from Gallup published on 6 February 1980 asked people whether they agreed with 'Abortion on Demand', and the results seemed to show that most people were in favour of restrictions. The *Daily Mail* carried the following report:

Make Abortion Rules Tougher

Most people believe there should be tighter controls on abortion, according to a Gallup Poll out yesterday. When questions were asked on various issues raised in the Corrie Bill to amend the law on abortion, a substantial majority supported each measure.

The fact that within six days Gallup had published polls with contradictory findings raised questions on the problem of wording. And since Members of Parliament were obviously confused, ALRA produced a background paper analysing the major findings and explaining the apparent contradictions (Francome, 1980b).

Apart from polls and lobbying, both sides used other techniques to show support. On 25 January Willie Hamilton, MP for Fife Central, put down an 'early day motion' pointing out that the Bill intended to change the criteria for abortion (*Times*, 29 January 1980). The opposition put down an alternative motion showing support. The medical profession continued its opposition to the Bill, and Doctors for a Woman's Choice on Abortion organised their own lobby at the House.

These ways of influencing the climate of opinion were obviously important, but it was clear that time was going to be a crucial factor. The future for the Bill looked very uncertain when the Speaker selected twenty-eight groups of amendments for debate (Ferriman, 1980). Jo Richardson, Labour MP for Barking, told a group of women gathered to protest at the Bill that with that number of amendments,'I could keep going every Friday until July' (8 February 1980). On 8 February only two groups of amendments were debated, and it was clear that clauses needed to be dropped. However Corrie was reluctant to do this, and he decided to carry on. The Members voted for a number of changes. They raised the time limit from twenty to twenty-four weeks, liberalised the grounds to a degree, and removed the proviso that would have made it easy to reduce the time limit further at a later date. There was also evidence that Members of the House were moving against support of the Bill. On 14 March 1980 Corrie was given an extra day, but when a vote was taken to close the debate it was lost by seven votes. At this point it was clear that the Bill was dead, and the following week Corrie announced he was going to withdraw it. The opponents of the Bill were surprised that they had succeeded in stopping it. The supporters were shocked at their failure, especially on the vote for the closure.

Almost immediately following the failure of Corrie, David Alton, a Liberal Catholic MP from Liverpool, attempted to introduce a ten-minute rule Bill to reduce the time limit to twenty-four weeks. This failed (22 April 1980) and many within the pro-choice groups felt they had blunted the opposition's attack. The *Breaking Chains* editorial (April 1980) read:

> After many months of hard fighting against the Corrie Abortion (Amendment) Bill, one can now feel for once that we have really defeated the anti abortion lobby. The extent of opposition to this attack on the 1967 Act has been so great that in the end the Bill did not run out of time in Parliament, it also clearly lacked the political and public will for it to succeed . . . Of course we are not so naive as to believe that this will be the last we'll hear of the anti abortionists. But their two serious failures will inevitably hinder any future plans they may have.

The confidence amongst pro-choice groups that they had temporarily defeated the anti-abortion lobby was strengthened when Timothy Sainsbury dropped the idea of introducing an anti-abortion Bill in 1981. It seems that he was advised not to stir up the issue again, and for the first time in a number of years pro-choice groups felt that they were winning the long-term battle.

Two events in 1982 seemed to confirm this fact. The first was the failure of the Pope's visit to galvanise the anti-abortion movement. Many within the pro-choice camp were concerned that the Pope's popularity would stimulate anti-abortion feeling. The day before he arrived, however, a poll was published which showed that the British support for the right to choose an abortion was at an all-time high of 80 per cent (Francome, 1982). It also showed that Catholics in Britain did not agree with official Church doctrine, and the *Daily Mail* (27 May 1982) reported that 'The survey contains some bad news for the Pope who arrives in Britain tomorrow. Seven out of ten Roman Catholics support the woman's right to choose, in opposition to the official teachings of the Church.' With this kind of evidence receiving wide publicity, the Pope's statements on the abortion issue could be seen in a wider context. SPUC attacked the poll in its newspaper (*Human Concern*, Summer 1982) and Phyllis Bowman was quoted as saying: 'The pro abortion Gallup poll was published in the week prior to the visit of John Paul II to Britain and was obviously intended to undermine anything which the Pope said on ethical issues'. The report continued by attacking Gallup, a little unfairly in my opinion, as the major questions had all been asked before, and the date of publication was my decision and not Gallup's.

In 1982 MPs at the top of the Ballot (including Corrie) refused to introduce an abortion Bill. However, on 6 December 1982 a restrictive Bill was introduced into the House of Lords by Lord Robertson, an Independent hereditary peer, and received its Second Reading. For the anti-abortionists it was their major opportunity to prepare the ground for another move into the House of Commons. The Bill sought to introduce two words into the statistical grounds for abortion and make abortion legal when two medical practitioners were of the opinion 'that the continuance of the pregnancy would involve *serious* risk to the life of the pregnant woman, or of injury to the physical or mental health of the pregnant woman or any existing children of her family, *substantially* greater than if the pregnancy were terminated'.

Table 7.4   *Vote on Abortion Restrictions*

	For restrictions	Against restrictions
Labour	3	30
Liberal	2	4
Conservative	19	5
Independent	12	5
Social Democrat	0	11
Communist	0	1
Bishop	5	1
Ex Law Lord (Lord Denning)	1	0
Total	42	57

Source: Abortion Review, no. 6, December 1982.

The opposition was led by Lord Houghton, whose wife Vera had been a prime mover of the 1967 Act. He drew attention to the Labour Party's support of a liberal law and the opposition of the medical profession to any change. Numerous speakers drew attention to the public opinion on abortion, and the Bill was defeated by 57 votes to 42. The breakdown according to party is shown in Table 7.4. The earlier differences according to party were confirmed by the vote. Labour supporters were opposed to restriction by a majority of ten to one, while Conservatives were in favour by a ratio of four to one. However, a higher proportion of Conservative peers abstained. A headline in *Doctor* (16 December 1982) read 'Profession blamed for the failure of abortion Bill' and continued by quoting Lord Robertson to this effect. However, the debate mirrored the first vote on the Steel Bill, in that many Catholics were missing. Phyllis Bowman pointed out that seventy Catholic peers had been written to five times, but only fifteen voted, and one opposed the Bill (*Universe*, 17 December 1982). The anti-abortionists do have plans for more campaigns, even after such reversals.

8
The United States After the Supreme Court Decision

There are a number of reasons for the strength of the opposition to abortion in the United States. After the 1973 Supreme Court decision even states most opposed to liberal laws were prevented from keeping such legislation. Further, much of the general population is very conservative. The strength of the feeling in one area can be gauged from the fact that in the legislature of the Mormon stronghold of Utah, the Supreme Court's decision was condemned by 66 votes to 1. Opinion poll results show that about one person in five agrees with the abolition of legal abortion (*New York Times*, 22 January 1982) indicating a sizeable minority totally opposed to the activities of the abortion clinics.

Furthermore, the right-wing pressure groups have had increasing success. Three issues – capital punishment, homosexuality and women's rights – show this clearly. It seemed in the early 1970s that there were going to be liberal laws in all these areas. The Supreme Court struck down all the death penalty laws in 1972 and some thought that that would be the end of capital punishment. However, in 1976 it ruled that the death sentence could be constitutional if the law concerned gave the jury or judge discretion in imposing the penalty. In the period 1972–6, thirty-five states enacted new laws on capital punishment, although they were unconstitutional and could not be enforced. On the matter of homosexual rights there has also been a great deal of controversy. Logically, the right of privacy established during the birth control cases should make laws against sodomy unconstitutional (Barnett, 1973). However, in May 1978 the Supreme Court allowed the North Carolina law to stand and so retreated from the logic of its earlier rulings. A third area where the right wing has been effective is in its opposition to the Equal Rights Amendment (ERA). In order for ratification to occur, thirty-eight states needed to support it, and by January 1977 thirty-five had done so. However, in the next eighteen months, in the face of skilfully organised opposition, no further states gave their assent and furthermore four states voted to rescind their earlier approval.

Although these issues show a movement towards the right in political terms, the question arises as to how far this is due to public opinion and how far to better organisation by right-wing groups. While the evidence is fragmentary, it does appear that the general population has not become more conservative. Polls on issues such as the ERA and abortion have shown, in fact, a movement towards liberalisation. In July 1978, at a time when the ERA was stalled, Harris poll reported that it had increased support in the population, which was 55 to 38 in favour of the amendment (*Newsday*, 17 July 1978). Various polls on abortion have also shown a steady movement towards a more liberal position (NARAL, 1978). There is even evidence of a decline in the support of some of the conservative forces in US society. For instance, Fr Andrew Greeley reported that in 1963 73 per cent of Catholics went to mass every week; by 1974 the percentage had declined to 50 and by 1978 to 42 (*Long Island Catholic*, 20 April 1978). Although this trend seems to be levelling out somewhat, there is clear evidence that American Catholics do not accept the Church's teaching on fertility control. By 1975 94 per cent of Catholics using contraceptive methods were using those forbidden by the Church, and it was not just the irregular Church attenders who were not following the teaching (Westoff and Jones, 1977). Furthermore even the Church hierarchy seems to be taking a more liberal line on sexuality since the events in the 1960s, with the *Long Island Catholic* (20 April 1978) noting a change as follows: 'Unlike pre-Vatican days when the bishops automatically condemned a film if there was any nudity in it, official Catholic policy today allows nudity when artistically merited and when not used gratuitously or sensationally'. Such clearly-stated movement within the largest conservative force, whilst it is by no means conclusive, does suggest that the victories against liberal measures are due mainly to improved organisation amongst the right-wing forces. Paul A. Brown, of the Life Political Action Committee, was quoted as saying in the *New York Times* (22 September 1981): 'It really doesn't matter what the polls says. Whoever can deliver politically is the group that's going to get its way.'

Social Composition of Opposition to Abortion

The Church

Despite the support of right-wing groups, the Mormons and some other religious groups, there is no doubt that it is the Catholic Church which has been the major driving force of the anti-abortion campaign. A study of National Right to Life campaign members found that 70 per cent were Catholic (Granberg, 1981). One possible point of conflict is that Church members do not share the official Church view on the subject. Various polls have shown a wide disparity between official doctrine and the beliefs of the laity. For example, Fr Andrew Greeley reported in the *Long Island Catholic* (26 January 1978) that 66 per cent of Catholics said they would have an abortion or encourage their wife to have one if there was a chance of a defective child, and 76 per cent said they would favour one if there were a serious threat to the mother's health. Similarly, Gallup found in 1977 that only 23 per cent of Catholics felt that abortion should be 'illegal in all circumstances', compared to 32 per cent in 1975 (*New York Evening News*, 4 March 1978).

A study I carried out amongst students on Long Island suggests reasons why the Church pressure can succeed. Only a quarter of my sample of nearly 600 Catholic students were opposed to abortion on request in the early months of pregnancy (Francome, 1978c). However, those who were regular Church attenders were much more likely to support the official teaching. Amongst those who had been in Church in the previous week, 41 per cent disagreed with the right to legal abortion in the early months of pregnancy compared to 17 per cent of those who had been to church in the previous month, and 16 per cent of those who had not been to church in the previous month, showing wide differences between the regular attenders and the rest. Regular churchgoing, then, is one factor which allows the Catholic Church to keep up its pressure. A second is its hierarchical structure. The power to make decisions is concentrated in the higher levels of the bureaucracy, and the lay members are expected to follow. Furthermore, the support of the Church's position is a question of numbers. Only 20 per cent of Catholics may believe fully in its position, but with 50 million Catholics this amounts to around 10 million. Once a proportion of these have become organised, they are bound to make an impact.

The bishops have been very involved in the politics of abortion, and have upheld a very restrictive point of view. A key development was in November 1975 when the Conference of Catholic Bishops pledged to help organise a campaign for a constitutional amendment that would proscribe abortion. The *Minneapolis Star* (22 November 1975) reported:

> A budget of $3.9 million, estimated to include $400,000 for anti abortion activities, was adopted by the Bishops for their national organisation . . . The Anti abortion campaign to be mounted by the Bishops includes establishing specific anti abortion agencies within every state Catholic conference, every Catholic diocese and every Catholic parish. Most of the Bishops' debate, however, focused on the proposal to stimulate formation of nonsectarian anti abortion lobbies in every congressional district. The plan asserts such a lobby is not to be an agency of the church nor is it to be operated, controlled or financed by the Church.

It then provided a detailed, twelve-point description of how such an organisation was to operate, stating amongst other things that it was to persuade all residents in the congressional district that permissive abortion was harmful to society, that some restriction was necessary, and that it was 'to maintain an informational file of the pro life position of every elected official and potential candidate'. This direct involvement of the bishops was a very important factor in organising the political power of the Church behind the anti-abortion movement.

The Moral Majority and the New Right

The Moral Majority was formed by Jerry Falwell in 1979. It was against 'sin', abortion and communism and for Reagan and South Africa. 'We are fighting a holy war,' said Falwell, 'and this time we are going to win' (Goreau, 1981). One of the most prominent political supporters, Senator Jesse Helms, wrote in a fund-raising letter: 'Right now your tax dollars are being used to pay for grade school courses that teach our children that cannibalism, wife swapping and murder of infants and the elderly are acceptable behavior'.

The fact that this kind of rhetoric can find favour shows the appeal of the simple solution to parts of the United States society. Hunter (1981) notes that both Wallace and Nixon put forward the idea that the vast majority of people were 'hard-working, sober, tradition-minded patriots fed up with welfare handouts, "peace-creeps", hippies, black militants and street violence'. They also stressed law and order and posed the image of an eastern establishment out of touch with the people. It was this feeling that the new right aimed to galvanise, and single-issue topics such as abortion were useful to add dynamism to the movement. 'Our success is built on four elements – single issue groups, multi issue conservative groups, coalition politics and direct mail,' wrote Richard Viguerie in *The New Right* (1981). 'There are an estimated 85 million Americans; 50 million born again Protestants, 30 million morally conservative Catholics, 3 million Mormons and 2 million Orthodox and Conservative Jews; with whom to build a pro family, bible believing coalition.' One of the weaknesses of this assessment, of course, is that at this number it is still a minority of the population in the United States. However, on some issues the new right does have public support. For example, an opinion poll conducted for *Time* magazine (May 1981) found that 71 per cent agreed that 'The Supreme Court and Congress had gone too far in keeping religious morals and values like prayer out of our laws, our schools and our lives'.

The National Conservative Political Action Committee (NCPAC – pronounced Nik Pak) founded in 1975 is the largest of the new right PACs and it funnels money to conservative candidates and targets liberals for defeat. Its programme, apart from the abolition of abortion, calls for support for prayer in state schools and other 'pro family' issues. It is controversial even amongst the right because it claims to be an 'independent' political organisation and is able to finance campaigns without breaking election laws limiting contributions – it says it does not support candidates but opposes them. Interestingly, there is opposition to the religious right from traditional conservatives, the most prominent being former Presidential candidate Barry Goldwater who feared that the moral majority and allied groups could succeed in dividing the country: 'I will fight them every step of the way if they try to dictate their moral convictions to all Americans in the name of conservatism' (Goreau, 1981). As we might expect from our knowledge of the difference in perspective of anti-abortion Catholics and the right (pp. 9–14), liberal Catholics have doubts about the developments in the new right. The fact that NCPAC targeted Edward Kennedy for defeat in 1982 has obviously not endeared them to some. Another liberal Catholic, Senator Leahy of Vermont, has expressed concern that 'The Church we love is being used in a dangerous way. It has allied itself with those who would turn aside nearly all that the Catholic leadership and laity have stood for in this century.' He continued by outlining the traditional opposition of Catholics to capital punishment and their concern with social justice, views not shared by the new right (Isaacson, 1981).

Other Right-Wing Support

There are differences in political perspective at all levels of the government, with the republicans naturally more inclined to support restrictions. The divide between left and right on particular issues can be shown by an analysis of voting patterns. On 28 April 1976 the Senate voted by 47 votes to 40 to table and so kill the Helms motion to amend the Constitution to outlaw abortion under any circumstances. The vote according to party is shown in Table 8.1. This vote shows that a majority of the Republicans were for a total ban on abortions whereas a majority of the Democrats were opposed to it. It also shows a clear divide between the Northern and Southern Democrats. Those from the North were in favour of abortion rights by a ratio of three to one whereas those from the South were opposed to them by a ratio of two to one.

Table 8.1 *Vote to Ban Abortions by Party*

	Against a ban	For a ban
Republicans	15	20
Northern Democrats	27	9
Southern Democrats	5	11
Total	47	40

Source: New York Times, 2 May 1976.

A number of other more detailed studies of members' voting patterns have been made. One in 1977 analysed the position on the

Hyde amendment to restrict government help for poor women to have abortions. It noted that many of those opposed to finance declared their willingness to provide pregnancy support and other family-related needs. However,

> An examination of House members' support for typical welfare policies, like food stamps, child nutrition, and legal services for the poor, raises doubts about this claim. Of those firmly opposed to Hyde on abortion, a clear majority, 114 out of 209, consistently voted for cutbacks in welfare programmes. Meanwhile 112 of the 163 members seeking a lenient abortion policy took a liberal line on welfare matters too. (Eccles, 1978)

The report continued by saying that of fifty-seven liberals joining Hyde, forty-five were Catholics, a finding very much in line with my research on British politicians. This showed that there was more opposition to abortion than to homosexuality and the abolition of the death penalty because, in addition to right-wing opposition, there was also that of the liberal Catholics (Francome, 1978b).

Politics of the Right to Life Movement

The modern anti-abortion movement seems to have begun in 1970, and its origin was closely linked to the Catholic Church in New York State. In a candid description Arlene Doyle has explained its beginnings: 'For publicity purposes, the Catholic Church in New York State had put together the names of some people and placed them on a New York State Right to Life letterhead. In fact, however, the people involved never held a meeting and most of them never even met each other' (Doyle, 1977).

The anti-abortion movement grew strongest in opposition to the New York law. However, the National Right to Life Committee (NRLC) did not evolve in its present form until after the Supreme Court decision. Six months later in Detroit it finalised a completely restructured organisation. Each state named its own member to the Board of Directors which in turn elected a nine-member executive committee. *Right to Life News* (vol. 1, no. 1, 1973) reported the change as follows: 'The National Right to Life Committee, which had operated for several years as a loosely knit information clearing house for state and local groups, working in cooperation with the Family Life Division of the United States Catholic Conference, became a completely independent, democratically structured and incorporated organisation'. An estimate in 1981 was that NRLC had 13 million members (Isaacson, 1981). A separate organisation, March for Life, was set up to arrange among other events a regular demonstration in Washington each year on 22 January, the anniversary of the Court's decision. The major work in Congress was carried out by the Life Amendment Political Action Committee.

Although the sources of strength of the anti-abortion movement are clear, there is a question of tactics. The major aim is a constitutional amendement. However, there are several kinds that can be chosen, and various methods of trying to get one accepted. The amendment could, for example, be relatively moderate. One suggestion put forward by Coffey (1976) in a journal orientated to Catholic doctors was for a restriction based on the length of gestation: 'Perhaps in the United States today the best pro lifers can realistically expect is the establishment of an amendment giving the unborn protection against unjust homicides from the end of the first trimester onwards'. However, calls for moderate change did not carry much sway in the anti-abortion movement, for the membership wanted a very tough law.

The two organisations, March for Life and Right to Life, seem to outsiders to take a very similar position, but Nellie Gray, the President of March for Life, told me that her organisation took a firmer line than Right to Life. She wanted to stop all abortions and was unwilling to compromise (personal interview, 14 August 1978): 'Once you tolerate a little bit of abortion the abortionist steps in and walks right through the law'. Others supported this position. Michael Schwartz, a director of March for Life and Associate Executive Director of the Catholic League for Religious and Civil Rights, wrote a series of articles in the *National Catholic Register* in April and May 1978. He said: 'We know that a potential or even an actual threat to the life or health of a mother cannot justify killing her baby. We know that rape, incest or any other crime, personal or social, cannot justify the commission of another crime, particularly against an innocent victim.' He continued by arguing that the pro-life movement might only have one chance to change the law, and so it was better to aim for everything it wanted at this time rather than live in the vain hope that other changes would come at a later date. He criticised some of those within the movement for raising legal difficulties (16 April): 'The deep thinkers object if we simply leave the personhood of the child open ended and unqualified, our enemies will invent all sorts of legal complications. They might say that this means preborn babies will have to be counted in the census.' He commented that if those in favour of legal abortion produced these kinds of arguments they would become a laughing stock. 'Besides, what's wrong with counting babies in the census.'

In one of the articles Schwartz considered the problems raised by inter-uterine devices (IUDs) and took the view that they should be made illegal (30 April, 1978):

> The IUD produces abortions. Their number and specific cases cannot be accurately determined, and therefore cannot be prosecuted. But, if only in principle, we want those babies who are killed by IUD's to be protected by our basic law, our statement of rights, our constitution. The IUD is an invention perhaps unique in human history. Prostaglandins, rat poison, guns, even tactical nuclear weapons can all kill people, but all of them (with the possible exception of the neutron bomb) can be used for some other, less malign purposes. The IUD has no other conceivable purpose than to kill innocent, defenseless people. It cannot prevent conception or as we must put it, fertilisation. It cannot remedy any pathological condition. It can kill and only kill. Therefore, it would not be unreasonable to declare an absolute ban on the manufacture, sale, distribution or use of the IUD. There is no legitimate reason why any person should have such a device.

This position of Schwartz appears to be the dominant viewpoint within the March of Life Movement. The refusal to compromise seems to be against the usual rules of politics, and a disadvantage is that it is likely to reduce the basis of support. Furthermore, by going for total change they may not get lesser amendments that would be more easily available. However, there are advantages to a group in taking an extreme position. Schattschneider (1960) has pointed out that the success of pressure groups depends not merely on what their members want but also on their priorities. If the activists are willing to give a high priority to their issue, the work can be made much more effective.

A second question to be resolved by the movement was what attitude to take to contraception. When NRLC met in Detroit in June 1973 Senator Mark Hatfield, a sponsor of the Constitutional amendment to prohibit abortions, took the view that NRLC should support family planning clinics and 'do everything to insure that those who do not wish to bear life will have every protection against conception'. This statement did not appeal to the audience and *Triumph* magazine (July 1973) criticised the Senator for asking the NRLC to 'ignore their own moral convictions' by encouraging contraceptive usage. It would have been problematical for Right to Life to take such a position when so many of its activists had religious beliefs against it. Furthermore, it was also facing pressure from the other side. Father Paul Marx, the most outspoken priest within the Right to Life Movement, wanted the organisation to come out against contraception as well as abortion. However, he was opposed for political reasons, clearly set out by the writer of a letter to the *National Catholic Register* (27 August 1978): 'I don't think he [Marx] understands what would happen if Right to Life took an official position against birth control. As it is, the pro abortionists accuse Right to Life of being exclusively linked to the Catholic Church. If we come out against all forms of birth control this would only strengthen their accusations.' This kind of argument told against Fr Marx and contributed to his resignation from the Right to Life movement, although he had been one of its most active supporters.

Another question of some contention was whether the Right to Life movement should show its debt to the Catholic Church. Father Marx had argued that it should. As the *Wanderer*, a conservative Catholic newspaper, reported in 1978 (25 May): 'Catholics have wasted too much energy trying to hide their prominence in the pro life movement, says Fr. Paul Marx. The Benedictine priest and sociologist says that until recently Catholics have generally tried too hard to disguise the fact they are the backbone of the pro life movement, but that many now feel there is nothing to be gained by such a tactic.' This view seems to have gained ascendancy, for after two non-Catholic presidents NRLC appointed Dr Willke, best known for his *Handbook on Abortion* (Willke and Willke, 1975).

One of the problems for anti-abortion groups is that the refusal to compromise can easily lead to great splits in the organisation.

These are well documented by Arlene Doyle in her pamphlet 'Do You Need Permission to Save an Unborn Baby?' She argued that the movement had, in one period at least, spent 90 per cent of its time on bureaucratic matters. She documented the split between Long Island Right to Life and the rest of New York State and also a similar battle in the nationwide movement (Doyle, 1977, p. 13). 'I have checked the minutes of all of the 1973 National Right to Life meetings, including a number of conference phone calls by members of the executive committee. Less than 2% of the time was spent on productive efforts relating to a Human Life Amendment. 98% of the time was devoted either to bureaucratic concerns or to the internal power struggle going on within National Right to Life.' There has also been a great deal of tension between March for Life and Right to Life. March for Life members claim that they walked into a press conference when Right to Life was claiming that it had organised the march; that Mildred Jefferson, the then President of Right to Life, boycotted the march even when in Washington that Jack Willke had encouraged people to take National Right of Life banners on the march so that it would get the credit with television audiences (Doyle, 1977).

A further problem for the right to life groups is how far to join with others on related issues, for by helping right-wing movements they will be able to form alliances and so obtain reciprocal support. Their most active alliance so far has been with the anti-ERA movement. On 28 March 1978 March for Life called on its members to write to their senators and ask them to fight for a change in the law to allow states to rescind a prior ratification of the ERA and to oppose changes allowing for an extension of the time limit. Similarly Lawrence Lader noted that Phyllis Schlafly, the leading anti-ERA campaigner, had many conspicuous anti-abortion groups at her rally in Houston (*New York Times*, January 1978). At first sight there does not seem to be any particular logic behind this alliance. In fact, a document published in 1978 by a sub-committee of the National Conference of Catholic Bishops called for support of the ERA. However, when the full Conference met it refused to endorse this report after pressure had been applied by anti-abortion groups (*Newsday*, 9 May 1978), these taking the view that the Amendment would constitutionalise abortion.

There has also been a certain amount of collaboration with those who were opposing gay rights. In September 1978, Oneida

County Right to Life sponsored a congress at which anti-gay activist Anita Bryant was invited as the principal attraction. The speakers at the event included Nellie Gray and Paul Marx (*The Wanderer*, 7 September 1978). Also in 1978 there was a 'rosary campaign' in New York to oppose both the Homosexual Orientation Bill and the state funding of medicaid abortions. A letter in the *Long Island Catholic* (18 May) said: 'Commitment to the crusade means saying a special Rosary for the stipulated intentions every day without fail. Groups or families are urged to say the Rosary together whenever possible . . . Remember what the Rosary has done in history against all the odds and what Our Lady has promised.' This kind of alliance with those attacking gay rights has not occurred in Britain, but in the USA it has helped anti-abortion groups to muster extra support at key periods.

Sources of Support for Abortion Rights

After the 1973 Supreme Court decision, many of those who had been active for abortion rights moved off into other areas of political concern. There were a few who predicted a great deal of further opposition but these were a minority, and in a sense this is understandable. There are, for example, no organisations pressing for rights to other operations, and one can understand the logic of the comments of one activist: 'We do not fight for the right to have blood donations because the Jehovah's Witnesses are not trying to legislate their morality. If they did make this attempt organisations opposing them would be formed' (personal communication). On this line of reasoning it is to be expected that, while a liberal law is in operation, its supporters will only be successfully mobilised when that law is threatened. At such a time the general sources of support are likely still to be those who were involved in the debate for legalisation.

Women's Movement

As the Catholics have led the groups against abortion rights, so the women's groups have led the campaign in their favour. The major organisation in this respect is NARAL (now standing for the National Abortion Rights Action League) which has monitored legislation, helped co-ordinate the work of various organisations, and developed a system of contacts in each state. The survey of membership (Granberg, 1981) showed it to be 78 per cent women, compared to 67 per cent in Right to Life. It was 17 per cent Jewish and only 4 per cent Catholic, yet one in five went to church each week. NARAL is the major single issue group on the subject of abortion with a membership of 80,000 in 1980 and 125,000 in 1981, but it also draws a large measure of its support from the general women's movement. For example, the National Organisation for Women (NOW) has abortion rights as one of its prime targets. Planned Parenthood is also important and has been particularly impressive in highlighting the problems of teenage pregnancy.

Other Groups

Various religious groups also support the right of women to have abortions. The Unitarians have probably been the most outspoken in this direction, but their numbers have been relatively small. A number of groups have worked together under the Religious Coalition for Abortion Rights which has helped to organise their campaign against restrictions. Amongst the more prominent members are the American Baptist Church, the Disciples of Christ, the Lutheran Church of America, the Presbyterian Church, the United Church of Christ, Reform Judaism, Conservative Judaism, the Unitarian Universalist Association, the United Methodist Church, the United Presbyterian Church and the YMCA.

There are also two Catholic organisations in favour of abortion rights, which may in part explain the low percentage of Catholics in NARAL. The best known is Catholics for a Free Choice, a Washington-based group which includes amongst its membership Joseph O'Rourke, a former Jesuit priest. The second group is Catholic Alternatives based in New York, which calls itself a 'Catholic Lay organisation that supports Catholics in their use and choice of birth control methods and/or termination of pregnancy'. These two organisations not surprisingly cause problems for the Catholic membership and hierarchy as was shown by the following letter in the *Long Island Catholic* (9 March 1978)

Recently some NOW members and other women interviewed on a TV news program protested New Jersey's refusal to pay for elective abortions. A Catholic Priest, the Rev. Joseph O'Rourke, was also interviewed. In Roman collar and clerical garb, a big 'Catholics for a Free Choice' button on his lapel, this Priest said he favoured abortions, that many Catholics had abortions, that 88 % of Catholics favoured abortions . . . What a terrible scandal his statement caused . . . Why is such an abomination, a priest crusading for abortion allowed to continue in the priesthood?

A priest taking a radical line on abortion certainly divides the Catholic ranks, and the literature of these two organisations also draws out certain inconsistencies in the historical position of the Church, such as that it was not until 1869 that it totally opposed abortions.

These, then, are the major pressure groups involved in abortion rights and, as discussed, they get majority support from the liberal politicians and from those in the population who take a liberal point of view. When Harris in July 1977 asked a sample if they agreed with the ban on use of medicaid funds for abortion, only 36 per cent of liberals agreed compared to 53 per cent of conservatives (*Harris Survey*, 1977).

General Tactics of the Groups

In their book on politics in the United States, Hathorn, Penniman and Zink (1963) suggest that pressure groups can work at at least five different levels. They can use media communication, participate in campaigns, influence the content of the platforms of the political parties, write letters and telegrams to members of Congress, and can try and influence the administration of existing laws by challenging interpretation in the courts. In the American campaign there has been action at all of these levels, but this section considers the general tactics of each side and their attempts to influence public opinion through education and the media.

There have been two well publicised murder trials involving late abortion. The first of these was in February 1975 when a Boston doctor, Kenneth Edelin, was found guilty of murder after a hysterotomy at twenty-four weeks. This was, however, reversed on appeal, and the case is discussed in a book by an anti-abortionist (Nolen, 1978). The second concerned another doctor, William

Waddill, Jnr, who was charged with murdering a baby who survived a saline abortion at possibly twenty-nine weeks' gestation. He was tried twice and both times there was a hung jury. The trials, however, gave an opportunity for anti-abortionists to use the case to call for the abolition of all abortions. Joseph Breig commented in his syndicated column in the *Pittsburgh Catholic* (7 July 1978):

> Dr. Waddill's troubles stem from the fact that his saline injection did not kill Baby Girl Weaver in the womb ... it is legal today (not moral; legal) for a physician to slay a child in the womb at any time in the nine months of development. BUT to cause the death of a child even seconds after natural birth is murder. Such is the legal madhouse into which the Supreme Court plunged the American people. It is an insane situation which must be corrected no matter how long we must work for restoration of the right to life of every human being from the moment of conception to the time of the natural death.

This argument moved from attacking late abortions to attacking all abortions, and is a good illustration of the way that an extreme example can be used to support a wider case. On the other side, the pro-choice groups publicised the death of a woman in Mexico who had travelled with two others for a cheap illegal abortion in the absence of medicaid. A memorial service was held in Washington and a biography entitled 'Rosie' was written.

Anti-abortionists use blown-up pictures of late abortions in their publicity, while those who favour legal abortions have pictures of women who have been found dead after they have tried to operate on themselves. Both sides also attempt to use the arguments of the other side against each other. For example, the 1963 Planned Parenthood/World Population statement 'An abortion kills the life of a baby after it has begun' is used time after time in anti-abortion literature (Marx, 1971). Pro-choice groups use statements which show the link between the Church and the anti-abortion movement in order to attack on the grounds of separation of Church and state. They also like to expose financial arrangements between the Right to Life groups and the Catholic Church (*Village Voice*, 28 November 1977; NARAL, 1978). This is important, as it is illegal for tax-exempt organisations to participate in a political campaign on behalf of a candidate for public office. So there are various allegations and counter-allegations between the opposing groups.

Both sides use the usual methods of campaigning such as writing letters, lobbying and holding marches, but a marked feature of the Right to Life campaign is its increased militancy. One of the most important developments in this respect is the growth of abortion clinic 'sit-ins' largely organised by a group calling itself PEACE (People Expressing a Concern for Everyone). These grew in number in 1977 and especially at the beginning of 1978. They were aided by a ruling in Fairfax County when a judge decided that six persons were not trespassing in May 1977 when they blocked halls and doorways at a clinic to try and stop eighteen abortions taking place that day (*Washington Star*, 19 October 1977). He reasoned that they believed that they were acting to save lives, and his decision was based on common law principles of self defence and necessity. Other judges have refused to allow this argument, but if the invaders are found guilty it gives them an opportunity to go to prison for their cause. This action highlights the strength of feeling and its proponents' conviction that they are able to save lives.

Focus of Right to Life Action

The anti-abortion groups have tried to restrict abortion rights by acting at several levels. They have tried for changes in the Presidency, the Supreme Court, Congress and in the states.

The Presidency

At the 1976 election the Republican platform supported 'the efforts of those who seek enactment of a constitutional amendment to restore protection of the right of life for unborn children' (*New York Times*, 18 August). The Democratic platform opposed this. In 1980 Ronald Reagan was quoted as saying: 'I strongly believe that the rights of unborn children must be protected in a civilised and humane society. Therefore as President, I will ask Congress to pass a constitutional amendment to protect the rights of all innocent human life' (*Catholic Herald*, 14 November 1980). However, the anti-abortionists overlooked the fact that Reagan, as Governor of California, had approved a measure liberalising abortion, and he assured them he had changed his mind and now opposed it.

The morning after the election Terry Dolan of NCPAC appeared on Breakfast Television to remind the President of his responsibility to carry out the policies of the new right. Two days after he was inaugurated Reagan met with Dr Willke and other anti-abortionists in the Oval Office, and Willke commented that 'It was a signal because we were the first citizens group in the White House. The one historical parallel is when the civil rights leaders were brought into the White House under Kennedy' (Isaacson, 1981). However, the early euphoria seems to have passed away. When Reagan kept his promise to appoint a woman to the Supreme Court he chose Sandra Day O'Connor, a past supporter of abortion rights. Paul A. Brown described the anti-abortion forces as 'devastated', and she had to pass anti-abortion pickets to get to the Confirmation Hearings (*New York Times*, 10 September 1981). However, the Senate supported her appointment by a vote of 99 to 0. This action distanced Reagan from the Right to Life groups and many of the anti-abortion leaders were concerned that he was not proving a reliable ally. They were therefore extremely relieved when at last on 8 September 1982 the President strongly supported (though unsuccessfully) anti-abortion legislation.

The Supreme Court

Although the Court Decision of 1972 had legalised abortion under a wide variety of circumstances, it left a number of issues open for opponents of abortion to use to try to restrict rights. Some of the areas not ruled on in the decision were as follows:

1   What extent could the states regulate abortion in the second trimester?
2   What regulation could be forced upon abortion clinics?
3   What restrictions could be placed upon the distribution of information and advertisements?
4   How far could the woman be forced to find the consent of other parties such as her husband or parents?
5   Could the states prohibit abortions by non-physicians?
6   May public hospitals refuse to perform abortions?

7   Must medicaid payments be made to women who want abortions?
8   May the states require records to be kept?
9   Can the woman be forced to take note of certain information before she makes her decision?
10   Should a doctor try to save the life of a viable foetus?

With all these areas of doubt there was obviously wide scope for court cases, and the following were particularly important:

a)   On the consent of the husband the court rules in 1976 by 6 to 3 (Danforth v. Planned Parenthood) that since the government has no authority to veto an abortion, it cannot delegate such authority to the woman's husband. The decision stated: 'It is difficult to believe that the goal of fostering mutuality and trust in marriage . . . will be achieved by giving the husband a veto power exercisable for any reason whatsoever or for no reason at all' (*New York Times*, 2 July).

b)   The Supreme Court overthrew attempts to restrict rights of under 18s to an abortion in 1976 and 1979. However, it set out guidelines for a law controlling minors' rights and this was confirmed by 6 to 3 in 1981.

c)   In June 1978 the Court agreed to review the Pennsylvania law, struck down by a lower court, that required a physician to try to protect the life of a foetus in an abortion if they thought it could survive (*Twin Circle*, 25 June 1978). However, on 9 January 1979 the Court voided the law by a 6 to 3 margin.

d)   The decision which had the most important implications was that of 20 June 1977 when the Supreme Court by 6 votes to 3 held that the states were not required to pay for elective abortions, and effectively returned to Congress and the states the decision as to whether or not to pay for abortions. In 1980 by a 5 to 4 vote the Court ruled that the federal government was not obliged to fund abortions for poor women even when such abortions were medically necessary.

Thus the Court has supported some restrictions wanted by the anti-abortionists, and for this it has been strongly attacked by pro-choice supporters such as Jaffe, Lindheim and Lee (1981, p. 196) who said that the attack on rights of poor women represented 'a hazardous retreat from the philosophy of pluralism on which this democracy is based'.

Congress

In the months immediately following the 1973 Supreme Court decision two Senators and a Congressman introduced Constitutional amendments to oppose abortions, this still being the main aim of the anti-abortionists.

Although Congress has not yet supported an amendment banning abortions, it has been more encouraging towards right to life plans to cut off public funding. The Supreme Court decision of June 1977 led to a five-month stalemate on the conditions under which federal funds would be granted. The House took a more conservative view than the Senate in the struggle which involved twenty-six roll calls excluding votes on rules (Eccles, 1978). The pro-choice groups attacked the fact that poor women were being discriminated against, but their campaign largely failed, and the American Civil Liberties Union reported that medicaid abortions declined 98.2 per cent in twenty-two states that adopted federal standards (*New York Times*, 24 October 1978).

In order to support their case in Congress both sides on the abortion issue have tried to oust members who do not share their views. A NARAL newsletter in 1978 (vol. 10, no. 1) set out its campaign as follows:

Our election year plan starts off with the process of targeting candidates using the following procedures:

1   identifying pro choice incumbents who will need our help to be re-elected.
2   identifying anti-choice incumbents who have a strong challenge from a pro-choice candidate.
3   identifying pro-choice candidates with a good chance of winning open seats.

Anti-choice groups, however, seem to have had the greater success in influencing members of Congress. *Congressional Quarterly* reported in February 1978 that first-term Congress members favoured strict curbs on abortion by more than a 2 to 1 margin. Forty-three of them backed the Hyde amendment to cut off funds for poor women, nineteen opposed him. In contrast, amongst the sophomore class a clear majority (37 to 47) were opposed to him. This is not what would be expected from demographic factors, as the young tend to take a more liberal position on abortion. It suggests that at that time anti-abortion groups had been most effective. They had either been able to get candidates supporting their position elected or managed to persuade the new members to support their views.

Anti-abortionists have also targeted certain members: as Senator Bob Packwood stated, 'If the Right to Life groups can defeat 8 or 10 House members, and maybe one or two senators, others will get the message' (Eccles, 1978). One person they were particularly keen to unseat was Fr Robert Drinan of Boston, as can be seen from the advertisement (Fig. 8.1) published in the *Wanderer* on 7 September 1978. In this campaign the anti-abortionists were unsuccessful, but Fr Drinan was 'retired' under instructions from Rome. Furthermore, several well known pro-choice Senators targeted by anti-abortionists have lost their seats. Dick Clark lost after being placed on the 1978 'hit list'. In 1980 a similar fate befell George McGovern, Frank Church, Birch Bayh and John Culver. However, it is a matter of debate how far abortion was the critical issue in these defeats.

Although a number of pro-choice members of Congress have been eliminated, there is still not the necessary two-thirds majority in both Houses to push through an amendment banning all abortions. By 1982, therefore, two alternative strategies were being put forward. The first was the Human Life Statute, which aimed to take advantage of a section of the Supreme Court which had made the decision that it was unable 'to resolve the difficult question of when life begins' (Isaacson, 1981). The Bill would simply state that 'For the purpose of enforcing the 14th Amendment not to deprive persons of life without due process of law, human life shall be deemed to exist from conception'. This Bill would only need simple majorities in both Houses, but there were doubts about its constitutionality. There was therefore an alternative strategy put forward by Senator Hatch. He proposed a 'Human Life Federation Amendment' which would authorise Congress and the states to regulate or prohibit abortion in order to 'restore to the representative branches of government the authority to legislate with respect to the practice of abortion' (Donovan, 1981). The proposed wording was: 'The right to abortion is not secured by this constitution. The Congress and the several States shall have the concurrent power to restrict and prohibit abortions, provided, that a law of a state more restrictive than a law of Congress shall govern.' The idea was that this constitutional amendment would have an easier chance of passage and ratification by three-quarters of the states. Then restrictions could be imposed constitutionally.

In March 1982 the Senate Judiciary Committee endorsed Hatch's proposal by 10 votes to 7 – the first time that a full Congressional committee had supported a Constitutional amendment (*New York Times*, 11 March 1982). Willke called this 'a major victory', but recognised a tough fight was in prospect since many anti-abortionists would say that it was not strong enough. In fact two of the members of the Committee who voted with Hatch said that they would try and change the amendment so that it just referred to 'States Rights', which would allow women to travel to states with liberal laws. In April 1983 a new Hatch Amendment which simply read 'A right to abortion is not secured by this Constitution', failed to get the support of a Senate sub-committee as the vote was tied 9–9. In a press release (19 April) the National Abortion Federation (NAF) said the pro-choice groups had grown considerably in strength from the previous year. So the proposed amendment looks unlikely to succeed.

States

The anti-abortion groups have tried to persuade the states to pass laws restricting funding for abortion, and also to reduce rights in areas where the Supreme Court was not specific. After the Hyde amendment became law the states had several options:

1 They could decide to pay the full cost of abortions for poor women unless barred from doing so by the state's legislature.
2 They were forced to discontinue funding of the state laws or regulations prohibited using state monies without matching federal funds.
3 They could stop funding altogether or only allow it in restrictive categories such as rape or incest.

These possibilities meant that the conflicts that occurred at the federal level were often replayed in the states. In New York, for example, in most sessions there is a fierce debate as to whether to continue funding.

By September 1981 only nine states including New York voluntarily funded medicaid abortions. In addition, Massachusetts and California paid for them because their state constitutions provided for equal treatment, and Pennsylvania and New Jersey funded abortions during court proceedings. Overall, the government's Centre for Disease Control reported that 85 per cent of needy women who might get medicaid abortions lived in states that have continued paying (*Newsday*, 5 September 1981). Since the anti-abortion lobby persuaded the Supreme Court to allow them to restrict the rights of minors, many states have passed such laws. These restrictions on abortion rights have only affected vulnerable groups such as the young and the poor. However, some anti-abortionists have been looking to the states to make a move to ban all abortions. Apart from action in Congress, the United States Constitution allows two-thirds (34) of the states to call a Constitutional Convention, but any decision this may make will have to be ratified by three-quarters of the states. Since 1787 all the twenty-six amendments to the Constitution have been proposed and ratified through the Congressional route and only the original Constitutional Convention has ever been called. By May 1980 nineteen states had called for a Constitutional Convention; but this approach seemed to have fallen out of favour with the Right to Life leadership as they concentrated their efforts in Congress. It could of course be revived at a later date.

Attacks on Birth Control and Abortion Centres

Given the fact that many members believe that abortion is murder, it is not too surprising that some of them have taken hostile action. Nellie Gray, head of March for Life, told me in August 1978: 'Our people are extremely frustrated so they think we have got to do something'. Pro-choice groups have claimed that the Church has promoted hostility, and it is true that the Catholic press has not always been seen to be opposing violence, as the *National Catholic Register* (7 May 1978) implied:

> CATHOLIC BISHOPS OPT FOR ACTION
> Washington – a pro abortion organisation has appealed to all concerned about abortion 'to refrain from violence and unlawfulness in any form'. The appeal of the Religious Coalition for Abortion Rights was signed by 26 religious leaders, according to the April edition of Options, the RCAR's official publication.
> 'Let our differences be settled by debate', the statement urged, 'our disagreements be fought with words'.
> Each of the 270 Catholic Bishops was asked to sign the appeal. None did.

The interpretation of the Catholic leaders' refusal to sign as a call to action is not the only one possible and might be regarded as provocative. The Right to Life groups have however distanced themselves from such action, and when Dr Carolyn Gerster took over as President of the National Right to Life her first official action was to offer $5,000 reward for information leading to the arrest and conviction of any persons responsible for the burning or destruction of abortion clinics.

In the two years to February 1979 twenty-five clinics had been fire-bombed. In Omaha on the day that one bomb caused $35,000 worth of damage, the *Omaha World-Herald* received an unsigned letter that read: 'You'd bomb a concentration camp, why not abortion centres', which suggests a link to Right to Life propaganda. The first time a person was arrested for a fire-bombing was at the Bill Baird Center at Hempstead in February 1979. The frequency of such attacks appears to have declined since that time.

Overall, the lack of success of the anti-abortionists in restricting abortion rights has led to frustration in their ranks. For those who sincerely believe that abortion is the same as killing babies it is obviously a matter of great concern that they have not been able to outlaw the operation, and so far have only been able to restrict rights for the poor and the young. They were particularly upset when on 15 June 1983 the Supreme Court reaffirmed its decision in Poe v Wade.

9
Future Developments

The period since the Second World War has shown an amazing increase in availability of legal abortion, but it has also seen a large increase in the size of the world population. Table 9.1 shows the increase for the thirty years 1950–80. These figures indicate that the world's population has been growing by about 75 million a year. From 1950–5 the annual increment was about 46 million. The highest rates of growth were in Latin America, Africa and Asia, and the lowest rates in Europe. If these trends continued some countries in Africa and Asia would between 1980 and the year 2000 have twice as many people to feed, house and care for. Furthermore, although many women have gained the right to choose how many children they want, there are still great problems for others. In 1980 a press release from the World Fertility Survey, the largest social science research project ever undertaken, gave preliminary reports from fifteen Third World countries (Francome, 1980a). It showed that half the married women of reproductive age did not want any more children, yet about half these women were not using effective methods of family planning. The main reasons for this were lack of knowledge and the fact that birth control methods were not available.

Table 9.1 *Trends in World Population*

	1950 (millions)	1980 (millions)	1975–80 Rate of increase (%)
World	2,501	4,432	1.7
Africa	219	470	2.9
North America	166	248	0.9
Latin America	164	364	2.4
Asia	1,368	2,579	1.8
Europe	392	484	0.4
Oceania	13	23	1.5
USSR	180	265	0.9

Source: United Nations, 1980b, p. 7; United Nations, 1976, p. 8.

There have been some determined efforts leading to great reductions in the birthrate. Costa Rica has halved its rate in sixteen years. In Sri Lanka birthrates declined from 5.6 per woman in 1960 to 3.5 in the early 1970s. There was also the 30 per cent decline in China, although in some cases it was produced by infringing the freedom of choice (Kendall, 1979). The rate of world population increase declined from 1.9 per cent in 1970–5 to 1.7 per cent in 1975–80, but even at this rate would double every forty-one years. So there is still a long way to go both to give people individual control over their lives and to prevent associated problems of over-population.

We have seen that in recent years many governments including Italy, Israel, Holland and Norway have been brought to crisis point by the abortion issue. In other places such as the United States it has led to politicians being driven from office. There is no sign of the worldwide debate ceasing or becoming less acrimonious. This chapter therefore considers the possibilities for further change, either to give women more freedom or to lead to restrictions.

Britain and the United States

In Britain the failure of the Corrie Bill was a great setback for the anti-abortionists. Its defeat in the face of all its advantages led to them being in a worse position than if no attempt had been made. The degree of opposition evident around the country has made Members of Parliament much more hesitant about becoming involved in the issue. It also showed pro-choice groups how to hold up action in Parliament, which means that no Bill is likely to succeed except in the unlikely event that the government gives it time. From the votes on the Corrie Bill, such as to increase the time limit from twenty to twenty-four weeks, it seems that even if a Bill were to pass through the House it would be watered down, and of course when the compromises began to enter, SPUC and LIFE would lose interest.

On the other hand, it is even more unlikely that a Bill could be passed to give women the right to choose in the first three months of pregnancy. It seems therefore that the best target for action is the courts. One possibility that could be used by pro-choice groups is to set up cheap abortion clincs giving abortions by doctors under the 1861 Act. The use of the word 'unlawfully' is sufficiently ambiguous for it to be argued that any abortion carried out by doctors is legal. The fact that abortion was openly available on request, as reported at the British Medical Association conference in 1926, indicates that even at that time there was wide interpretation. Furthermore, the evidence brings the exact meaning into question. It therefore seems likely that in a test case a British jury might well refuse to convict a doctor who performed an abortion at the woman's request. This is suggested especially by the Gallup Poll carried out in March 1982 which found that 80 per cent of British adults believed that the decision on an abortion should be left to the pregnant woman and her doctor (Francome, 1982). Furthermore, the evidence from Australia and New Zealand suggests that such a challenge would have been made in Britain had the 1929 Infant Life Preservation Act not been passed. There would of course be the danger in such an approach that once the law had been broadened in the courts, the government might support a more restrictive measure. In that case the composition of Parliament would be important, since right-wing politicians have in virtually all societies taken a more restrictive position than left-wing ones. This is particularly relevant in Britain and the United States. Ironically, as far as Britain is concerned, poll after poll has shown that Conservative supporters are either equally in favour of abortion rights or more in favour as compared to Labour voters. In the 1982 Gallup Poll, for example, 75 per cent of Conservatives believed abortion should be free on the National Health Service compared to only 69 per cent of Labour.

The most plausible explanation for this difference is that, while Conservative voters believe in personal freedom, the politicians are concerned with social order. They may well feel that they have a duty to protect people from a freedom they may misuse. Further light is thrown on this issue by considering the evidence of capital punishment. In Britain and New York politicians in favour of abortion rights are more likely to be opposed to capital punishment and vice versa (Francome, 1978 a and b). However, no such relationship existed amongst 1,000 New York students (Francome, 1978b). In fact, there was a slight but not statistically significant tendency for students who favoured abortion rights to be in favour of capital punishment. This result suggests that there is no necessary inverse correlation between the two attitudes, but that the nature of politics tends to cause beliefs to cluster. Right-wing politicians tend to believe that capital punishment is necessary for the social order, as are restrictions on sexuality. They also support their political allies and expect support in return. Consequently their beliefs tend to correlate in ways not found in the general population. Thus, the future of abortion rights depends in part on the extent to which politicians believe that the social order is threatened. The longer rights exist, the less threatening they will seem. We have seen that right-wing politicians now generally support birth control rights.

The situation in the United States is made more complicated by the fact that politicians can be targeted in a way not possible in Britain. The polls show three-quarters of the population opposed to a Constitutional amendment to ban all abortions. However, the politicians, fearful of their seats, have voted to ban federal money to women even if their abortions were medically necessary, and members of Congress could possibly vote to ban all abortions. A crucial question is how long this gap between the politicians and the people will remain. One problem for the pro-choice groups is the finding of Granberg (1981) that the anti-abortionists are much more likely to vote against a candidate on this single issue alone. This fact, and the money they can raise, suggests that politicians may continue to be defeated on the abortion issue. However, it is unlikely that abortion rights will be totally withdrawn. If an anti-abortion amendment were to pass through Congress there would be a great deal of time for opposition to grow in the states.

Italy and France

These two countries having both introduced the right to choose in the early months of pregnancy, now seem unlikely to lose it. However, one point Greenwood and Young (1976) make is that countries which pass laws allowing abortions on certain grounds are vulnerable to attack which eliminates the number of categories of women allowed to receive terminations – as happened in Israel. However, France and Italy do not have that problem, and so the limit of the debate is likely to be over the gestation period, the rights of minors, or bureaucratic obstacles in terms of licensing. In other countries of Europe it seems that the changes that have been made are likely to remain.

Spain

Spanish law is important not only for its citizens but also for the possibilities of further change that could occur in former Spanish colonies. Under Franco, abortion, birth control and divorce were illegal, and women found guilty of adultery could be sent to prison for up to six years. After he died a new Constitution was set up which paved the way for birth control to be legalised in 1978 and divorce in 1981. A court case effectively repealed adultery as an offence (*Guardian*, 28 March 1977; *Catholic Herald*, 8 October 1982).

Abortion, however, remained outside the changes. As early as 1974 the Spanish Council of Scientific Investigations had come to the conclusion that the law was inadequate and should be revised. However, a television debate between leading doctors and priests was abandoned on advice from the religious advisory council (*New Humanist*, October 1974). With the setting up of a democratic system the parties split as elsewhere with the Socialist (PSOE) and Communist (PCE) parties supporting a change in the law, if not too enthusastically (Anderson, 1980). The Centre–Right Governing party resisted any change and the Prime Minister was reported in *Newsweek* (5 April 1982) as saying that abortion would never be legalised while he remained in office.

The major pressure for change has come from the women's movement. There have been many trials for abortion. In 1975 there were 151, for example, and in December 1979 *Spare Rib* reported that a woman had received ten years' imprisonment. It was, however, the twice-suspended trial of eleven women in Bilbao which mostly galvanised opinion. Nine of the women had undergone abortions and almost all of them already had several children. The tenth person was the abortionist and the eleventh her daughter who had helped. The trial began in October 1979, re-opened in June 1981, and concluded amidst many protests in March 1982. As in France and Italy, one of the most effective protests was from 4,300 well-known women, including a respected dramatic actress, the Eurovision Song Contest winner, and a former Miss Spain. In October 1979 they signed a public manifesto admitting that they had had abortions, which said, 'Spanish justice is condemning women because they do not have the £250 which it costs to go to England for an abortion' (*Guardian*, 25 October 1979). This protest brought great publicity to the trial, and in the end ten of the eleven women were cleared. The abortionist, Ms Julia Garcia, was found guilty but was recommended for an immediate pardon (*Guardian*, 26 March 1982).

In some ways there are parallels between Spain and the developments towards legalisation in other European countries. The number of women travelling to England, for example, jumped from 191 in 1971 to 4,230 in 1975 and then to 18,300 in 1980 and over 20,000 in 1981 (OPCS, 1973, 1978, 1981). Overall it estimated that in Spain there are 300,000 abortions a year (Anderson, 1980).

In January 1983 the newly elected Socialist government published plans to liberalise the law in cases of rape, foetal deformity and risk to the life of the woman (*Daily Telegraph*, 28 January). Although the Archbishop of Oviedo was quoted as saying that the proposed liberalisation was 'a grave step towards dismantling the morals of Spanish society', the proposal was so mild that it could hardly be expected to have much effect.

Portugal

With the setting up of a democracy in 1974 it was clear that women's rights were going to be a crucial issue. The new Constitution introduced in 1975 recognised the right to a 'conscious parenthood', but abortion remained a crime. In 1976 the Family Planning Association was founded and the abortion issue was brought to prominence by a film called, ironically, 'Abortion Is Not a Crime'. It showed an abortion by use of a Karman's canulla and bicycle pump, and made it reasonably clear how to carry one out. The programme also included a discussion in a dimly lit room with a group of women who explained why they had had abortions. The journalist who wrote the script, Mario Palla, was charged in 1979 with an 'assault on public morals' and incitement to crime. *Peace News* reported (6 July 1979) that none of the others associated with the programme were charged. Palla's position on the issue was clear: 'To legalise abortion is a real, concrete way to make women more free. People who are against the liberation of women are against abortion.'

A 22-year-old nurse became the first person to be charged with having an abortion after the 1974 change of government. In response to these cases the National Campaign for Abortion and Contraception was set up and lobbied Parliament with a 9,000-signature petition. The nurse's trial was postponed to October 1979 and when it occurred 1,000 demonstrators, mainly women, protested outside the court. The activists also used the technique of other European countries when they released the names of 200 prominent women who had had abortions and announced that the total list included 3,000 people (*Daily Telegraph*, 25 October 1979). The case was quickly ended when the Judge said that there was no proof that an abortion had occurred. He also made it clear that he was influenced by the national controversy.

Although the demand for abortion seems high, with a Family Planning Association estimate of 180,000 a year, there are very few women coming to England. In 1980, for example, only forty-one Portuguese women had terminations in Britain, which suggests that abortion services in Portugal must be relatively efficient. Support of this view is provided by one of the activists, Madelena Barbosa, who was quoted in the *Guardian* (11 July 1979): 'Some of the midwives are really quite good, they use proper medical instruments and operate in sterile conditions'.

An opinion poll published in the weekly magazine *Expresso* (21 February 1982) showed that only 29 per cent of Portuguese thought abortion was always wrong, 71 per cent agreed with it in some circumstances, although 56 per cent were against general legalisation. An attempt at change was made in March 1982 with a Communist party-sponsored Bill, but there was great opposition from the ruling right-wing groups. It is expected that a leftward movement in the political spectrum is needed to produce liberalisation (*Morning Star*, 22 February 1982).

Ireland

In both the North and South of Ireland the 1861 Offences Against the Persons Act is still in operation. Northern Ireland was specifically excluded from most of the British liberalising measures in the 1960s, for example, capital punishment was not abolished, and male homosexuality not legalised. So the law is left with the amendments brought in by the 1929 Infant Life Preservation Act and the Bourne trial.

Public opinion in Ireland on social issues is very different from the rest of Europe and the United States. A survey in 1973/4 made by a research unit sponsored by the Irish Bishops Conference found that in Eire 53.7 per cent agreed with the statement 'Divorce should never be allowed', and seven out of ten regarded sex before marriage as 'always wrong'. The survey was not carried out in the North because of the unsettled conditions (*Belfast Telegraph*,

21 June 1977). The survey also found that 91 per cent of Catholics went to mass each week, and a quarter more frequently than that. On the question of abortion, 74.3 per cent regarded it as always wrong and 21.1 per cent as 'generally wrong'. Only 1.3 per cent viewed it as 'generally right'. Attitudes to artificial birth control were more liberal, however, only one-third seeing its use as 'always wrong'. A further third felt it was generally wrong, and 25 per cent felt it was right (*The Universe*, 22 July 1977). Later opinion polls are useful for comparative purposes. In 1980 Gallup in Britain, Ireland and the United States asked a very similar question. In the United States and Ireland the question was 'Do you think abortion should be legal under any circumstances, only under certain circumstances or illegal in all circumstances?' In Britain the phrase 'legal under any circumstances' was substituted by 'available on demand', but otherwise was identical. The results (Table 9.2) show a great difference in opinion between Ireland and the other two countries. Whereas four out of five of the Irish thought that abortions should be illegal in all circumstances, only one in five Americans and one in eight British residents shared that view. Catholics in the North of Ireland seem to be more liberal than the South, and 35 per cent would allow abortions in certain circumstances (Francome, 1981). Although abortion does not have public support, increasing numbers of Irish women are coming to Britain for abortion (Table 9.3).

Table 9.2 *Attitudes to Abortion in Three Countries*

	USA (per cent)	Britain (per cent)	Ireland (Eire) (per cent)
Legal in all circumstances (on damand)	25	23	2
Legal in some circumstances	53	61	13
Illegal in all circumstances	18	12	80
Don't know/no opinion	4	4	5
Total	100	100	100

Source: Francome, 1982.

Table 9.3 *Irish Women Having Abortions in Britain*

	1970	1972	1974	1976	1978	1980	1981
Northern Ireland	199	775	1,102	1,142	1,311	1,565	1,441
Eire	261	974	1,406	1,821	2,548	3,320	3,603

Source: OPCS *Monitor* Series.

The figures show that between 1972 and 1981 the number of women from Northern Ireland having abortions in England nearly doubled, and the number from Eire more than trebled. Even these are reckoned to be an under-estimate, as many women give English addresses.

Northern Ireland

Doctor (12 January 1978) reported that abortions were available in the North if the woman was mentally subnormal, if there was a substantial risk of handicap, or if the pregnancy would be a danger to her life or health.

The Ulster Pregnancy Advisory Service was started by An English woman, Lorna Goldstrom, in 1971. In 1978 its director Joan Wilson was quoted as saying: 'If those who condemn abortion so loudly and with such a considerable amount of energy would put their resources towards campaigning for better sex education programmes . . . then perhaps the need for abortion which they so vigorously oppose might be decreased considerably' (*Pulse*, 4 March).

The birthrate in the first quarter of 1977 in Northern Ireland was 16.3 per thousand compared to 11.6 for England and Wales. Coward (1981) reported that in 1973–4 Catholics had a larger family size than Protestants: in the age group 18–34 years Catholics had a family size of 4.1 and Protestants 2.8. Overall, Catholics aimed to have an average family size 1.1 children higher than Protestants. However, it could be the case that this difference is narrowing. The proportion of Catholics applying to the Ulster PAS for abortions increased from 21 per cent in 1971–3 to nearly 30 per cent in 1978. Roughly 35 per cent of women of childbearing age are Catholic, and so there may be a merging of fertility rates as has occurred in other countries (*Belfast Telegraph*, 26 May 1980).

The first Northern Ireland abortion conference was organised by the Northern Ireland Abortion Campaign (NIAC). This organisation was set up in the spring of 1980 soon after a woman died from a back-street abortion. It was opened by Madeleine Simms who asked, 'Can there really be many people left who believe that any good is achieved by compelling women to have unwanted babies?' (*Morning Star*, 13 October 1980). In October

1981 NIAC sent letters to all MPs at Westminster giving facts about abortion in Northern Ireland and enclosing a coat hanger to symbolise illegal abortion. Labour MP Jo Richardson receiving the delegation said that many MPs were shocked to find that abortion was not available on the same basis as in Britain (*Breaking Chains*, January 1982). However, eleven out of twelve Northern Irish MPs oppose the extension of abortion rights, and the Minister of State for Northern Ireland said (17 November 1981) that since direct rule in 1972 the government has felt that it shouldn't change the law 'unless such a measure was likely to command broad support among the people of the province'. Progress for NIAC is therefore likely to be difficult.

Eire

Wilson-Davies (1980) reports that wives had a higher ideal family size in Eire than in other countries. At 4.3 it contrasted with 2.3 in West Germany, 2.6 in Italy, 2.9 in Britain, and 2.7 in France and Belgium. However, Eire is changing, as is shown by an important Supreme Court decision in 1974 which ruled that a law forbidding the import of contraceptives was unconstitutional. Polls showed a vast majority in favour, and a group of campaigners went by train to Belfast and came back waving their purchases, with the police just standing by. The law continued to bar any sale of devices, but clinics were able to get round this by giving them for free and asking for a donation.

An attempt to legalise birth control was made in 1974 but ended in farce as Liam Cosgrave, the Prime Minister, voted against the government's own Bill. In 1979 Charles Haughey introduced another Bill which went into operation on 1 November 1980. This allowed the legal sale of contraceptives for the first time, but raised a number of objections. For example, even non-medical birth control was only to be allowed on doctors' prescription and then purchased at a chemist. Doctors objected to this, as did patients faced with two sets of fees. In February 1980 the Women's Right to Choose Campaign was set up. Four months later British SPUC sent two representatives and an Irish SPUC was launched.

The international aspects of the abortion issue were brought to a head in February 1981 when the EEC Parliament debated a document on women's rights produced by its women's group. It accepted the need for safe legal abortion as a last resort (Holland, 1981). Thirteen of the fifteen Eire members voted against the document because of the section on abortion, and two abstained. A Northern Ireland deputy, John Taylor, voted in support and described the scenes in the Parliament as Ireland's day of 'Holy Terror'. Archbishop Dermot Ryan of Dublin warned that the endorsement of abortion by the EEC might force Ireland's withdrawal. Holland reports that the Irish bishops were alarmed lest abortion should become a live issue. In April 1981 a campaign was launched to insert an anti-abortion amendment into the Constitution. The Pro-Life Amendment Campaign (PLAC) initially proposed to guarantee 'the absolute right to life of every unborn child'. However, it had to be modified as it did not allow for abortion in circumstances like an ectopic pregnancy which was allowed by the Church. A reason for introducing this amendment at a time when abortion was already illegal was provided by anti-abortion activist John O'Reilly who said: 'The Pro Life amendment to the Constitution was the answer to the abortion problem in Ireland. It must be won while the vast majority of the Irish people were still opposed to abortion and while abortion was not too politically divisive' (*Irish Catholic*, 1 April 1982).

Paradoxically, the amendment campaign does seem to be raising great conflict. The anti-amendment lobby feels that tying the law so closely to the doctrines of the Catholic Church will damage the chances of an agreement with the Protestants of the North. It also pointed out in a press release (30 June 1982) that the referendum was opposed by all the major Protestant churches in the Republic and by the Chief Rabbi. So the amendment will certainly keep abortion in the forefront of the debate.

Moslem Countries

A number of predominately Islamic countries have liberalised their laws. These include Morocco (1967), Tunisia (1973), Iran (1976 – possibly reversed) and most recently Kuwait. In January 1982 this became one of the first Arab nations to permit abortion. The all-male parliament voted by 27 votes to 3 to allow abortion if the pregnancy would result in gross physical harm to the woman or if the foetus had brain damage 'beyond hope of treatment' (*New York Times*, 31 January).

The legislation in other Islamic countries will to a large extent depend on the relationship between the Church and state. The International Planned Parenthood Federation organised the first Islamic conference of family planning and the participants decided that birth control was permissible in Moslem law but that sterilisation and abortion were prohibited (*New York Times,* 1 January 1972).

Turkey is one Moslem country where change might occur. It has by far the highest population growth in Europe. According to the 1980 census it was 21 per 1,000 population. The *Financial Times* (17 May 1982) reports that it also has increasing unemployment, overcrowding in the cities and the highest infant mortality in Europe. These factors have combined with the high rate of deaths from illegal abortions to encourage the military government to take action. A programme of family planning was introduced in the army; advertisements for smaller families appeared on television, and a Bill legalising abortion on social grounds is being considered. However, the *New York Times* (7 February 1982) reports that an attempt at liberalisation in 1978 was prevented by Moslem religious groups and right-wing parties, so a change in the law may be thwarted again.

Change seems less likely in Nigeria, a country with strong Moslem and Catholic religious groups, although there is known to be a great amount of illegal abortion. In 1975 the Nigerian National Council of Women's Societies opposed an attempt to change the law on the grounds that it would lead to 'moral laxity'. There was a further attempt to change the law in 1981, and on 15 February the *Nigerian Sunday Times* instituted a great debate on the subject. The wording of the Bill followed that of the British 1967 Act, but it was strongly opposed. The head of the Catholic secretariat, Monsignor Inyang, claimed that 'This is a move to legalise abortion and turn our women, old and young, into a business commodity'. A Moslem leader said that the *Koran* had no place for abortion and the Bill was rejected without debate. A surprising development was reported, by Rebecca Cook, a specialist in Commonwealth law (personal communication, 16 September 1982). She said that Northern Nigeria and Pakistan (and India) have a law dating back to 1860 which states that a woman cannot be prosecuted for aborting herself unless pregnancy is proved. This law presumably makes modern techniques such as menstrual extraction legal.

Latin America

Table 9.1 showed that this area had the highest population growth rate of the seven tabulated. Tietze (1979) reported that of the twenty-two Latin American countries with populations of more than a million, in seven abortion was illegal in all circumstances, in six it was allowed to save the life of the woman, and in nine it was available on broader medical grounds. In 1973 Guatemala and El Salvador liberalised their laws to allow abortion in cases of foetal defect, rape and to save the life of the woman. In Costa Rica future health as well as life can be a reason for termination, and Uruguay allows abortion for serious economic stress in the first three months of pregnancy (Potts *et al.*, 1977; Tietze, 1979). Only in Cuba is abortion available on request.

However, although abortion is not generally legally available there are many illegal abortions. An early indication of this came in 1963 from Chile (*New York Times*, 8 October) which reported that, despite the fact that the country was 90 per cent Catholic, the government was going to support birth control clinics because of the high rate of deaths from illegal abortions. In 1961 there were 49,195 admissions to hospital because of abortion, and for every one of these, two more were estimated. In outlining the plan for nine clinics the government spokesman, Dr Adriasola, said that abortion accounted for 35–40 per cent of all pregnancies and was a cause of 40 per cent of the maternal deaths. Furthermore, despite this high level, the population was growing more than twice as fast as the increase in food production. This sorry picture, with women unable to control their fertility and being forced either to have children they could not afford or to resort to the back-street abortionist, was not unusual for Latin America. Potts *et al.* (1977, p. 95) give data from surveys in sixteen countries and show that abortion was common in the vast majority of them.

Brazil is the largest Catholic country in the world with an estimated population of over 125 million in 1982. Even so, the *New York Times* (28 May 1977) reported that about half of all pregnancies were terminated and that there were 2 million illegal abortions each year. In 1974 Brazil's delegate to the World Population Conference said that birth control should be available to all couples who wanted it, but the *New York Times* reported that it had only been provided in four of the twenty-two states.

Bolivia has moved to greater restriction. *People* (1976, vol. 3, no. 3) reported that 60 per cent of hospital costs in obstetrics and gynaecology were due to illegal abortion. Despite this fact in 1977 the government increased its stand against birth control. Mr Dorian Gorena, the Under-Secretary of Health, said that any attempts to curb births artificially were 'an attack against the country itself' and that the government would punish anyone advocating birth control (*Catholic Herald*, 19 August 1977).

A study of 1,273 patients for treatment for incomplete abortions at the El Salvador maternity hospital found that 93.4 per cent of the women had used no method of contraceptive. Illegal abortions accounted for 23.8 per cent of deaths at the hospital (*People*, 1976, vol. 3, no. 3) of whom the great majority were married Catholic women with an average age of 26 and at least two children. Thus it would seem that Latin American women have great problems: but there are some hopeful signs.

In Argentina the annual increase in population is half that of Latin America as a whole and the rate of illegal abortion seems less than some other places. Surveys in Buenos Aires found that less than a quarter of all pregnancies ended in illegal abortion, and some evidence of a fall in the rate (Sainz, 1976). These two facts together suggest that birth control use must be reasonably effective.

In Mexico a family planning programme was started in 1975 and since that time there has been pressure to liberalise the abortion laws. In the *New York Times* (17 December 1979) Anilu Elias, a leader of the women's movement, asserted: 'It's a woman's right not to die because of a clandestine abortion'. The government estimated that there were 10,000 deaths a year from illegal operations, and that only 8 per cent of terminations were carried out under medical supervision. The Communist party introduced a Bill in November 1979 and, although the President opposed it, the fact that such pressure exists could produce change in the future.

Two factors are likely to influence future developments. One is the political nature of regimes. Any liberalisation of military dictatorships is likely to produce a movement, for example in Chile under Allende where legal abortions began to be performed in Santiago and the President announced that the law would be changed. The results of 3,250 hospital abortions were analysed and there was a measurable decline in admissions for incomplete abortions and a fall in infant mortality. After the military coup there was a cut-back on abortion and other rights of women such as the wearing of slacks (Potts *et al.*, 1977, p. 442). A second factor is the role of the Catholic Church, which itself seems to be divided as to what action to take. The *Catholic Herald* (22 August 1976) reported that the bishops in Bolivia had sent a pastoral letter calling birth control 'genocide' and saying that the rich countries were trying to keep the population down in the poor areas to use them as reservoirs of raw materials. However, elsewhere it has seen the need for family planning. This is true of the Church in Britain and the United States, and in the Philippines it has promoted its free natural family planning clinics on the national Catholic radio station. The *Catholic Herald* (19 August 1977) said that the Catholic Church acknowledged that fewer children meant a better future for them and a lighter economic load for the parents. Certainly, the degree of opposition to change from the Church is going to be crucial.

A final point is that menstrual extraction is not illegal in Latin America as it is in countries where the law derived from Britain. This is because the pregnancy must be confirmed for an offence to be committed. It could therefore be the case that even within existing laws the deaths from illegal abortion could be reduced by using this method.

Conclusion

This book has shown evidence of widespread changes in abortion laws. These have been influenced by a variety of factors including the role of the women's movement, the views of the courts and the influence of religion. Women have been involved not only through pressure groups but also at an individual level. We have seen that they have often had to travel to other countries to get abortions. British women went to France in the early part of the twentieth century and French women came to Britain in great numbers in the mid-1970s. Swedish women went to Poland, New Zealand women went to Australia and up to 1970 American women came to Britain. After 1970 Canadian women went in great numbers to New York State, and after the United States imposed restrictions on financial help for the poor, some women sought cheaper abortions in Mexico. German and Belgian women go to Holland and increasingly Spanish and Irish women come to England. So women have had to travel extensively to circumvent restrictions their own society has placed on their personal choice.

The British Abortion Act 1967 has been an important development for many reasons. It has provided a haven where rich women at least could have a safe, legal abortion, and this has led to greater political pressure in countries whose women have been forced to travel for their abortions. Supporters of change could therefore argue that rich women had rights of control of fertility which poor women were denied. Furthermore, the legal systems of the United States and the British Commonwealth were based on English law, so when the British Act was passed it was certain to draw attention to the restrictive laws in other countries. We have seen how the logic of the British Act was important in the judgement of the United States Supreme Court, and was earlier important in the changes in Hawaii and New York.

There are still many countries of the world with laws which force women to have unwanted babies. By late 1980 28 per cent of women lived in countries which prohibited abortion without exception or permitted it only to save the life of the pregnant woman. A majority of countries in Africa, almost two-thirds of the countries of Latin America and a majority of the Moslem countries of Asia fall into these two categories. These restrictions also apply to five countries in Europe – Belgium, Ireland, Malta, Portugal and Spain (Tietze, 1981). The possibility of further change depends on a number of factors. The historical analysis has shown that there is a relationship, albeit an imperfect one, between the climate of opinion on sexuality and the laws on fertility control. Countries which move away from repression of women and towards greater freedom in general are more likely to be sympathetic to abortion rights.

Throughout this book the term 'pro-choice' has been used rather than the term 'pro-abortion' to emphasise the fact that the advocates of free choice have consistently argued that the number of abortions should be reduced by education and birth control. The total number of abortions worldwide is extremely difficult to determine, but one estimate was of 55 million a year, or three out of every ten known pregnancies (IPPF, 1974). There are those who believe that this number cannot be reduced by an extension of freedom, for this will make people 'abortion minded' and they will neglect birth control. Such people see the solution as returning to tight controls on sexual expression. However, there is evidence that birth control education can work to reduce the number of unwanted pregnancies. In Britain, for example, the number of births amongst teenagers of 16–19 years dropped by 40 per cent between 1970 and 1979 and less than one-third of the decline was due to an increase in legal abortion (Francome, 1983). This kind of fact suggests that birth control can take over from abortion as a means of controlling births. Other evidence such as the low level of birth control in Italy, where only 5 per cent of women use the pill and many use coitus interruptus, suggests that a campaign for improved contraception could greatly reduce the abortion rate estimated (legal and illegal) at 800,000 a year (*Doctor*, 22 October 1981). There are contrasts between countries such as Italy, Japan and the Soviet Union which have low use of birth control and high abortion rates, and countries such as Holland and Britain with better birth control programmes and low abortion rates. These differences show a clear need in certain countries to extend their family planning programmes.

Developments in rights of control of fertility will obviously not solve the deep economic and social problems facing the world. However, they will give people greater control over their lives and more opportunity to have the number of children they want and at a time of life when they are best able to care for them.

Bibliography

List of Journals in the Abortion Field and Where Available

Abortion Research Notes Transnational Family Research Institute, 8307 Whitman Drive, Bethesda, Md 20034

Abortion Review Published by the Co-ordinating Committee in Defence of the 1967 Abortion Act, 27 Mortimer Street, London W1N 7RJ

ALRA News Published by the Abortion Law Repeal Association of Western Australia, PO Box 143, Claremont, WA, 6010

Breaking Chains Published by Abortion Law Reform Association, 88a Islington High Street, London N1 8EG

Birth Control News Published by the Society for Constructive Birth Control, available at British Newspaper Library, Colindale, London

Conscience Journal of Catholics for a Free Choice, 2008 17th St, NW Washington DC 20009

Family Planning Perspectives Published by Alan Guttmacher Institute, 360 Park Avenue S., NY 10010.

Human Concern Published by the Society for the Protection of Unborn Children, 7 Tufton Street, London SW1P 3QN

Journal of Biosocial Science Published by the Galton Foundation, 7 Downing Place, Cambridge, England

LIFE News Published by LIFE, 35 Kenilworth Road, Leamington Spa, Warwickshire

The Malthusian (from 1922 known as the *New Generation*) Published by the Malthusian League and available at the British Library, Russell Street, London WC1

Medico-Pharmaceutical Critic and Guide (which went through several slight name changes until ceasing publication in 1936) Published by Critic and Guide Company and available at the New York Academy of Medicine, 2 East 103rd Street, New York, New York 10029

NARAL News 1424 'K' St, NW Washington DC 20005

People Published by IPPF, 18 Lower Regent Street, London SW1Y 4PW

Public Affairs Bulletin Published by NAF, 201 Mass. Ave, NE Washington DC 20002

Right to Life News Published by National Right to Life Committee Inc., Suite 341, National Press Building, Washington DC 20045

Studies in Family Planning Published by the Population Council, One Dag Hammarskjold Plaza, NY, NY 10017

The Wanderer Published by the Wanderer Printing Company, 201 Ohio
  Street, St Paul, Mn, USA

Many boxes of primary material such as historical documents,
campaigning leaflets and Parliamentary Reports have been placed at
Middlesex Polytechnic Library, Queensway, Enfield, Middlesex where
they are available for reference (Tel: 01-804 8131 Ext. 497).

References

Akingbar, J. B., and Gbajumo, S. A. (1970), 'Procured Abortion: counting the cost', *Journal of the Nigerian Medical Association*, vol. 7, no. 2, pp. 1–12.

Anderson, H. (1980), 'Abortion in Spain', *Peace News*, 25 January.

Armytage, W. H. G. (1964), *Four Hundred Years of English Education* (Cambridge University Press).

Baker, M. (1974), *The Folklore and Customs of Love and Marriage* (Shire Publications).

Banks, J. A. (1954), *Prosperity and Parenthood* (Routledge).

Barnett, W. E. (1973), *Sexual Freedom and the Constitution* (University of New Mexico Press).

Benfield, B. B. (1972), 'The spermatic economy: a nineteenth century view of sexuality', *Feminist Studies*, vol. 1, no. 1 (Summer), pp. 341 ff.

Besant, A. (1877), *Law of Population* (Freethought Publishing).

Birkett, W. N. (1939), *Report of the Inter-Departmental Committee on Abortion* (HMSO).

Birth-Rate Commission (1917), *The Declining Birth Rate* (2nd edn.) (Chapman and Hall).

Borden Harriman, J. (1923), *From Pinafores to Politics* (Henry Holt).

Bowles, T. G. A., and Bell, M. N. M. (1979), 'Abortion, a clarification', *New Law Journal*, vol. 129 (27 September), pp. 944 ff.

Boyer, P. S. (1968), *Purity in Print* (Charles Scribner's Sons).

British Medical Association (1936), 'Report on the Committee on Medical Aspects of Abortion', *British Medical Journal* (25 April), pp. 230–8.

Brittain, V. (1934), *Testament of Youth* (Gollancz).

Brouardel, P. (1901), *L'Avortement* (J. B. Bailliere et Fils).

Buck, P. S. (1968), *The Terrible Choice* (Bantam) (Buck introduced the Conference Report).

Bunker, J. P. (1970), 'Surgical manpower', *New England Journal of Medicine*, vol. 282, no. 3, pp. 135–44.

Calverton, V. F., and Schmalhausen, S. D. (1929), *Sex in Civilisation* (Macaulay).

Carmen, A., and Moody, H. (1973), *Abortion Counselling and Social Change* (Judson Press).

Carstairs, G. (1962), *This Island Now* (Hogarth Press).

Cartwright, A. (1970), *Parents and Family Planning* (Routledge).

Cavadino, P. (1976), 'Illegal abortion and the Abortion Act 1967', *British Journal of Criminology*, vol. 16, no. 1, pp. 63–7.

Chance, J., Edge, M., and Ryan, M. (1947), *Back Street Surgery* (ALRA).

Churchill, W. S. (1972), *My Early Life* (Fontana: 1st edition 1930).

Cisler, L. (1970), *Abortion Law Repeal (Sort Of)* (New Yorkers for Abortion Repeal).

Coffey, P. (1976), 'When is the killing of the unborn a homicidal action?', *Linacre Quarterly*, vol. 43, no. 2, pp. 85–93.

Coleman, J. (1966), *Equality of Educational Opportunity*, Department of Health, Education and Welfare, US Government).

Cook, R. J. (1976), 'Abortion laws in the Commonwealth', *International Planned Parenthood Federation Medical Bulletin* (April).

Cook, R. J. (1978), 'A decade of change in the Abortion Law 1967–77', *People*, vol. 5, no. 2 (a supplementary chart).

Cook, R. J., and Dickens, B. M. (1983), *Emerging Issues of Commonwealth Abortion Laws* (Commonwealth Secretariat).

Cowan, J. (1880), *The Science of a New Life* (Cowan and Co.).

Coward, J. (1981), 'Ideal family size in Northern Ireland', *Journal of Biosocial Science*, vol. 13, pp. 443–54.

David, H. P. (1982), *Eastern Europe: Pronatalist Policies and Private Behaviour* (Population Reference Bureau).

David, H. P., and McIntyre, R. J. (1981), *Reproductive Behaviour* (Springer).

de Bruijn, J. (1979), *Geschiedenis van Abortus in Nederland* (Van Gennep).

Dekker, H. (1920), 'The ethical grounds of abortion', *The Medical Critic and Guide*, vol. 23, pp. 336–40.

Dickens, B. (1976), 'Crusader or criminal', *People*, vol. 3, no. 3, p. 27.

Donovan, P. (1981), 'Half a loaf: a new anti abortion strategy', *Family Planning Perspectives*, vol. 13 (December), pp. 262–8.

Doyle, A. (1977), 'Do you need permission to save an unborn baby?' (Committee to Defend Pro Life Groups).

Drinan, R. F. (1967), 'The inviolability of the right to be born' in *Abortion and the Law* (ed. D. Smith) (Western Reserve University Press).

Eccles, M. E. (1978), 'Abortion: how members voted in 1977', *Congressional Quarterly*, vol. 36, no. 5 (4 February), pp. 258–67.

Ehrlich, P. R. (1976), *Population Bomb* (Ballantine).

Ehrlich, P. R., and Ehrlich, A. H. (1970), *Population Resources and Environment* (W. H. Freeman).

Elderton, E. M. (1914), *Report on the English Birthrate* (Eugenics Society).

Ellis, H. H. (1928), *Studies in the Psychology of Sex*, Vol. VI (F. A. Davies).

Ellis, H. H. (1933), *Psychology of Sex* (Heinemann).

Eppel, E. M., and Eppel, M. (1966), *Adolescents and Morality* (Routledge).

Facer, W. (1978), 'Initial consequences of the 1977 New Zealand Abortion Law', *New Zealand Nursing Forum*, vol. 6, no. 2, pp. 9–12.

Ferriman, A. (1980), 'Women clash with police at Commons', *The Times* (9 February).

Field, M. G. (1956), 'Re-legalisation of abortion in Soviet Russia', *New England Journal of Medicine*, vol. 255, pp. 421–7.

Friedan, B. (1963), *The Feminine Mystique* (W. W. Norton).

Francome, C. (1976a), *Youth and Society*, unpublished MA thesis (University of Kent, Canterbury).

Francome, C. (1976b), 'How many illegal abortions?', *British Journal of Criminology*, vol. 16, no. 4, pp. 389–92.

Francome, C. (1977a), *First Report of the Select Committee on Abortion: Counter Report (ALRA)*.

Francome, C. (1977b), Correspondence in *British Journal of Criminology*, vol. 17, no. 4, p. 416.

Francome, C. (1977c), 'Estimating the number of illegal abortions', *Journal of Biosocial Science*, vol. 9, pp. 467–79.

Francome, C. (1978a), 'Abortion and the death penalty', *Breaking Chains*, no. 9 (September), p. 7.

Francome, C. (1978b), 'Abortion: why the issue has not disappeared', *Political Quarterly*, vol. 49, no. 2, pp. 217–22.

Francome, C. (1978c), 'Catholics – sex , contraception and abortion', *Breaking Chains*, no. 10 (November).

Francome, C. (1979), 'More teenage sex', *Breaking Chains*, no. 11 (January).

Francome, C. (1980a), *Birth Control: A Way Forward*, pamphlet to celebrate centenary of Marie Stopes's birth (Marie Stopes House).

Francome, C. (1980b), *Public Opinion on Abortion* (ALRA).

Francome, C. (1980c), *Social Forces and the Abortion Law Ph.D. Thesis*, Council for National Academic Awards (CNAA).

Francome, C. (1980d), 'Abortion policy in Britain and the United States', *Social Work*, vol. 25, no. 1, pp. 5–9.

Francome, C. (1980e), 'Abortion politics in the United States', *Political Studies*, vol. 28, no. 4, pp. 613–21.

Francome, C. (1981), 'Religious attitudes . . . US and Ireland', *Breaking Chains*, no. 24 (October), p. 8.

Francome, C. (1982), *Gallup on Abortion: 1982* (ALRA and Doctors for a Woman's Choice on Abortion).

Francome, C. (1983), 'Unwanted pregnancies amongst teenagers', *Journal of Biosocial Science*, vol. 15, no. 2.

Gavron, H. (1966), *The Captive Wife* (Penguin).

Gillie, O., Wallace, M., Ashdown-Sharp, P., and Zimmerman, L. (1975), 'Abortion tales revealed as fantasies', *Sunday Times* (30 March), p. 1.

Glass, D. V. (1940), *Population Policies and Movements in Europe* (Frank Cass).

Godwin, W. (1793), *An Enquiry Concerning Political Justice* (Paternoster-Row).

Goode, E. (1970), *The Marijuana Smokers* (Basic Books).

Goodhart, C. B. (1973), 'On the Incidence of Illegal Abortion', *Population Studies*, vol. 27, pp. 207–34.

Goodhart, C. B. (1974), *The Lane Committee on the Working of the Abortion Act: Comments by the Society for the Protection of Unborn Children* (SPUC).

Gordon, L. (1977), *Woman's Body, Woman's Right* (Penguin).

Goreau, A. (1981), 'Book burners: the threat to literature', *New Statesman* (25 September).

Granberg, D. (1981), 'The abortion activists', *Family Planning Perspectives*, vol. 13, no. 4, pp. 157–63.

Greenwood, V. and Young, J. (1976), *Abortion on Demand* (Pluto Press).

Guttmacher, A. (1959), 'Therapeutic abortion: one physician's viewpoint', *Quarterly Review of Surgery, Obstetrics and Gynaecology*, vol. 16, p. 235.

Guttmacher, A. (1967), *The Case for Legalised Abortion Now* (Diablo Press).

Hair, P. H. E. (1966), 'Bridal pregnancy in rural England', *Population Studies*, vol. 20, pp. 233–44.

Hair, P. H. E. (1970), 'Bridal pregnancy in rural England further examined', *Population Studies*, vol. 24, pp. 59–70.

Hall, A. (1905), 'The increasing use of lead as an abortifacient', *British Medical Journal*, vol. 1 (18 March), pp. 584–7.

Hall, A., and Ransom, W. B. (1906), 'Plumbism from the ingestion of diachylon as an abortifacient', *British Medical Journal*, vol. 1 (24 February), pp. 428–30.

Harris Survey (18 August 1977) (*Chicago Tribune*).

Hathorn, G. B., Penniman, H. R., and Zink, H. (1963), *Government and Politics in the United Stated* (Van Nostrand).

Heron, A. (ed.), (1963), *Towards a Quaker View of Sex* (Society of Friends).

Himes, N. E. (1930), 'Robert Dale Owen, the pioneer of American neo-Malthusianism', *American Journal of Sociology*, vol. 35, pp. 529–47.

Hindell, K., and Simms, M. (1971), *Abortion Law Reformed* (Peter Owen).

Holland, M. (1981), 'Ireland's bishops decide', *New Statesman* (3 April).

Hunter, A. (1981), 'In the wings', *Revolutionary Socialism* (Summer).

Illman, J. (1976), 'Abortion distortion', *General Practitioner* (6 February).

IPPF (1974), *Survey of World Needs in Family Planning* (International Planned Parenthood Federation).

Isaacson, W. (1981), 'The battle over abortion', *Time* (6 April).

Jaffe, F. S., Lindheim, B. L., and Lee, P. R. (1981), *Abortion Politics* (McGraw Hill).

Jenkins, A. (1964), *Law For the Rich* (Charles Skilton).

Jenness, L. (1976), *Socialism and the Fight for Women's Rights* (Pathfinder Press).

Kendall, M. (1979), *The World Fertility Survey* (Johns Hopkins University).

Kennedy, D. M. (1970), *Birth Control in America* (Yale University Press).

Ketting, E., and Schnabel, P. (1980), 'Induced abortion in the Netherlands: a decade of experience 1970–80', *Studies in Family Planning*, vol. 11, no. 12, pp. 385–94.

King, L. R., and Moser, C. (1979), *The Impact of Robbins* (Penguin).

Kommers, D. P. (1977), 'Abortion and the Constitution: United States and West Germany', *American Journal of Comparative Law*, vol. 25, no. 2, pp. 225–85.

Lader, L. (1966), *Abortion* (Beacon Press).

Lader, L. (1973), *Abortion II: Making the Revolution* (Beacon Press).

Lane Report (1974). *Report of the Committee on the Working of the Abortion Act*, Cmnd 5579 (HMSO).

Lauter, P., and Howe, F. (1970), *The Conspiracy of the Young* (World Publishing Co.).

Lewis, J. (1981), 'Has the Church overplayed its hand?', *Catholic Herald* (15 May).

LIFE (no date), *Fifteen Errors of the Abortionist* (LIFE).

Lindsey, B. (1925), *The Revolt of Modern Youth* (Boni and Liveright).

Linner, B. (1968), *Sex and Society in Sweden* (Cape).

Litchfield, M., and Kentish, S. (1974), *Babies for Burning* (Serpentine Press).

Malinowski, B. (1929), *The Sexual Life of Savages* (Routledge).

Malthus, T. (1978), *Essay on the Principle of Population* (Everyman's University Library).

Marsh, D., and Chambers, J. (1981), *Abortion Politics* (Junction Books).

Martin, D. (1967), *The Sociology of English Religion* (Heinemann).

Marx, K. (1976), *Capital*, Vol. 1, trans. from 3rd German edn. in 1887 (Penguin).

Marx, P. (1971), *The Death Peddlers* (St Johns University Press).

McGovern, J. (1968), 'The American woman's pre World War I freedom in manners and morals', *Journal of American History*, vol. 55 (September), pp. 315–48.

McGregor, O. R. (1957), *Divorce in England* (Heinemann).

McLaren, A. (1978), *Birth Control in Nineteenth Century England* (Croom Helm).

Mead, M. (1943), *Coming of Age in Samoa* (Penguin). Originally published in 1928.

Means, C. (1968), 'The law of New York concerning abortion and the status of the foetus 1664–1968: a case of cessation of Constitutionality', *New York Law Forum*, vol. 14, pp. 411–515.

Means, C. (1971), 'The phoenix of abortion freedom', *New York Law Forum*, vol. 17, pp. 335–410.

Mohr, J. C. (1978), *Abortion in America* (Oxford University Press).

Moody, H. (1967), 'Man's vengeance on women', *Renewal Magazine*, p. 7.

Muhua, C. (1979), 'Birth planning in China', *Family Planning Perspectives*, vol. 11, no. 6, pp. 348–54.

Myrdal, A. and Klein, V. (1968), *Woman's Two Roles* (Routledge).

NARAL (1972), *Newsletter*, vol. 2, no. 2 (March).

NARAL (1976), *Abortion Questions and Answers*, undated leaflet (National Abortion Rights Action League).

NARAL (1978), *Newsletter*, vol. 10, no. 3 (May).

Neville, A. (1976), 'Inside West Germany', *Glasgow Herald* (13 January).

Nolen, W. A. (1978), *The Baby in the Bottle* (Coward, McCann and Georghegan Inc.).

Noonan, J. (1967), *Contraception* (Mentor-Omega Edition).

Office of Population Censuses and Surveys, *OPCS Monitor* Series AB (Notifications) (HMSO).

OPCS (1974), *Statistical Review, Supplement on Abortion* (HMSO).

OPCS (1978), *Abortion Statistics 1975*, Series AB No. 2 (HMSO).

OPCS (1981), *Abortion Statistics 1980*, Series AB No. 7 (HMSO).

Osofsky, H. J., and Osofsky, J. D. (1973), *The Abortion Experience* (Harper & Row).

Parish, T. N. (1935), 'A thousand cases of abortion', *Journal of Obstetrics and Gynaecology of the British Empire* (December), p. 1107.

Parry, L. A. (1932), *Criminal Abortion* (Bale; Carswell).

Paxman, J. M. (1980), *Law and Planned Parenthood* (International Planned Parenthood Federation).

Perrin, N. (1970), *Dr. Bowdler's Legacy* (Macmillan).

Pierce, R. (1963), 'Marriage in the fifties', *Sociological Review*, vol. 11, no. 2, pp. 215–40.

Place, F. (1930), *Illustration and Proofs of the Principles of Population: Including an Examination of the Proposed Remedies of Mr. Malthus and a Reply to the Objections of Mr. Godwin and Others* (Allen & Unwin).

Planned Parenthood (1945), *Planned Parenthood's Campaign for 1945*, Pamphlet.

Planned Parenthood (1963), *Plan Your Children for Health and Happiness*, anonymous pamphlet.

Pomeroy, H. S. (1888), *Ethics of Marriage* (Funk and Wagnalls).

Pope, T. A. (1888), 'Prevention of conception', *Medical and Surgical Reporter*, vol. 59, pp. 522–5.

Potts, M., Diggory, P., and Peel, J. (1977), *Abortion* (Cambridge University Press).

Potts, M., and Selman, P. (1979), *Society and Fertility* (MacDonald & Evans).

Reed, J. (1978), *From Private Vice to Public Virtue* (Basic Books).

Robinson, J. (1963), *Honest to God* (SCM Press).

Robinson, W. J. (1928), *Sex, Love and Morality* (Eugenics Publishing Co.).

Robinson, W. J. (1933), *The Law Against Abortion* (Eugenics Publishing Co.).

Rongy, A. J. (1933), *Abortion: Legal or Illegal* (Vanguard Press).

Rostow, W. W. (1971), *The States of Economic Growth*, (2nd edn., Cambridge University Press).

Rowntree, B. S., and Lavers, G. R. (1951), *English Life and Leisure* (Longmans Green).

Royal Commission on Population (1949), *Report*, Cmnd 7695 (HMSO).

Royal Commission (1977), *Contraception, Sterilisation and Abortion in New Zealand* (New Zealand Government Publication).

Russell, B. (1929), *Marriage and Morals* (Allen & Unwin).

Sainz, S. G. (1976), 'Abortion research in Latin America', *Studies in Family Planning*, vol. 7, no. 8, p. 918.

Sanger, M. (1915), *Family Limitation* (Rose Witcop).

Sanger, M. (1932), *My Fight For Birth* (Faber & Faber).

Sanger, M. (1969), *Woman and the New Race*, 1st edn. 1920 (Maxwell Reprint Co.).

Scarisbrick, J. J. (1971), *What's Wrong With Abortion* (LIFE).

Schattschneider, E. E. (1960), *The Semi Soverign People* (Holt, Rinehard and Winston).

Schur, E. M. (1965), *Crimes Without Victims* (Prentice-Hall).

Select Committee (1976a), *First Report of the Select Committee on Abortion*, Vol. 1, HC 573–1 (HMSO).

Select Committee (1976b), *First Report of the Select Committee on Abortion*, Vol. 2, HC 573–11 (HMSO).

Simms, M. (1975), 'The compulsory pregnancy lobby, then and now', *Journal of the Royal College of Medical Practitioners*, vol. 25, p. 716.

Society for the Suppression of Vice (1874), *Annual Report.*

Steinhoff, P. G., and Diamond, M. (1977), *Abortion Politics* (Hawaii University Press).

Stopes, M. C. C. (1918), *Married Love* (The Critic and Guide Company).

Sutherland, H. G. (1922), *Birth Control* (Harding and More).

Taussig, F. J. (1910), *The Prevention and Treatment of Abortion* (George Keemer).

Taussig, F. J. (1936), *Abortion – Spontaneous and Induced* (C. V. Mosby).

Thomas, D. (1969), *A Long Time Burning* (Routledge).

Tietze, C. (1979), *Induced Abortion 1979*, 3rd edn (Population Council).

Tietze, C. (1981), *Induced Abortion: A World Review* (Population Council).

Tietze, C. (1983), *Induced Abortion 1983*, 5th edn (Population Council).

Tietze, C., and Dawson, D. A. (1973), *Induced Abortion, a Factbook* (Population Council).

Titmuss, R. M. (1963), *Essays on the Welfare State* (Unwin University Books).

Treffers, P. E. (1965), *Abortus en Anticonceptis* (Haarlem).

Treloar, S., Snyder, E., and Kerr, C. (1977), 'Effects of new services on women's abortion experience', *Journal of Biosocial Science*, vol. 9, pp. 417–27.

United Nations (1976), *UN Statistical Yearbook*.

United Nations (1980a), *Annual Review of Population Law 1980*.

United Nations (1980b), *World Population as Assessed in 1980*, UN Department of International and Social Affairs.

Van Os, M. (1977), 'Den Vyl to resume coalition attempts', *Financial Times* (2 September).

Van Praag, P. (1977), 'Population problems in the Netherlands 1918–1939', *Population Studies*, vol. 32, no. 2, pp. 251–65.

Viguerie, R. (1981), *The New Right* (Caroline House).

Wainer, B. (1972), *Isn't It Nice* (Aplan Books).

Walbert, D. and Butler, J. D. (1973), *Abortion Society and the Law* (Case University Press).

Watson, J. (1979), 'Italy – latest report', *Breaking Chains*, no. 13 (June), p. 7.

Weber, M. (1968), *The Protestant Ethic and the Spirit of Capitalism* (Allen & Unwin).

Westoff, C. F., and Jones, E. F. (1977), 'The secularisation of United States Catholic birth control practices', *Family Planning Perspectives*, vol. 9, no. 5, p. 203.

Willey, D. (1975), 'Reform Italian style', *People*, vol. 2, no. 3, p. 26.

Willke, B. and Willke, J. (1975), *Handbook on Abortion* (Hiltz).

Wilson-Davies, K. (1980), 'Ideal family size in the Irish Republic', *Journal of Biosocial Science*, vol. 12, no. 1, pp. 15–20.

Wulf, D. (1980), 'The Hungarian fertility survey, 1977', *Family Planning Perspectives*, vol. 12, pp. 44–6.

Wynn, M. and Wynn, A. (1973), *Some Consequences of Induced Abortion to Children Born Subsequently* (Foundation for Education and Research in Childbearing).

Young, J. (1971), *The Drugtakers* (McGibbon & Kee).

Yusuf, F. and Briggs, D. (1979), 'Legalised abortion in South Australia: the first seven years', *Journal of Biosocial Science*, vol. 11, pp. 179–92.

Index